ANN M. ISR

ADVICE
FOR THE
LAWLORN

CAREER DO'S AND DON'TS FROM
ONE OF THE MOST SUCCESSFUL
LEGAL RECRUITERS IN THE INDUSTRY

18 17 16 15 14   5 4 3 2 1

Library of Congress Cataloging-in-Publication Data

Israel, Ann M., author.
  Advice for the lawlorn : career do's and don'ts from one of the most successful legal recruiters in the industry / Ann M. Israel.
      pages cm
  Includes bibliographical references and index.
  ISBN 978-1-62722-204-4 (alk. paper)
  1. Corporation law—United States—Vocational guidance—Miscellanea.
2. Corporate lawyers—United States—Handbooks, manuals, etc—Miscellanea.
I. Title.
  KF299.I5I835 2014
  340.023'73--dc23
                              2014020257

Dedication
This book is dedicated to all those attorneys who endlessly toil away at the law.

Contents

▌▮▌

▌▮▌

Preface

Hon. Steven S. Honigman

One of the great books about boxing is *My View From the Corner*, by Angelo Dundee. It recounts the role, skills, and satisfactions of a premier trainer and cornerman who forged neophyte boxers into champions. In the gym he taught them moves, strategy and endurance, and from the corner of the ring he salved their cuts, gave them tactical instructions and encouragement, and sent them back into the fray to prevail.

Ann Israel is a lawyer's cornerman, and *Advice for the Lawlorn* is a cornerman's book. During thirty-five years as a legal recruiter, Ann has counseled soon-to-be first year associates on what to wear to an interview, the best way to describe their skills, how to radiate enthusiasm about working for the interviewer's firm, and the need to realistically match their aspirations to what the market is looking for. For lawyers in the midst of their careers, she has given advice about when to move from one firm to another and managing the departure without burning a bridge, the best time to ask for a raise, shrugging off the backbiter in the office down the hall, maintaining a healthy skepticism about promises of advancement, gracefully accomplishing the metamorphosis from associate to partner, and wringing every possible advantage from an unhappy termination.

At every turn, Ann has emphasized the bedrock need for honesty and candor. For those confronted with potentially life-changing career or personal choices, she has recommended an illustrious precedent—the decision-making approach codified by Benjamin Franklin. And for everyone thinking about making a change, she describes the process and rewards of working with the right recruiter.

I have lawyered with BigLaw, small and medium-sized firms, as a military judge advocate in the Navy, and as a political appointee. As a board member and company advisor, I have also been a client. At some point in every stage, I would have benefited from Ann's wealth of experience and sage counsel.

It is with great pleasure that I offer this advice—take Ann into your corner. Read her book and let her guide you to becoming a law firm champion.

The Honorable Steven S. Honigman has served as the General Counsel of the Navy.

Foreword

As we in the legal community all know, the nature of the practice of law has changed radically in the past ten years. From the reduction of state and federal budgets for judicial clerks to the hourly billings that clients will no longer tolerate, the changes have generally been motivated by economic factors and their trend has been to compel the achievement of more with less.

No part of the legal world has been hit harder by these changes than hiring. And no one I know of has had more to say about hiring—more to say from the inside looking out and the outside looking in—than Ann Israel.

Ann is among the most highly respected and sought after legal search professionals in the largest and most competitive legal market in the United States—the New York City metropolitan area. She enjoys long-standing relationships among top-tier and mid-tier law firms in Manhattan, Long Island, Connecticut, and New Jersey. And a startling tribute to her is that even in tight markets, even when the inboxes of hiring partners are overflowing with unwanted resumes of skilled and hungry lawyers, the hiring partners still come to Ann with the specifics of their wishes and she is able to deliver.

Ann also hears the tales of woe of young folks on the move and mid-level folks unhappy and looking to relocate. I know this not only from my general familiarity with the market in the northeast, but because many years ago, after I left the bench in New Jersey and before my work at Fox News became full time, I, too, utilized Ann's services. My experiences with her were so salutary and charming, so informative and intriguing, that we became good friends; and when she asked me to write this brief Foreword, I immediately agreed to do so.

Before I wrote this Foreword, I thought I knew the marketplace. I had my eyes opened.

I was reminded that engaging Ann to find the right job for you is like talking to your mother and father, your priest or rabbi, your financial backer and career counselor all at the same time. She demonstrates in these pages, as she did to me in person and to countless others who became frustrated with rejection, that the more she knows about her client—whether it be the law firm or the candidate—the sooner the deal will close.

But while learning about her client, she is shrewdly educating the client—perhaps to lower his sights, perhaps to raise them; and she is doing so with such a soft touch that the process is not only almost always rewarding, the process is enjoyable as well.

If you think that process is only troubling and cannot be enjoyable; or if you want to see a professional at work who has great command of her field and of human nature, turn this page and you will be captivated by *Advice for the Lawlorn*.

Advice for the Lawlorn is Ann's compilation of some of the anecdotal highlights and lowlights from a newspaper column that she wrote which appeared in the *New York Law Journal* over the column's 20+ year history, and within her 35 years as a legal search professional. There is no question or concern or issue that is left unanswered or unaddressed—and because of the anonymity of her readers' letters, they are candid to the extreme. Some of these letters will make you laugh and some will make you cry. And Ann's replies reveal an iron fist of knowledge inside a velvet glove of understanding.

Ann condenses the wealth of experiences relayed by 20+ years of these letter writers to her column and the treasure trove of advice she's provided in that same time into this single handbook for lawyers. She supplements her greatest hits from her column with contemporary reflections that when you read them will make you ponder at her introspection.

Her advice ranges from the tactical to the practical and covers the entirety of a lawyer's career—from law school through partnership and even to the winding down of a legal career. Much of her advice is timeless, but some of it is specifically useful for today's bear market.

The subjects of her insight—either attorneys she's worked for, firms she's searched for, and even the writers to her column—run the gamut from insightful to embarrassing (don't worry, there are no proper names here). Yet, Ann draws from all of those experiences to provide salient advice that I have not seen presented in such a fascinating way. Ann's wisdom is more necessary now than ever given the massive shifts and realignments taking place in the legal market.

In my nearly 40 years at the bar, I have been a litigator, a general counsel of a billion dollar corporation, a life-tenured trial judge, a professor at three law schools, and a television commentator on the nation's legal, political, and economic affairs. Nearly every week, someone asks me to help a relative or a friend land a nice job in the legal profession. I guess they think I know how to get this done just because of my varied legal career. Yet, Ann has probably forgotten more about this than I have ever known. And what she has not forgotten is right behind this Foreword in a rollicking new book that every lawyer concerned about our shrinking legal community can benefit from reading.

Go ahead, see if I am right. Turn the page . . .

Hon. Andrew P. Napolitano
Senior Judicial Analyst
Fox News Channel
New York City
Summer 2014

Introduction

Twenty years ago I received a phone call from Jimmy Finkelstein, then the publisher of the *National Law Journal* and the *New York Law Journal.* Jimmy was about to launch a website for the *New York Law Journal*—the first of its kind—and he wanted to know if I would be interested in doing a weekly advice column for lawyers. It sounded like fun, so of course I agreed. The column, initially called "Asked and Answered," started up the following Monday and the first question came from a friend. But after that first column, it was never necessary for friends to send in questions: the floodgates opened, and each day my e-mail inbox would be overflowing with questions from attorneys and law students alike. The questions were from all over the United States and eventually from all over the world.

After more than twenty years of receiving questions, I still haven't heard it all! The questions continue to roll in and I continue to respond. Although my style of giving out advice remains the same, the name of the column was changed many years ago to "Advice for the Lawlorn" and I have been dubbed the "Dear Abby of the Legal Community."

My practice as a legal search consultant is focused on BigLaw attorneys, those who wish to become BigLaw attorneys, and law students from the top-tier law schools. Some people have asked (and criticized) why seemingly I am only interested in this very finite world of lawyers in the corporate law firm environment. The reason is simple: I am in the business of primarily placing BigLaw lawyers to satisfy my clients' needs, and this is the type of attorney they are looking for. I certainly have no bias against part-time attorneys; graduates from second-, third-, and fourth-tier law schools; and attorneys working in firms other than corporate-minded ones. It just so happens that my world is about BigLaw. However, the advice I give certainly can be applied not only to non-BigLaw attorneys but also to anyone who is out there seeking career advice.

I truly believe that every attorney is employable, but not every attorney is employable with a fee attached to his/her candidacy. It has been questioned why I don't fight back against the bias of my clients and start presenting candidates from lower-tier schools or in different practice areas. Unfortunately, as much as I would love to represent everyone who is interested in my help, the clients have myriad search firms to choose from that agree to search under the law firms' guidelines. I would be out of business in a flash if I started representing candidates who do not fit the search parameters given out by my clients. And so, I represent the candidates with the BigLaw profiles in my search business, but I believe my column applies to anyone and everyone—and not just attorneys—seeking career advice.

I love writing this column and am delighted to share some of the standout questions that have been published over the past six years, during the time when we have witnessed a difficult and tremendous change in the way law firms and corporations do their hiring. Although every question is always new and different to me, I have sorted them into categories by subject. I hope you enjoy reading these columns as much as I have enjoyed writing them. Keep the questions coming! And, as I always say, best wishes!

Ann M. Israel
January 2014

CHAPTER 1

Why Should I Become/ Stay a Lawyer?

Why to become or stay a lawyer is not a frequent question, but when it is posed to me, it is always heartrending. It is such an awful scenario to be in a situation where you hate what you do. But I often think—and advise—that it is necessary to give your profession a little more time or change your practice area, or perhaps just change the environment in which you are working. The problem might not be the profession but instead the place where you work each day or perhaps the type of law you are practicing.

Of all the columns I have written over the years, there is one that stands out among the rest for me. The first time I published this answer to the question of "What are the benefits of being a lawyer?" was in 1994. The second time was in 2004 and the last time was in 2012. I wondered if a recruiter of lawyers could be objective in answering this question, as those of us in this field believe there is no nobler profession than that of an attorney. But, as I started to write down all the wonderful benefits of being an attorney, I realized that the best answer would not come from me but rather from a response to an article entitled "Misery," both published in *The American Lawyer*. Now I share with you what has always been my favorite column, followed by a few others on this same topic.

▮▮▮

What are the benefits of being a lawyer?

Dear Readers,

A law degree is extremely versatile. If you were to take a long, hard look at the credentials of the CEOs of companies, you might be very surprised to see how many of these "captains of industry" have a law degree, whether or not they ever intended to practice law.

Of course, an MBA is also extremely valuable. Perhaps the conclusion to be drawn here is that a graduate degree is always a good thing, whether it is a law degree, an MBA, a medical degree, and so on. However, earning a law degree does help to discipline your mind and teach you to look at things in an analytical light. There are so many other good reasons to earn a law degree—you certainly cannot go wrong by earning your JD. However, if you do not intend to practice law, just be aware of how difficult those three years of law school are going to be and how expensive it is going to be to earn that degree.

If you are a leader and possess the skills necessary to make you powerful and savvy, and if you are in the right place at the right time, then yes, a law degree may very well help to lead you into a powerful and lucrative position outside of the law-firm world. But then again, if you are a leader possessing those necessary skills to make you powerful and savvy, and if you do happen to find yourself in the right place at the right time, your success in the world outside of the law might happen with or without that JD degree.

Many years ago—October 1993, to be exact—an attorney wrote an article for *The American Lawyer* titled "Misery." The author of this article was very unhappy with his profession as an attorney and was incredibly disillusioned and dissatisfied, much in the same way as you have described the attorneys practicing at your law firm. This author made it very clear that he would not want his son or daughter to suffer this same fate and hoped that his children would not become attorneys.

In the January/February 1994 issue of *The American Lawyer*, a response to this article appeared in the Letters to the Editor section. Stanley Komaroff, the then-chair of Proskauer Rose Goetz & Mendelsohn (now known as Proskauer Rose LLP) in New York, wrote the letter. I was so very moved by Mr. Komaroff's response to the "Misery" article, and I never forgot how he described his passion and love for the practice of law.

When I received your question, I picked up the phone and called Mr. Komaroff. He graciously offered to share that article with me, and I now share it with you. I hope you will read it and then read it again. Perhaps you will realize that, even though the practice of law is not for everyone, the benefits of being a lawyer are innumerable for those who find a true love in the profession. Read on—this is a wonderful holiday gift courtesy of Mr. Komaroff for those attorneys or attorneys-to-be who are questioning their choice of profession.

∎

The Pros Outweigh the Cons
By Stanley Komaroff
Chair, Proskauer Rose Goetz & Mendelsohn

By this letter I happily accept the invitation to respond to your Head-notes article entitled "Misery," which appeared in the October 1993 issue. I write this in many capacities as a member of a large New York firm, the same firm I clerked at between my second and third years of law school, and joined following law school graduation in 1958; as a lawyer with 35 years filled for the most part with gratification and more than fair financial reward; as the father of a young litigator in a large firm; and as a friend and colleague of dozens and dozens of proud and happy lawyers in large and small firms all across the country.

The enthusiasm I bring to the practice has not diminished. Each year remains more stimulating and intellectually challenging than the preceding one. Each client's problems present new issues, the need for a variety of increasing skills, and the constant requirement to grow, improve, and learn. No, I am not miserable. No, I do not want to change jobs, teach law school, run a book store in Vermont, or, except for a few weeks here and there, bask in the sun in Palm Beach or on the ski slopes of Vail.

I am far from alone in my love for the profession. One of my partners thrives on "the constant intellectual stimulation, the excitement of litigation, the fun and satisfaction of winning, the feeling that I've made a difference, and the camaraderie of practicing in a large law firm with people I consider my friends and with clients with whom I have long-term relationships."

Another, who, contrary to Wesley Williams, would be very happy if his son or daughter became a lawyer, said, "While I would caution them about the long hours and, at times, tedious work, I think the high points clearly outweigh the drawbacks. I love the chess match between myself, on behalf of my client, and the opposing side. Given my competitive nature, the trial process suits my personality well."

Others used words like "exciting," "invigorating," "challenging," "interesting," and "rewarding." Indisputably, practicing top-quality, cutting-edge law, satisfying knowledgeable, sophisticated, and demanding clients, keeping up with complex changes, being a "good" partner, contributing some pro bono time, conferring with colleagues, teaching associates or younger partners, and, yes, filling out reports and time sheets, billing and collecting, all require sacrifices and long hours, and often involve intense pressure, immense energy, and unselfish commitment. The demand for better service seems ever increasing. The technological innovations of word processing, faxing, video conferencing, electronic transfers, etc., often make response times frightening and nerve-racking. Competing and succeeding as a lawyer today seems to require greater legal competence and more business acumen than ever before.

Still, these changes do not go to the core of what we do. They do not eliminate or outweigh the essential attractions of the profession.

Instead, I believe that a part of the problem is caused by a failure to recognize that the financial rewards of the profession have increased substantially over the last 25 years—a partner at one of the most profitable New York firms told me that last year the lowest paid partner in his firm received more money than the highest paid partner in that firm received ten or so years ago. There is a price to pay for this "success."

Moreover, I believe that a good part of the dissatisfaction is caused by a nostalgic look backward rather than a mature look forward. Nostalgia has no place in analyzing the profession. As former New York City mayor Edward Koch once was reported to have said to a voter longing for yesterday: "We cannot make it like it was!" We cannot make it like it was, and it probably was not that much better. I do believe that in the legal profession there are good news days ahead. The challenge is to be creative and visionary. The challenge is to adapt. The challenge is to do things differently and better. We should not be fearful of the opportunity to reshape the profession. We need to reform ourselves to provide better value to the client while at the same time preserving a balanced and harmonious life-style for ourselves. A balance is possible.

Perhaps I have been more fortunate than most. I continue to look forward to coming to work each day with the same zeal as when I first started to practice. I have been lucky in my choice of profession, my choice of firm, and my choice of specialty. Over the years, my friends have become my clients and my clients and partners have become my friends. I have enjoyed respect and appreciation—and probably even admiration here and there, and at the same time achieved financial security beyond my expectations.

After all these years, when a client telephones on a Sunday night with a seemingly insoluble problem, an unreasonable deadline, a disagreeable adversary, and an acute need for help, the juices continue to flow.

So, there it is . . . a nice reminder that the practice of law can be a stimulating and intellectually rewarding profession, and a lovely gift from Mr. Komaroff to all those who are celebrating the start of the Jewish New Year, those who are just beginning their legal careers, and those of you who perhaps just needed a reminder as to why you go to the office each day. Best wishes!

Sincerely,
Ann M. Israel

City: Pittsburgh

I am an associate working in a small general practice firm. I have been engaged in the practice of law for just over a year now. I am free to make my own hours and do not feel overworked. I have had the opportunity to work on many different types of cases. The only complaint that I have about my position is that I do not get enough guidance from my superiors. The problem that I am having is that I do not enjoy the work that I am doing. For the past few months I have had the feeling that the practice of law is not for me. I am seriously considering changing careers. My question is: How long should I continue to practice law before I can be certain that it is not for me? Is it too soon, or should I just bite the bullet and move on?

Moving On

Dear Moving On:

So, it sounds as if you have a pretty nice situation going on there—you can make your own hours, do not feel overworked, and are given the opportunity to work on all types of cases.

Unfortunately, it seems as if there are two problems lurking here, one being that you are not getting much supervision or guidance from the people working over you and the second one being that you don't like what you are doing.

I would have to say that no matter how nice your situation is at this firm, what good does it do you if you aren't learning anything and, most critical of all, you are not happy with what you are doing there? This just doesn't make any sense at all to me.

You have now been at this firm for over a year, which leads me to believe you have given it enough time to really determine that you are not happy. But instead of jumping the gun after only one year at just one small general practice firm, did it ever occur to you that it might not be the practice of law itself, but rather the actual place where you are practicing?

I am only saying this because I hate to see you having spent three long and hard years in law school and then this past year practicing law to only throw it all away without trying to figure out if it is the environment or the actual career path that is the problem.

It does sound to me that even though this firm offers a very casual environment, it is lacking several of the most critical factors for a junior associate, and those are supervision and mentoring. How in the world are you supposed to learn the practice of law without a senior associate and/or a partner there to guide you? It is no wonder that you are not enjoying what you are doing—it must be very frustrating and difficult to start practicing law without anyone there to instruct, supervise, or help you.

Before you give it all up to find a new career path, let me suggest that you try to find some solutions to your dilemma. If none of these work, perhaps the practice of law is not for you, as you have suggested. However, I do think it is far too early to throw in the towel.

First, before you begin a job search, have you spoken with a senior associate or partner at the firm regarding your concerns that you have not had any supervision over the work you are doing? As a junior associate, this is a very reasonable request. Explain to the senior associate and/or partner that you are delighted with the environment at the firm and the varied work you have been given, but as a junior attorney you would appreciate the opportunity to have a senior attorney helping to guide you along as you develop your practice.

If this is not a possibility at your current firm, then you have no choice but to begin a job search for a firm where being mentored is part of the job description. However, please be careful to keep your intentions of moving on as confidential and quiet as possible. You absolutely do not want your current employer to get wind of your job search and possibly terminate your employment. The last thing you want to have happen is to be unemployed in a tough job market.

I do believe it is too early for you to be certain that the practice of law is not for you. You need to find out if it is the career or the environment that is making you unhappy, and from what you have told us, I suspect that the problem lies with the environment. Try to get your current environment to make some changes and work for you, and if this does not happen, move on as soon as you can to a firm that will offer you the guidance, supervision, and mentoring that you so need and deserve. Best wishes!

And to everyone, I wish you all happy holidays and a happy and healthy New Year!

Sincerely,
Ann M. Israel

City: Los Angeles

Dear Ann,

After successfully weathering the economic storm of the past two years—including landing a full-time offer following my summer associate experience at BigLaw, keeping my GPA high enough during my 3L to keep my offer, and then finding a back-up job during my deferral year—I am now faced with the wonderful yet difficult decision of leaving BigLaw entirely. My firm gave us deferred associates a stipend and explained we could do whatever we wanted for the year. I landed a very prestigious temporary gig in-house and the company and I quickly clicked. Although my in-house job was supposed to be for my deferral year only, I was recently offered to stay full-time. The salary is comparable and the lifestyle is predictably much better. I have my weekends and evenings, and I'm learning tons from the general counsel, who is as much a mentor as one could ask for. My only reservation is leaving behind a path I worked so hard to create, and whether moving in-house as a first-year out of law school will close many doors that working for BigLaw would presumably open. I'm currently in a very niche industry, finance, and am unsure if I'd like to stay here for my whole career. I'm unsure when and if I decide to leave my in-house gig, if anyone besides a bigger company in my industry would consider the experience worthwhile. I feel ashamed to discuss this wonderful dilemma of having to choose between two great paths, but think it's a worthy discussion to have in this deferral age, no less. What exactly are the merits of the first couple years of BigLaw and do they truly train you for the legal world better than would a small in-house legal department with never-ending legal issues? In light of BigLaw's recent shake-ups, should the legal community be reconsidering their true value for junior lawyers aside from financially?

Many thanks,
Tough Luck

Dear Tough:

Don't feel ashamed—you should be very proud that you are in such a fortunate position. You must have a winning personality along with great credentials and a natural aptitude for the law to have two solid employers wanting you to work for them. It is a wonderful dilemma and you should be absolutely delirious with joy—or any ecstatic emotion other than shame—to be in this wonderful position.

Times are changing so rapidly that I really don't know what the law firm model is going to be down the road. However, at this time I still believe that if one is fortunate enough to be offered a position with a BigLaw firm, that is the best way to start off a legal career. The training and exposure you will have is priceless. Rotating through different departments, meeting partners of different levels of seniority and experience (and temperament), working with clients from diverse industries, forging relationships with other associates—these are all part of the BigLaw experience.

In your specific situation, where you are currently in a niche practice area, one that you are unsure as to whether or not you want to stay in for an entire career, I have to say to you that your first few years in practice will brand you as an attorney in this area should you want to move on to a different area. Staying in-house in this niche industry for those first critical years of practice will make it exceptionally difficult for you to interview at BigLaw firms down the road or to move to other in-house positions unless those jobs are in similar industries.

I do firmly believe that BigLaw firms (and other types of law firms) train you for the legal world in the beginning of your career much more than a small in-house legal department. The attorneys in-house still, even in this age of cost-cutting, farm out much of the work to their outside counsel. And the typical in-house legal department is not set up with a mentoring and/or teaching system, as is a law firm. Law firms hire large classes of first-year attorneys and expect that they need training and mentoring. In-house legal departments have very few, if any, junior attorneys. All you have to do is think about what all this means.

I know there are many successful attorneys who started out their careers in-house. However, given the choice you have been given, I would advise you to go for the BigLaw career path, if only for the first few years of your practice. At least then you leave yourself open for many choices. Best wishes!

Sincerely,
Ann M. Israel

<hr />

City: New York

After graduating from a good school with high honors, passing several bars on the first try, and surviving a number of first-year cuts at a big firm where I work, I have serious reservations about my career choice.

The reason: I am a parent of small children but barely get to see them, given the time demands of the big-firm lifestyle. Is there such a thing as a law-related job where you can leave at 6:00–7:00 and don't have to work weekends? I feel bad complaining, given the number of jobless lawyers out there, but there is very little balance between my home and work life, and from what I hear from my friends at other firms, the story is the same all over. Nor do the hourly demands change the more senior I become. What kind of job am I qualified for? I don't mind the cut in salary; I just need to be a part of my kids' lives!

Reserved

Dear Reserved:

And such is the life of a BigLaw lawyer.

Here's the bottom line—if you live in a major city and work for a major law firm earning a big six-figure income, the truth of the matter is you have chosen a career path that is extremely demanding.

You ask what kind of job you are qualified for. Clearly you are qualified to practice law in several states and in the practice area you are currently working in, obviously to good reviews.

However, the problem here is not what you are qualified to do; it is where you are doing it.

I will say, however, if you are a litigator or a transactional attorney involved in high-profile deals, it is extremely difficult to count on predictable hours or hope that you will always have your weekends to yourself and your family.

Litigators do have clients they must be responsible to—when there is a litigation that you must be prepared for, it isn't easy to say that you are going to cut off your workday at 6 p.m. and not respond to your client's needs until the next day. The same concept holds true for transactional attorneys. When a deal needs to be completed or else it isn't going to happen, you might be toiling away until 11:59 p.m. to satisfy that client's needs for a deal to close by a certain date. That's just the way it goes when you are an attorney.

However, a smaller practice does attract smaller clients with smaller deals, or smaller litigations and smaller needs. And that is probably the direction you should be headed at this time, as long as you have given this enough thought.

You say that you don't mind the cut in pay, and that is going to be one of the big differences you will see between the BigLaw life and that of a smaller, less stressful practice. You will also see a change in support in a smaller practice. You will have to take on a number of the tasks that you have taken for granted. The law library will not be as extensive as the one you have in a BigLaw firm. The mentoring aspect will not be as wide, nor will it be quite so available. Many small comforts that you have also taken for granted will no longer exist. But none of this should matter because you should be home by 7 p.m. each evening and the weekends essentially should be yours.

The biggest issue facing you right now will be finding this ideal job. It does exist, but with today's job market being what it is, the job you want might be harder to find. If you live outside of Manhattan, you might have better luck finding the "lifestyle" type of practice at the smaller firms in Westchester or on Long Island. However, with your credentials and BigLaw training, I would think that you are going to be a highly viable candidate for a smaller firm's practice.

Before you jump, make sure you carefully research the firm you are thinking about joining. Have some lunch or after-work interviews with other associates at the firm (if there are other associates!) to be sure that the hours really are what you think they are going to be and that the weekends really will be yours. Don't just stop there, though—make certain that this firm is financially sound and that the legal practices are sound as well. The last thing you want to have happen is that you leave your BigLaw firm and join a firm that suddenly doesn't exist any longer.

Lastly, and once again, before you jump firms, speak with the head of your department to see if there isn't some sort of mommy (or daddy) track that your BigLaw firm offers. Many of the AmLaw 100 firms offer this type of track for those attorneys who are not that interested in following a traditional partnership track but want to stay in the BigLaw environment. You may very well find that you are able to stay at your firm while at the same time reducing your hours and seeing your children grow up! Best wishes.

Sincerely,
Ann M. Israel

City: New York

Ann—I have a question similar to that of the individual who wrote and asked about leaving his/her job voluntarily. I am a third-year associate in New York, and my firm also has not laid anyone off. I am considering resigning in November too, completely voluntarily. The difference is, I hate the practice of law as it is currently carried on in law firms. I am far too entrepreneurial to sit and wait for work to be doled out. I am far too ambitious to remain unchallenged. I think the billable hour is the worst economic/business model ever to have come out of an office building. Most importantly, I want to make a career change and therefore see no reason to continue sitting in a law firm. Same answer, then, or is my line of thinking more reasonable? I don't care what a partner at a law firm will think when he hears that I left on my own because I don't want to work for the type of people that run law firms. What say you?

Ambitious

Dear Ambitious:

I say you are in a different situation from our exhausted friend in last week's column.

But before I address your situation, let me go back to that column for just a moment. While most people agreed with what I wrote, a few anonymous readers were quite upset with my response to Exhausted's situation. They thought I didn't understand his/her question and that this individual wanted to leave the firm before being laid off to look for a new job.

That really wasn't the case. S/he wrote, "Is it best to quit and take time off or be cut?"

In my experience, taking time off generally is the same thing as a vacation. It didn't make sense to me, particularly in this tough job market, to hang out for a while if the alternative is to be employed. If you don't like your employer but want to continue practicing law, I would suggest looking for a job while you are still employed, if you are so fortunate to be in that position. People who are employed are, unfortunately for those who are not, more viable candidates to potential employers. Is that fair or right? Probably not. Is it just the way things are? Yes.

Was I angry when I wrote that column? Yes, and I expressed that fact in the column. Why? Because as I speak to so many unemployed lawyers every day that would do anything to be employed, it just hurt me to read this question from someone complaining about having too much work.

But I must say that my favorite response came from the unknown individual who wrote, "You should be grateful that you have a job too, one with your own name on the door so you don't have to worry about when it will be pulled out from under you."

Yes, I am grateful that I have a job, especially one with my own name on the door. I have worked many long and hard years to maintain that position.

But if you think that there are no worries here simply because my name is on the door, then I suspect you must be a trust fund baby. I guess you haven't thought about the fact that my recruiters can't place associates any longer because there are no associate jobs for them to fill or that the payroll and taxes and advertising and rent and overhead and everything else still need to be paid even though the cash flow for the company isn't exactly what it used to be. And guess who has to take care of all of that? The person whose name is on the door.

And like Exhausted, there are times when I am so worried and exhausted that I throw my hands up and would just like to quit and take some time off. But you see, if I did, then it would be difficult to come back into the marketplace. It is the same thing in any other profession. You can't just take some time off because you are tired and then expect your profession to welcome you back with open arms. In the world of law (or in any business, for that matter), the partners in the law firms just don't understand that kind of mentality.

So, that takes us back to the question at hand. This person doesn't want to deal with those partners at the law firms. S/he wants nothing to do with billable hours and in fact, it sounds as if the practice of law has not been a happy experience for this individual as s/he claims that s/he would like a career change and intends to quit in November.

The only advice I can dole out here is to ask if you have thought about what you would like to do when you leave the practice of law. As you are a third-year attorney, I suspect you might still have some law school loans outstanding, and you do need to think about how you are going to continue paying off those loans once you leave your firm. Additionally, the job market is tough out there, not only for attorneys but in many different areas—business, advertising, sales, etc. You say you are entrepreneurial, so I am hoping that you have thought about starting up some interesting and exciting new venture that will bring in some cash while at the same time keeping you interested and enthused, since it does sound as if the practice of law is no longer a challenge for you. I just hope you have a sound business plan for whatever your next step is.

I wonder why you are waiting until November to give notice. Obviously you are not waiting to cash in on your year-end bonus or else you would stay through the end of December. Why not leave now if you are that unhappy? I hope you have really given this complete and thorough thought before you take this step (and I am certain that you have done so, right?!!).

The only reason I ask this question is because I think back to one of my very favorite placements that happened a number of years ago. An associate came in to see me who sounded a little like you. She was at a BigLaw firm and wanted to leave the practice of law. She hated being a lawyer and wanted a career change. However, after meeting with her, I began to get the feeling that it wasn't the practice of law that was the problem, it was the firm where she was practicing. I made her promise that she would interview at just one firm, and if she still hated the law, I wouldn't push any other interviews on her. Well, to make a long story short, she is the hiring partner at that firm today, and a very prominent partner to boot. I receive a holiday card from her every December, thanking me for making her go on that interview.

So, I ask you to really analyze the firm where you are currently working and make sure that the problem isn't the firm rather than the practice of law altogether. If it really is the law firm model along with the practice of law that you dislike, then I do support your decision and hope you have a good plan as to what you intend to do when you give notice. My only question remains, why November? Best wishes!

Sincerely,
Ann M. Israel

IⅢI

City: New York

I became a member of both the NY/NJ bars in January. I graduated from a poorly ranked law school. I learned too late in the game how I was playing the financial equivalent of Russian roulette, except with more bullets in the chamber. Of course, by failing to engage in the proper due diligence before attending said law school, perhaps I never had the requisite talent for this field. Accordingly, I only have myself to blame for ending up in no-fault, earning less in both real and inflation-adjusted dollars than I did in my think-tank job between college and law school, with obscene loans to pay. Everybody makes mistakes in life, except from my read of the landscape, Hester Prynne had better odds in shaking off her stigma than those of us with JDs from poorly ranked law schools. What is the best exit strategy from the practice of law?

Hester

Dear Hester:

Sorry about this mess. Just think, if only you could have done all of this about five years ago—oh, how different things might have been. Back then, firms were just about hiring anyone who could breathe for certain practice areas. If you had graduated from your very same "poorly ranked law school" with a B+ or better average and, having been admitted into the New York bar, you more than likely would have found yourself working into the wee hours of the night seven days a week at some New York BigLaw firm in their M&A or corporate finance department.

Oh, what a difference a few years make. That was then and this is now.

Not that this is going to make you feel any better, but those graduates from the top-tier law schools are not finding things much better than you at this time. Have you read the column that is now a blog titled "The Diary of a Laid Off BigLaw Corporate Attorney"? Or have you spent any time on the Unemployed Lawyers website? And I suppose there are lots of other similar websites put up by attorneys with what are considered to be impeccable credentials but who are unable to get hired at this time. I speak with them every day.

But as I wrote above, I doubt that makes you feel any better.

I suppose I could tell you that this too shall pass and eventually you will find a job. Hmmm, I'm not going to say that because my crystal ball is cloudy today and I can't see when this will all end.

What I can tell you is that there are alternative jobs for people with a law degree, and you should never, ever believe that those three years in law school were years wasted. That law degree will make you such a viable candidate for so many other professions, and no one will care where you went to law school.

Banking, politics, business affairs, legal aid, and teaching all jump out at me right away. Becoming a recruiter—in any area, not just legal recruiting, mind you—also is an option. Of course, with your law school background, legal recruiting seems to be a natural choice. Have you thought about any of these professions?

What have you been doing besides responding to ads and sending out your resume (which doesn't have any work experience on it anyway)? Have you been networking like crazy? Are you going to every bar event, speaking to everyone you know or have ever met, calling your law school's career services office frequently and then even more than that?

And, as I have mentioned several times before, if you do want to try to continue (or start, as the case may be for you) in the practice of law, have you looked at any of the branches of the United States Armed Services?

As I read on some website the other day (and said "ick" when I read it), your new job is looking for a job. That doesn't mean part-time or sometime or when you feel like it. It means full-time, all the time. So, if you want to leave the world of the law, sit down and figure out what you intend to do and then get going and find a job in that area. Perhaps you might want to sit down with a professional career guidance counselor to help determine what you are best suited to do besides practicing law.

But the main thing you need to do right now is stop blaming yourself for not knowing that your law school wasn't going to be good enough and that is the reason you must leave the practice of law. I just am not buying it right now. You passed both the New Jersey and the New York bars? Something sunk in during those three years sitting in a classroom. You may not get hired at Cravath, but before you leave the law you might want to reconsider all of your options. It's a tough job market out there, no doubt, but don't be a quitter just yet. There are jobs out there, and maybe it won't be your dream job right now, but this mess will eventually turn around. Best wishes.

Sincerely,
Ann M. Israel

CHAPTER 2

Law School Woes

Second only to law firm associates, the most complaints and problems come from law school students. It is understandable, as they are under tremendous pressure on so many levels. Grades are very important because what is on their transcript is permanent and will follow them for the rest of their legal career.

After making it through that first tough year of law school, they must return to their campus in the fall to go through OCIs (on-campus interviews) for what is known as their 2L summer employment (meaning the temporary job they will have during the summer following their second year of law school). And although it might be a lot of fun and games during that summer, the end result is critical since it is a black mark on a resume to not receive an offer of permanent employment (to start after graduation the following year) to become an associate with that firm.

Lastly, on top of all of this pressure, a large percentage of law school students also have the knowledge that they will graduate with over $100,000 in law school debt. Yikes! No wonder I receive so many questions from law students and potential law students.

City: Oakland, CA

I am a recently admitted law student with a wife and a child on the way.

I will be attending a good school, either Michigan or Cornell, depending on which gives me the best aid package. I cannot really afford to have a low-paying job over the summer. How can I maximize my chances of getting a 1L summer associate position?

Maximized

Dear Maximized:

First of all, congratulations on your acceptance to two great law schools. I hope you receive strong aid packages and that your biggest problem will be deciding which school to attend.

Maximizing your chances for getting 1L summer associate positions depends on so many factors, and some of them are completely out of your control. For instance: the economy. If things continue on the way they are right now, it probably will still be very difficult next summer to secure a law firm job after your first year of law school.

It is true that some of the BigLaw firms have started hiring 2L summer associates again and that the classes are not as devastatingly small as they have been during the last couple of summers. However, even in the best of times it has never been easy for 1Ls to find employment.

That is not to say that those jobs didn't exist. And certainly for some 1Ls, they still do. Right off the bat, you have a top-10 law school about to go on your resume, so part of the equation is there for you.

Your first semester in law school is going to be a great determining factor. Your grades will make a big difference in whether or not you are one of the viable candidates for the few 1L jobs that do exist out there. For instance, if you have all As on your transcript coming from your top-10 law school, chances become much better that those employers looking for a 1L clerk are going to look twice at you. However, a B– or C grade during your first semester is going to hurt your chances dramatically.

The old adage of location, location, location is going to play into this equation as well. I suspect there are not as many employers in and around Ithaca/Syracuse/Binghamton as there are in and around Ann Arbor/Detroit looking to hire 1Ls. Naturally, all the major law firms come to both Cornell and

Michigan for OCIs, but that is primarily for 2L interviews. For a 1L opportunity, it is wise to think strategically about what the surrounding geographic areas might have to offer simply to expand your options and have a better chance of securing a paying job during that first summer.

Also, I am thinking that since you do have a wife and will have a child by then, you probably will be settled in a house or apartment, and wouldn't it be easier to stay in one place for several years if at all possible? That's why the geographical location of the school perhaps should be a consideration if the financial aid packages are similar.

I also think that connections can play a large role in securing a 1L job. A letter from a professor, a law firm where a family member is a major client, a corporation where you worked during undergraduate school, any kind of connection you might think of—these are all contacts you want to utilize and network with to maximize your chances.

Hopefully the readers of this column who have secured 1L jobs will send on the secret to their success and I will pass it on in a future column in time for the fall semester!

Sadly, the 1L jobs are few and far between. Be realistic about this, and while you are working your way toward being a viable candidate for a 1L job during your first year of law school, you also need to be thinking about other types of opportunities you might be able to take on during that summer break. Best wishes!

Sincerely,
Ann M. Israel

City: New York

I am in my last year of law school. I have a solid resume of work experience in corporate human resources; I want to enter the field of labor and employment law. I am not on law review or any journals and was not able to secure a summer associate position in a major firm. I have average grades now with a 3.0 GPA, but my grades were terrible during my first year of law school, due to the deaths of two close family members and overall stress and confusion in my life. Is it still possible for me to obtain a first-year associate position in a large New York City firm, or should I just give up on that dream?

Dreaming

Dear Dreaming:

Never give up on your dreams. However, sometimes you need to work on other things and be realistic about what might be available to you while at the same time keeping your dreams alive but simply on the back burner for some time in the future.

We don't know certain things about you, but based on what you have told us, it does seem that you do not have a job secured for yourself upon graduation. We also do not know where you went to law school.

We do know that you had a really rough and sad time during your first year of law school. I am surprised that you decided to stay in school during this period instead of withdrawing and trying to work something out with the school where you might be able to start over again the following year. Although this is hindsight now, this is something that others in a similar position have done in the past or might consider in the future.

Losing—for example—a mother and a father at the same time is a horrible and very traumatic situation, one that could easily and understandably cause stress and confusion in one's life. Add on the stress and confusion of the first year of law school, and it all adds up to disastrous grades, ultimately no offer for a 2L summer job, and lastly, a less-than-attractive final transcript. Aside from all of that, this is also a time for grieving and being with other family members and taking care of oneself.

Here is the saddest part of all: you really can't discuss this in interviews because the partners, while sympathetic to your plight, really don't care. They don't want to hear about your personal problems. In fact, it is doubtful that you will even get to an interview stage at any of the large New York City law firms where you dream to go because they are going to view your transcript prior to anything else, see your "terrible" first-year grades, and not even consider your candidacy.

This may sound so cruel and unfeeling, especially considering your situation, but in the real world of work, this is what happens. It is necessary that the moment you walk out your door in the morning, your personal life should stay home and only your professional life goes with you into the office. Everyone has problems—some big, some small—but no one really wants to hear about them or to hear them as an excuse as to why work wasn't done or grades weren't good, etc.

So, how do you keep your dream alive? I suggest you send out your resume with the best cover letter possible indicating your extensive pre–law school human resources experience. I strongly recommend you do not discuss your personal problems that happened while you were in law school in the cover letter. You will have a chance to briefly cover this in an interview, when you inevitably will be asked why your first-year grades were so low.

At this point in time, you should be focused at getting experience in labor law at any firm that makes an offer to you. Down the road—and I am talking in terms of at least several years—when you have some experience in this practice area and perhaps have written or coauthored some published articles, you will have some practical experience to your name to add on to your resume and will be an expert in your field, and then you will be able to pursue your dream of practicing with the BigLaw firms.

The job market is so difficult right now for recent grads that basically it is all about the transcript. I am sorry that you had such personal tragedy during your first year of law school, but now you need to move on and find a way to make your dreams eventually come true. There is a way to do it—it just may take some time. Best wishes!

I hope everyone has a happy Labor Day weekend. I can't believe the summer is just about over!

Sincerely,
Ann M. Israel

∎

City: Unknown

Will I lose my opportunity to work at a large DC firm if I choose to start my career at a local firm in [my hometown]?
I [will spend my 2L summer] at one of the largest DC firms and anticipate receiving an offer of permanent employment. Now, I am contemplating moving to my small hometown and starting my career with a firm that has under 50 attorneys. At my DC firm I am only one of two summers that is not from a top-10 law school (I am from a school ranked in the 40s) and I graduated from a very small (lackluster) undergrad. However,

I know I will graduate in the top 10 percent of my class and as an editor on law review. Is there hope for someone that wants to move from a small market to a large market after two to four years of work? I would be taking a large pay cut (40 percent) at home, but what worries me more is that I would be bored with the level of work after a couple of years. My other options are to start in a DC firm and maybe move home in a year or two or to clerk and put off the decision entirely. Any advice?

Hoping

Dear Hoping:

Yes, I have some advice: Forget about all of these other options because based on what you want for your future, your decision is already made for you.

If this happened to be any other place or time, my advice to you might be different. I say *might* be different because in reality, I suspect I would advise you to take the DC job no matter what, based on what you have written to us. However, let's take a good long look at what is going on in your life.

You have told us that you eventually (meaning within two to four years after beginning your practice) want to work in a large DC firm. You will spend your 2L summer at one of those firms where you want to ultimately end up, and you believe that you are going to be given an offer of permanent employment, even in this day and age when so many summer associates are finding themselves left out in the cold.

Here is what I like about you—you are a very confident and self-assured individual and that is going to get you far in your career. However—and there are several *big* "howevers"—many of your predictions are just that . . . predictions. You can't count on anything just yet because so many variables can come into play that might change things. I do believe you should continue thinking the way you do, but you need to think about certain things carefully.

You are very fortunate to have an offer to summer at a top DC firm in this tough job market, especially considering that you are from a law school ranked in the 40s. Since the rest of your summer class—except for that one other summer associate—is all from top-10 law schools, you should be feeling very proud and confident. *However,* there are no guarantees these days (as if there ever were guarantees) that offers of permanent employment will be given out to everyone, including you. So I am telling you that should you be fortunate enough to get an offer of permanent employment from this top DC firm, the type of firm where you eventually would like to work, don't turn it down in the hope that you can return within two to four years after hanging out in small-town America.

Why are you even considering this when you point out all of the negatives about working in your hometown? The 40 percent pay cut is one thing, but are you listening to what you are saying about the fact that you are deeply concerned that you will be bored with the work? Why are you even thinking about doing this when you believe you have a sure thing about to be offered to you?

If you read through the archives of this column, you will find so many people complaining about a situation that you are liable to find yourself in—they started out at small law firms in small towns and now want to join BigLaw but are unable to even get an interview. You have an opportunity to do the BigLaw gig and then, if it doesn't suit you, you can always go home and end up at the smaller firm; you will be an incredibly viable candidate for that job market since you will have the big firm training, something that is always a desirable trait in a candidate. That's what is lacking in the candidates coming from the small-town firms trying to break into BigLaw and why they have such a difficult time trying to get an interview with those firms.

You, on the other hand, will probably have a chance to work in a fabulous city for a great salary at a top law firm and to be trained by big-name attorneys. Then, after a couple of years, if you decide that this is not the life you want to lead, you can head home with a nice savings account (and perhaps a good chunk of your law school loans paid off) and know that you are a top candidate for a clerkship or for the best law firm in your hometown. Or whatever it is that you think might be the next step in your career. So, if given this opportunity now, take it while it is offered. It may not be there later. Best of luck!

Sincerely,
Ann M. Israel

City: Los Angeles

I am currently a first-year student at UCLA Law School. Unlike many of my classmates, I don't really have any desire to work in corporate law. However, I am greatly interested in litigation and would like to clerk for a federal judge one day. What advice or strategy would you suggest for me to go about pursuing a federal clerkship? The word is that the federal courts only "really" consider those from, say, the top-10 schools, i.e., Ivy Leagues, etc. Is this true?

I really hope not!

Hoping Too

Dear Hoping Too:

Good for you! That's a lofty goal you have set for yourself and one that I believe you can definitely attain. That is, if you follow a very specific path beginning now all the way through the application process and then through your acceptance as a federal judicial clerk!

First of all, UCLA is a great law school regardless of which ranking system you utilize. No matter what, it is in the top 15 law schools and that's nice. You will be very surprised to know that although many federal clerks are on law review and are attending the top, top law schools, there are still a number of judges who are more interested in the entire picture of a law student than just the honors or where you are attending school.

Now, I am not suggesting that you can let your grades slip. It is critical that if your goal is to be a federal clerk, then you must be the best you can be and you must do whatever you can do to have the best possible grades. However, your application to clerk is going to present an entire package to the judge, and there are many federal judges who are looking for clerks with special interests rather than just coming from a specific school.

I understand that at this time in your life, you believe that you have no interest in corporate law, but it is early in your career. Clerking is not just a wonderful experience for litigators, but it is also beneficial for those who move on to transactional practices. For that very reason, you want to remain open to all kinds of federal clerkships and bear in mind that the more clerkships you are open to, the more job opportunities you will have.

For example, if you have an interest in bankruptcy law, then you might want to apply to the federal bankruptcy court clerkships. Explaining why you have this interest in bankruptcy as a practice area for your career will help you to stand out as a very viable candidate.

One thing you can do to help your application as a federal clerk is to apply to what some people might consider to be "out of the way" federal clerkships as opposed to the most popular ones. For example, instead of applying to clerkships in the 9th circuit in California, think about applying to clerkships in the 8th district, which covers Arkansas, Missouri, South Dakota, North Dakota, Minnesota, Iowa, and Nebraska. There can be literally hundreds of clerkships in certain states, and you might want to be open to location if you aren't number one in your class or graduating from the number one law school in the country.

By the way, that doesn't mean you shouldn't apply to the 2nd and the 9th circuits as well. And considering the fact that you are right there in the 9th circuit, of course you should apply there. I'm just saying that you need to cover as much territory as possible.

Incidentally, the website you want to be intimately familiar with is OSCAR (Online System for Clerkship Application and Review), located at https:// lawclerks.ao.uscourts.gov/index.php?_tab=home. Here is your one-stop site for registering, learning all about, and applying for clerkships. It's all here, and this is where you will learn everything you need to know about federal clerkships and appellate court staff hiring. Although you are only a first-year law student at this time, it is never too early to familiarize yourself with what you need to know. I recommend you going to this site and taking a look at it.

By the way, another career path—and an excellent way to go—is to think about starting out with a state clerkship or beginning your career at a law firm; after a couple of years in the state clerkship or two or three years as an associate in a litigation department, then apply for a federal clerkship. This is a very common and typical career path and another sensible way to approach your goal.

Whatever you decide, you really can become a federal clerk if you take this as a very serious goal and realize that the next two years of law school will make the difference as to whether or not you will achieve your goal. Let nothing deter you and focus on the brass ring—work as hard as you possibly can and get the best grades that you possibly can get. That's how you are going to do it. Let your professors know what you are aiming for, and in fact, network whenever possible, letting people know that this is your goal. Letters of reference are always important. I hope to hear back from you in two years telling us about the wonderful federal clerkship you have just been awarded! Best wishes!

Sincerely,
Ann M. Israel

Dear Readers:

Thank you to so many of you for sending in suggestions and ideas for Beyond Discouraged. In the weeks to come, I will reprint from time to time some of the more interesting e-mails that have been sent to this column. The following e-mail is from an individual who decided to take his/her despair and turn it around by reevaluating his/her goals and plans. I like the way s/he tells us that s/he informed his/her parents that s/he was moving back in with them "due to not having a job lined up." Good for you!

Beyond Discouraged wrote that all this wasn't supposed to be happening to him/her. Our friend from Newark decided that a pity party simply wasn't the way to go so instead just changed plans. The new job-hunting strategy obviously worked out, and even though it may not have been exactly what had been in the overall scheme of things initially, it seems that all's well that ends well for this individual.

So, here is just another suggestion from a fellow reader that might work for those of you who are trying to find a job following law school graduation. Best of luck!

Sincerely,
Ann M. Israel

City: Newark, NJ

Dear Ann,

I'm responding to Beyond Discouraged. My road to a midsized law firm was very nerve-racking, to say the least. I found out in February of my 3L year that I was not offered a position at the firm where I did my 2L summer and had been working during my 3L year. Of course, I was discouraged and upset in the days following this rejection. However, I decided I needed to reevaluate my goals and job-hunting strategy. This is how I turned it around (and granted, this was 2006):

1. I decided to switch from taking the MA bar to taking NY and NJ bars and to move back to the NYC area, where I'm from.

2. I informed my parents of having to move back in with them due to not having a job lined up.

3. I decided to pursue a clerkship to buy me a year of job hunting and at least one year of a salary. I called/searched online for the list of judges in the NJ courts who had not yet hired a law clerk—Trenton has the list. There were at least 50 judges still looking, and this was February 2006. I did a mail merge and sent out my resume to about 100 judges—superior, appellate, and supreme court levels.

4. I got my interviews during my final exam period and drove to NJ from Boston during finals to do interviews.

5. I got my job offer the day *after* my last final in May.

6. I actually continued to get calls for interviews into June from judges looking to hire a clerk.

7. In the fall of 2006, while waiting for bar results, I did another round of applications to the big and midsized firms in Newark, Roseland, Morristown, etc. I did not apply to NYC firms. I got many interviews based upon my clerkship, which I would never have gotten without it.

8. And here I am. My firm is actually hiring and interviewing all levels of entry-level and laterals. Beyond Discouraged may want to consider NJ, both for clerkships and firms. Job hunting as a 3L is much harder than as a judicial clerk. Tell him/her good luck. And keep trying.

[This column was written long before we learned that the law schools were definitely manipulating their statistics on employed attorneys. Just call me Pollyanna . . . read on.]

City: New York

Ann, Do you think second- and third-tier law schools attempt to attract students by failing to paint an accurate portrayal of the job prospects of those not in the top 15? My experience is that they do manipulate their job placement statistics. What are your thoughts?

Manipulated

Dear Manipulated:

Oh my, that is so Machiavellian. I hate to believe that the law schools out there are standing behind a curtain like some old Wizard of Oz, working together to manipulate statistics so that they might be able to fill their class ranks with unsuspecting students. How would it be possible for all of those law schools to fool around with their statistics, year after year, and graduates would never band together and stop the craziness?

There is no question that the schools want to portray the job prospects for their law school graduates as favorably as possible. But I really don't see how they can stretch them to a point where they are completely and utterly manipulated to total inaccuracy.

I do know that I hear from graduates over and over again that their law school's career services office has done absolutely nothing for them. But then, when I question these individuals who complain about the lack of help from the career services offices, I generally find that the expectations have been unreasonable.

The career services offices definitely want to help in whatever way they can to get as many graduates and alumni into the best jobs possible. The statistics are formed directly out of their office. However, it is not their job to get everyone hired. Again, it is their job to help in whatever way they can. Each individual must get out there and do whatever s/he can do as well.

Right now we are going through a hiring crisis the likes of which we have never seen in our lifetime. It is going to be very difficult for every single law school graduate to get the job of his/her dreams. The law school career services office at each school is going to be going crazy trying to save its job statistics so that the school will be able to attract new students for the upcoming years.

And so, if there is some manipulation going on with statistical numbers right now, I suppose I wouldn't be totally surprised. But let's face some facts: if you are going to choose a law school based solely on how many of their graduates were able to get jobs upon graduation, then you need to be doing your own due diligence before you sign the acceptance letter. All you have to do is go on the Internet and check out www.martindale.com to see how many graduates of a certain law school—and their class year—are working at any particular law firm. That's a really quick fact check that should take you about ten minutes at the most to find out if the statistics are correct.

Call the career services office and ask them where their graduates are being placed—find out if the graduates are going to law firms (and what kind of law firms they are working at) or if they are going to corporations or to government jobs. *Do your own due diligence.* If you are concerned that schools are manipulating figures just to get you to attend, don't rely on what they are telling you. Take it upon yourself to find out the truth! Best wishes!

Sincerely,
Ann M. Israel

I▮I

City: New York

I am a 2L (rising 3L) at a tier-2 regional law school. I did well as a 1L and just started my summer associateship at BigLaw NYC. I am a little concerned that almost everyone at the firm has better credentials than me (or, at least, went to better schools). Would it be worth it to me to sacrifice my full scholarship and attempt to transfer to Columbia or NYU for the completely useless third year of law school, just for the resume stamp? I am more than a little concerned that even though I am obviously qualified to summer at this firm, I don't really have the pedigree necessary to succeed here.

I am completely ignorant of the transfer process. Is it too late to even be thinking about this?

Best,
Concerned about Pedigree

Dear Concerned:

Although I am always the first one to recommend transferring to the higher-ranked law school, in your particular case I don't think you will reap the greatest benefits if you transfer at this point in your law school career, particularly in light of the fact that you will be sacrificing your full scholarship.

The reason I am saying this for your situation is due to the fact that when you transfer law schools after your second year, although you will be able to put down that you attended Columbia or NYU during your third year of law school, your JD will not be from one of those schools. Rather, it will be from the school where you spent your first and second years.

So yes, it will look very spiffy to show that you were able to transfer to a top-10 law school during your last year, but really, what are you ultimately accomplishing here? Let's look at the facts. Apparently you must be doing quite well at your tier-2 regional law school or I doubt that you would have been invited to be a 2L summer associate at a BigLaw New York firm. I don't see any reason to give up that full scholarship except to show that you were able to transfer to an Ivy League law school for your 3L year.

Some people might encourage you to transfer for the professors you will meet at Columbia and NYU as well as some of the contacts you will make with the students in your class. Granted, you might come in contact with some lifelong influential friends at Columbia or NYU.

And, the truth of the matter may very well be that many of the other associates at the firm have "better" credentials than you in terms of the ranking of their law school. However, you would not be at a BigLaw summer program unless your grades were high enough to put you at the top, or close to the top, of your class.

But take a look at the Martindale's of all of the major firms—and I have discussed this over and over again in many of my previous columns. All of the BigLaw firms—the major law firms of the world—have graduates from almost all the law schools in the four tiers. What you will find is that partners and associates from the lower-ranked law schools all have stellar transcripts. Generally they will have been in the top 5 percent of their graduating class, if not higher.

You said it yourself: you are obviously qualified to summer at this firm, and believe me, if the powers that be have decided that they want you to be associated with the firm, then your "pedigree" is just fine. You might be very surprised to learn that some of the most powerful rainmakers in some of the greatest firms come from the lesser law schools.

In the final analysis, when all is said and done, I still believe that you really do not need to give up that full scholarship and transfer to Columbia or NYU for your third year of law school to be ultimately successful at the BigLaw firm and beyond.

Don't put yourself down . . . you are to be congratulated for being the best that you can be! You have earned a full scholarship and you are clearly working very hard to get top grades, grades that have put you in the highest echelon of your class, allowing you to compete with those other law students from schools that you label "pedigreed." Good for you! Keep going and don't look back . . . you have a great future waiting for you, and don't ever let anyone tell you otherwise. Best wishes!

Sincerely,
Ann M. Israel

IIII

City: Nashville

I just finished my 2L year at a top-15 law school and will be spending the summer at a top law firm. I have substantial law school debt and am married with a child. I am considering applying for a federal judicial clerkship, but the economy has me worried. Should I get into BigLaw and start paying off my loans ASAP, or should I pursue the clerkship? My biggest fear is not being able to get a BigLaw job after clerking for a year if the economy tanks.

Nashville

Dear Nashville:

I have only good news for you!

It seems to me that no matter what you decide to do here, you are in a win-win situation. Your choices are such winners that I don't see how you can lose, even with a sinking economy.

You are finishing up your second year at a top-15 law school and will now be doing your 2L summer at one of the top law firms. Unless you really do something off the wall, or the firm decides to close its doors (I'm kidding—this is not going to happen!), you are probably going to receive a lovely offer of permanent employment to commence after you graduate from law school next year. So, there is goal one accomplished—you have a BigLaw firm job almost guaranteed, with the commensurate BigLaw salary that will help you to start paying off those loans.

But let's say that you do decide to apply for that federal judicial clerkship and lucky you, it comes through! Here's the good news: you can have your cake and eat it too in this particular case!! My guess is that your BigLaw firm that has offered you a job upon law school graduation will be more than happy to defer your start date to after you finish that federal judicial clerkship.

You might wonder why a firm would be so happy to hold your employment and defer your start date, but the answer is simple. Law firms are delighted to have federal clerks listed on their rolls—so prestigious!

Even if you decide not to return to the firm where you have spent your 2L summer, you will still be a viable candidate to many top BigLaw firms if you have a federal clerkship on your resume.

So, work hard during your 2L summer and be the best summer associate that you can possibly be so that you can be certain to get your offer of permanent employment from the BigLaw firm. Keep your grades up during your third year of law school, and then, when the time comes, if you do receive an offer for a federal clerkship, you will be able to accept this wonderful opportunity if you so choose, knowing full well that you are in a win-win situation. Best wishes!

Sincerely,
Ann M. Israel

∎

City: Chicago

I am a 2L preparing for on-campus interviews for summer associate positions, but all the big firms look alike. Do you have any suggestions on how I should focus my efforts?

Prepared

Dear Prepared:

What a great question! I have a feeling you are not alone in thinking that all the BigLaw firms look the same at this point in your career. I thought it best to go to an expert to find the answer to your question, so I went to Beth Silberstein, who is an attorney as well as someone who during her career has been in charge of recruiting attorneys for a number of BigLaw firms, including Milbank Tweed Hadley McCloy LLP and Paul, Hastings, Janofsky &

Walker LLP, two AmLaw 100 global law firms. Ms. Silberstein was exceptionally generous with her knowledge and experience, and I think you will find her advice to be very helpful:

> This is a common problem since all "big firms" seem to say the same things in their literature, on their website, and in their NALP (The National Association for Law Placement*) forms. Starting with the basics, assuming you have already decided to go to a big firm for the summer, where do you want to live when you graduate? What area of law are you the most interested in? Then look to see which firms really have a "presence" in the marketplace both in geography and practice area. For instance, many New York firms have a litigation department, but who are really the players with the best partners and matters (check the American Lawyer "A List" for that information)? With a narrower list, find out from your career services office who was a summer associate at each firm and talk to them. 3Ls are usually more than happy to tell you about their experience last summer. You can also refer to the American Lawyer's Summer Associate surveys for the rankings of almost all the summer programs.
>
> Check also the Vault synopsis of each firm. For a small investment, you can become a Gold Member and find out more in-depth information on each firm or again, check with your career services office, which probably has a hard copy of the Vault book. Then it would be a good idea to go back to the NALP forms and websites to look at the details as to each firm's training programs including whether or not the firm has a first-year training retreat, pays for CLEs outside the office, has a technology allowance, and other things that will contribute to your success as an entry level associate. Since almost all summer associates tend to go to the firm where they spend their second summer, you should make sure that this is the place you really want to end up.

I hope you will find this advice helpful as you focus on the BigLaw firms and try to differentiate one from the others. Law firms are just like people; each one has a distinct and different personality and philosophy. If you follow Ms. Silberstein's advice, the differences in each firm will slowly begin to take shape and you will narrow your list down to the firms that have a closer fit with your career goals. Best wishes!

Sincerely,
Ann M. Israel

*If for some reason your career services office does not have the NALP Directory of Legal Employers, you can purchase it by going to http://www.nalp.org.

The NALP website is located at http://www.nalp.org.

I

City: Chicago

Dear Ann:

I am a rising 3L at one of the top six law schools in the country, and I had few summer associate offers as compared to the rest of my classmates. The problem was that I bombed my first semester of law school and finished my 1L year with three Cs on my transcript. My grades improved a good bit after that. In my 2L year I got one A and all the rest Bs. How marketable would you say I am if I decide to interview again after this summer? Do you think firms will overlook my three Cs my 1L year? Or will these bad grades at the beginning haunt me forever?

Bombed

Dear Bombed:

This is an issue I have discussed in many previous columns, but clearly I am not coming through loud and clear. Your law school transcript is something that stays with you throughout your legal career. It is very true that some of our most prominent attorneys did not attend the top law schools, but you can be sure that their grades were stellar.

It is not surprising you did not have the amount of offers for your 2L summer that the rest of your classmates had, even though you are attending one of the top law schools. Certainly the economy had something to do with it, but more than anything else, the fact that you had three Cs on your transcript was the killer.

Indeed, your grades did improve in your 2L year, but you need to be realistic about what that improvement means to hiring partners. One A and all the rest Bs will not endear you to the hiring committee. This is a very painful column for me to write, but you need to be aware of the reality of your situation based on the job market today and your transcript.

Your marketability is not high if you are planning to look for interviews with the BigLaw firms. I doubt that you will be able to find any firms that are going to be interested in setting up any meetings with you at all. I am afraid that is the harsh reality of the situation.

Perhaps—and even this presents a big question mark—five years ago, when the economy and therefore the job market was quite different, you would have been able to wrangle some interviews simply because of where you were attending law school, but that just doesn't work these days. As you must be well aware, many recent law school graduates have been deferred from their start dates, and because of this, law firms aren't hiring as many first-year associates as they used to do. With your low grade point average, I suspect you are not going to be at the top of lists of people the firms want to interview when there are so many viable candidates out there. Again, this is the harsh reality right now.

So, now what do you do? The first place you need to go is your law school's career services office and camp out at their door. What are they doing for you? How are they going to help you find your first job upon graduation? Trust me, they want to help their graduates with placement.

However, you did tell us that you had a few summer associate offers—what happened there? Did you actually go to work at one of those firms? Did you receive an offer of permanent employment after the summer? If so, I strongly urge you to accept that offer and don't look back. Whether or not you loved that firm, I submit to you that you have no other choice. Pick up the phone and accept that offer immediately and let that firm know you are thrilled to be coming to work for them.

If this is not a viable option (meaning you did not have an offer from a 2L summer employer), go ahead and try to set up other interviews, but be sure to cover all types of firms and opportunities, not just BigLaw firms, or else you are liable to be sorely disappointed. Best wishes!

Sincerely,
Ann M. Israel

CHAPTER 3

Do Law School Grades
Really Matter?

This is a frequent question, and no matter how the question is phrased, my answer is always the same. If you are hoping to be a part of the BigLaw group of firms, yes, yes, yes, your law school grades really matter. Your transcript will be a part of your law firm life for the rest of your career. As you will read, even a partner with millions of dollars of verified portable business is not exempt from the scrutiny of his/her transcript. Of course, reality tells us that there will always be 50 percent of any law school class in the bottom half. But that does not mean all is lost. You just need to adjust your dreams and goals and understand that you most likely will not start out your career at a BigLaw firm. Over the years I have told and retold the story of when I was representing a small group of two very experienced and seasoned partners in their 50s. They were bringing with them around $10M worth of portable business. Back in the early 1990s, this was a very impressive and large book of business for two partners to be generating. It seemed as if an offer was about to be made when the potential employer asked for their law school transcripts. After all their years of practicing, and with such an established and impressive book of business, their law school transcript was still carrying a tremendous amount of weight.

I remember making the phone call during which I had to ask these two rain-makers for their law school transcripts. I held the receiver away from my ear as the astonishment and anger erupted through the phone. Understandably, they could not believe they would have to produce transcripts from more than 25 years earlier. Fortunately for all concerned, they really wanted to be partners at this firm and so, begrudgingly, they produced their transcripts and, once their grades were scrutinized, they were at long last invited into the partnership.

I have noticed a recurring theme of a sick or dying parent being the cause of poor grades in law school. Naturally, everyone is sorry to hear of a loss, but that doesn't excuse those poor grades. Either take a year off from school to care for the sick family member or be determined to get high grades if you decide to stay in school. Excuses just don't cut it in the world of BigLaw. Say what you will about this, but it is the nature of the beast.

One thing I would suggest is if you do get a C in one of your classes, don't accept it blindly if you feel it was unwarranted. Go speak to your guidance counselor, or even better, the professor, and find out the reason for the grade and if there is any possibility of an appeal. Just remember to treat law school as a precursor to your career as an attorney and be diligent in your studies. Don't cut class or study groups. If you don't understand something, get help until you do understand it. As I always say, be the best you can be during law school because your transcript will have a lot to do with determining your future.

Sincerely,
Ann M. Israel

I⬛I

City: New York

I graduated from a top Ivy League law school, but I am ranked in the bottom 20 of my class. What are my prospects of getting hired by the likes of Cravath, Sullivan & Cromwell and Davis Polk?

Thanks,
Marginal

Dear Marginal:

The bottom 20 of your class puts you in a very difficult position, even though you graduated from a top Ivy League law school. I suspect that your chances for a job with Cravath, Sullivan & Cromwell or Davis Polk are probably not great.

The main reason for this is due to something that I have discussed in many previous columns. If you were in the bottom 20 of your class, it would stand to reason that your transcript is loaded with Cs and perhaps even a D grade from one or two of your classes.

I can tell you right now that the Davis Polks (and Cravaths and Sullivan & Cromwells) of the world are far more concerned with your transcript than with your law school.

Basically, here is how the major law firms look at potential candidates: if a candidate has attended one of the top Ivy League law schools, s/he will be granted an interview with a lower GPA than someone who attended a second-, third-, or even fourth-tier law school. However, there is a cutoff point, even for an Ivy Leaguer. The bottom 20 is just not going to make it for the major law firms.

If you look at the Martindale Hubbell listings for the major law firms, you will see partners and associates from just about every accredited law school out there. However, the lower the ranking of the school, the better the transcript of the attorney.

Nevertheless, this is just a rule of thumb for interviewing potential candidates. For the most part, even the Ivy Leaguers at the BigLaw firms have outstanding transcripts from law school.

I am afraid that you are going to have just about an impossible time getting hired by the firms you have named unless you have some special skill, a major client to bring with you, or some other way to get into the firm—and that still isn't going to guarantee you a spot.

I don't think anyone should abandon their dreams, but in your particular situation you need to be more realistic about the types of firms that are going to be interested in hiring you. I would suggest that you ask for advice from your law school career services office as to which major law firms are more interested in where you went to law school than in your law school transcript. Those firms are out there, and your Ivy League law school degree should be very attractive to certain firms. Best of luck.

Sincerely,
Ann M. Israel

City: New York

I graduated four years ago in the lower half of my class from a third-tier law school. While I have excelled in the jobs I have had since law school, I am only able to find employment at one- to two-attorney firms that pay about one-third of the salary of a first year at a large firm and do not offer any benefits. Am I stuck in "small" law forever? How can I find a better-paying employer? Are there any recruiters that would work with me? I would really appreciate any advice you may have to offer. Thank you.

Stuck

Dear Stuck,

First, the bad news. No, I do not believe that there are any recruiters out there that would work with you. It's not that we wouldn't like to work with you, especially since you are now a midlevel attorney and describe yourself as someone who excels at the practice of law.

The problem stems from the fact that recruiters work with a very specific group of clients who have very specific guidelines that they give to the recruiters regarding their searches. Why do we work with these specific groups of clients? Because they are the types of firms and corporations that are able to pay fees for the people they hire. It would be wonderful if we could work with every firm and company out there, but that is not a reality. A small firm such as the one where you are currently working more than likely cannot afford or is not budgeted—or is not willing—to pay a recruiter's fee.

So, when we work with the firms that are willing to pay the required fee, these clients spell out exactly what they want. They might very well hire someone from a third-tier school when they are hiring on their own, but when a fee is attached to the candidate's resume, the firm is looking for very specific credentials and experience. Recruiters work in a very competitive world and must satisfy the client's needs or else they will be replaced by another search firm right away. The client sets the tone; the recruiter serves the client.

Now the good news. There are firms out there that will be interested in your experience rather than your law school transcript. They will be happy to hear about your positive experiences as a lawyer and will not even ask to see your transcript. Some of these firms are quite large and have extensive and well-respected practices. The pay can be quite attractive, the benefit packages are strong, and these firms can offer a stable and secure future.

The issue here is how you find these firms, and that is something you are going to have to research yourself. As I always recommend, you need to get out there and network and meet everyone you possibly can. Attend bar association events, lectures, and meetings and contact your career services office—do anything connected with the legal community.

It would be great if you could fall back on a recruiter to find these firms for you and market your background, and then all you had to do was show up for an interview. But this is not going to happen. The reality is you went to a third-tier school, ended up in the bottom half of your class, and now work for a very small law firm. This is not the typical profile of a recruiter's candidate. So, don't dwell on the past—that's history and you need to move on. Focus on the great achievements you have had in your practice and be ready to discuss them in interviews. There are firms out there that will be happy to meet with you—you just need to find them on your own. Best of luck!

Sincerely,
Ann M. Israel

▮▮▮

City: Dreary Seattle

Can you sanitize poor JD grades with an LLM?

Dreary

Dear Dreary:

In a word, no. Sorry about that. Unfortunately, you can't run from or hide those grades.

As I have discussed in many, many past columns, your law school transcript will be a part of your history for the rest of your career. Trying to improve the appearance of your transcript with a high grade point from an LLM degree just doesn't work.

I have also discussed the general reasons for earning—or not earning—an LLM in a number of my past columns. In my experience over the years, I have found that unless you are a tax attorney or perhaps an international lawyer, an LLM does not enhance the way any employer will view your JD academics, class ranking, or school.

I've noticed lately that a number of attorneys from foreign law schools come to my firm with an LLM earned from one of the prestigious law schools here in the United States. I think in these instances it helps to show that they are able to understand the law in this country. However, it does not erase where they went to law school prior to arriving here, nor does the LLM transcript replace the grades earned at the law school from their home country.

An LLM is not a useless degree by any stretch of the imagination. It is an internationally recognized degree, one that some people compare to an MBA in the business world. It generally is earned in a relatively short period of time (one year), compared to the three years that it takes to earn a JD.

All of this I'm sure is quite fascinating to you, but the bottom line is that if you are thinking about spending more money and another year of your life earning an additional law degree simply because you think it will "sanitize" your law school transcript, perhaps you should rethink this idea. Best wishes!

Sincerely,
Ann M. Israel

∎

City: New York

Dear Ann,

I am a 2L at a "top 6" school and I have no offers. My transcript is all Bs and my interview skills are rather middling, though not exceedingly poor. Obviously, my on-campus interviews were a waste and I honestly don't know what to do now. I'd like to work for a firm that pays the market-rate salary, but I think my chances are quite low. What do you think?

Sincerely,
Considering Dropping Out

Dear Considering:

Your future for working at a BigLaw firm seems bleak, doesn't it? Well, I suppose I would have to agree with you on that, at least for the beginning of your career. But buck up, buddy—it doesn't mean your life as a lawyer is over, nor should you be dropping out of law school at this point.

First, let's look at the sunny side of the street for just a moment. You are at a top-6 school. This is great and something that will stay on your transcript forever. Obviously you didn't have the best first year of law school, but then again, you didn't have the worst year, either, because thankfully, you don't have any Cs or Ds on your transcript (we're still on that sunny side of the street). You're still early enough into your second year where you can change the next two years of your transcript if you really are determined to do so and produce some B+ and A grades. But that is really going to be up to you.

It's going to mean that you will need to be focused on and dedicated to your studies, and if you find that you need extra help, you are going to find a way to get it. You are going to speak with your professors and guidance counselors and any other person available to ensure your grades will go up. Nothing is going to matter right now except your studies.

Now we have to cross over to that darker side of the street. I am concerned that you have determined that all of your on-campus interviews were a waste due to a combination of a lackluster transcript *and* middling interviewing skills. As you are at a top-6 law school, I suspect that just about every major law firm was interested in setting up 2L interviews. Stellar interviewing skills might—and I am going to emphasize the word *might*—have produced at least one or two callbacks for you, which might then have brought about an offer for a 2L summer associate job.

Knowing that you don't have the greatest interviewing skills should have propelled you to get help prior to your interviews . . . why didn't you? Probably for the same reason that you didn't get any extra assistance during your first year with your studies and ended up with a transcript filled with all Bs.

How many columns do I have to write indicating that this is a tough job market? Just attending one of the top law schools doesn't give you an automatic job offer the way it might have done back in the go-go years. It's a different world out there now. Don't be afraid to ask for help and assistance with your studies or with something as critical as learning how to interview for a job. No one expects you to know how to do this. Your law school career services office is there for a purpose—use it.

Having said all of this, I still don't think you should throw in the towel. I think it is very important that you find some kind of job during your

2L summer—don't just hang out getting a tan, whatever you do. It doesn't appear that you will be working for the big-salary jobs, but then again, you never know. Sometimes people turn down offers or leave town or continue to apply for 2L jobs at other firms where you have not been rejected (I would speak with your career services office about how you might be able to do this) or whatever.

Additionally, there are many other firms out there that didn't interview at your law school and might be interested in someone with your pedigree. Perhaps you will be able to raise your grades, and by the end of the school year you will have a transcript that has quite a different look to it. You might have to take a job with a firm that isn't paying quite the salary you had hoped for, but at least you will have a job with a good firm. And that will make quite a difference when you start interviewing on-campus at the start of your third year for that all-important first-year associate position that begins after law school graduation.

Bottom line: Don't quit; work harder. You can do it—best of luck!

Sincerely,
Ann M. Israel

❚❚❚

City: New York

Dear Ms. Israel:

I read your weekly column in the *NY Law Journal,* but unfortunately I have not been able to benefit that much from your advice since most of your questions seem to come from people who graduated with honors and/or from a top-10 law school. That being the case, I am asking your advice for recent graduates like me who did not exactly have the best grades in law school needed to get even any kind of legal job these days, but who have a variety of experience. Thank you.

Varied

Dear Varied:

Ah, if only all those questions came from graduates with honors or JDs out of top-10 law schools. . . . First of all, that would be a headhunter's dream, and secondly, it certainly would make answering the questions so much easier since the questioner could just be directed to another BigLaw firm. Ho hum, and I suppose if that were the case, then this column wouldn't have seen 17 years of questions and still counting.

No, the questions that this column has received over the years have come from a broad range of people. Many have been in the same situation that you are finding yourself in at this time: not exactly the best grades in law school, and yet many of them have figured out how to enjoy a fulfilling and satisfying legal career. The main difference is that you now have one other issue to deal with that others did not have to face and that is the current state of hiring—it is much more competitive and difficult than it has ever been before.

You did not tell us where you went to law school. Did you receive your JD from a top first- or second-tier law school, or is your school ranked in the third or fourth tier? That, of course, makes a difference when coupled with those "not exactly the best grades."

The reason I ask this question is because many law firms use the law school ranking as a tool for how they will look at your GPA. In other words, if you have graduated from one of the top-10 law schools, then many of the law firms will allow you to have a bit of a lower GPA than if your JD is from a third- or fourth-tier school. It's a benchmark that has become an industry standard in lieu of experience.

However, even if you went to a law school that is ranked number one or two, you are still going to have problems getting interviews if you have Cs on your transcript.

My question to you is about the variety of experience that you claim to have. As you are a recent graduate, I don't know how you have any experience as an attorney, so obviously you are referring to other life or work experience. Although this is always valuable experience, it is unfortunate that when interviewing with law firms, this nonattorney experience really doesn't seem to help. As I have written over and over again throughout the years, for a recent law school graduate, the law school transcript is what the interviewers look at first and foremost.

As far as I can tell, the only time that previous work experience has an impact is when a recent law school grad has a technical degree, has worked in an applicable area, and is planning on becoming a patent attorney. Other than that, and as harsh as this sounds, other work experience may be very interesting in an interview but I have yet to see it overcome a transcript loaded with Cs.

So, what's the solution? Keep sending out your resume, continue to network, bug your career services office at your law school (their job supposedly is to help you find a job), speak to everyone you know, follow up on everything, answer every ad, do everything possible.

At this point, there is nothing you can do to change your transcript. It is what it is. From this time on, be the best you can be at interviewing, even if it means you need to find a professional to help you with your interviewing skills. Review your resume and your cover letter. And continue to have the right kind of attitude that allows you to interview for any kind of legal job. Best wishes!

Sincerely,
Ann M. Israel

City: Washington, DC

When advertisements for legal jobs state they want somebody from a top-10 law school, just how serious are they? What if you had mediocre to good grades at a top-20 law school? What if you had excellent grades from a top-40 school? What if you were summa cum laude from a second-tier school? Do you really have to be from a top-10 school in order to land the position? They're not trying to fill a vacancy on the Supreme Court, are they?

Top

Dear Top:

When you see an ad that states that the needed qualifications include a JD from a top-10 law school, this generally is a code for the type of candidate the employer is seeking.

Will the eventual hired employee absolutely have graduated from a top-10 law school? Perhaps not, but that certainly would be the preferred candidate.

Will this employer look at someone from a lower-tier school? My guess would be that they will not unless that person has graduated as the number one to five person in his/her class and surrounded by all types of honors, obviously including that summa cum laude you mentioned. Certainly if you are that person from a top-40 school, you are going to have a number of employers interested in meeting with you.

You asked if the employer would look at someone with mediocre to good grades at a top-20 law school . . . in this job market, I can tell you that is unlikely. Mediocre to good grades probably are going to include a C (or two or more) somewhere on your transcript, and that is going to hurt your chances dramatically.

As I have discussed a number of times before, the BigLaw firms have certain grade point levels for considering candidates from certain schools. In other words, if you have received your JD from one of the top five law schools, there is going to be some leeway in considering your application if your transcript has a few Bs on it (Cs still need not apply). It also helps if you are lateralling over from another prestigious firm (or from a major clerkship—here's where that Supreme Court comes into play).

As your law school ranking diminishes, your law school transcript must get stronger to be viable for these firms. So, the bar for a top-10 graduate is lower than it might be for someone from a top-20 school.

Do the firms prefer to hire someone with a pedigree from the top 10? Yes, there is no question that they would like their Martindale listing to read only top-10 schools. But given the choice to have all law review, Order of the Coif associates—and all other things being equal—I can assure you that any firm will hire someone with that background from a lower-tier law school as opposed to someone from a top-5 school with middling grades. Take a look at the Martindale listings of the BigLaw firms and you will see this to be true.

I have always advised that you should attend the highest-rated law school to which you are accepted. However, even more important than where you go to law school is how you do there. Your law school transcript will follow you for the rest of your legal career. Every time you think about making a job change, your new potential employer will ask to see your transcript.

I just spoke with a soon-to-be graduating law student at a top-20 (by *U.S. News*, top 30 by the Gourman Report) law school. She had a rotten first year and was not offered a 2L summer associate position at a law firm. She worked for a corporation but was not given an offer of permanent employment. I heard every excuse in the world from her about how she never really wanted to work for a law firm, that she really does want to work for a corporation, and that during her last two years of law school she really did bring up her grades.

The truth of the matter is that she partied hearty her first year and realized too late that her grades were going to hurt her in the future. She's graduating from a decent law school. Had she worked hard that first year and delivered top grades, she would be able to apply to firms that advertise for top-10 law school graduates, even though that is not where she received her JD. Unfortunately for her, that first year on her transcript is going to show up wherever she does apply throughout her career, and she will always have to answer for it.

Those good grades mitigate to some extent your law school ranking when you are ready to lateral to a new firm. If you have those grades, don't worry about those ads that scream out "top-10 law school." You've got nothing to lose by applying and everything to gain. You should be very proud of your accomplishments. Best wishes!

Sincerely,
Ann M. Israel

CHAPTER 4

Writing a Resume

A strong resume is your best shot at getting an interview. It really is your first impression, and, as I always advise, first impressions are critical. There are many rules you must follow in order to achieve the necessary strength in the resume. The first rule you must remember is to think of a resume as a key to unlock a door. Use it to gain entrance to the people you want to meet, but use it to just unlock the door, don't go all the way through it. In other words, don't give everything away on a resume so that the prospective employer feels that s/he knows everything about you and thus no longer needs to meet with you.

And what about a cover letter? Studies have shown that employers don't read cover letters. I can attest to the veracity of that study. I stopped reading cover letters years ago. Most of them are boilerplate copies of a sample cover letter, such as "I am writing to you today because I understand you are a leader in your field." Really? Where did you hear that? I think that cover letter says the same exact words that I have seen on hundreds and hundreds of cover letters. If you are savvy, you will write a short cover letter introducing yourself, explaining the reason for sending in your resume, and including your contact information. Let the potential employer get to your resume as soon as possible and don't bore him/her with a long cover letter extolling his/her virtues.

From a future employer's point of view, basically what they want to see on your resume is where you went to law school and undergraduate school, if you received honors, and your work history. Keeping this in mind will help you to write your resume, showing your education first and then your chronological work history, starting with your most recent or current employer. Don't omit or misrepresent anything, because if you do, you will eventually be found out and the consequences may very well be dire. If you feel it is necessary to put down your interests (do you really believe the person reading the resume cares if you like skateboarding or that you can perform magic tricks?), keep it to one very short sentence at the bottom of the resume. And at the very end of the resume—and the best resumes are only one page—the last line should read: "References upon request." Never list your references by name unless you want them called right away—a big mistake! Lastly, check and then recheck again for typos. That is a job killer. Check again! Use spell check! Check again!

▌▒▌

City: New York

I did not receive a summer offer from a law firm but have practiced at a different law firm after graduation. Do I have to include the law firm I summered at on my resume?

Summered

Dear Summered:

No, you do not have to include the law firm you summered at on your resume.

You also don't have to list your law school if you didn't attend a top-10 law school, and while you're at it, why bother listing your undergraduate school if you didn't attend some fancy Ivy League school?

The only problem with not listing things on your resume is that you are going to have to deal with them one way or another before you get hired, so you might as well be honest about everything from the beginning.

For example, if you are working with a recruiter, one of the first questions you will be asked is, "Where did you spend your 2L summer?" if the employer is not listed on your resume. And whether or not it is noted on your resume, the next logical question will be, "Did you receive an offer of permanent employment at the end of the summer?" The question will definitely be asked because you practiced at a different law firm after graduation and people who receive an offer but go to different firms always make a notation indicating that they did receive an offer; that notation will be absent on your resume should your 2L employer be listed.

Let's say you are not working with a recruiter but instead are representing yourself, and you are now interviewing with a partner at a law firm. Don't you think s/he is going to wonder what you did during your 2L summer? How do you think it looks to him/her when you are asked if you worked during your second summer and you answer yes but you decided not to put it on your resume because you didn't receive an offer of employment? I don't think that is going to be a point in your favor.

Now let's take this to the worst-case scenario, and that would be if no one asked what you did that summer. Are they assuming that you didn't summer anywhere? Were you a total deadbeat during your summers? Or such a loser that no firm wanted to hire you? Or do they know the truth and were they just waiting to see if you were going to confess during the interview?

If you have read my columns over the years, then you know I always urge you to be completely forthright and honest about everything on your resume and in your interviews. If you have gone to two law schools, make sure you list them both, indicating which school awarded your JD. If you haven't received an offer of permanent employment from your 2L employer, list that employer nevertheless. Trust me, these things will come out no matter what, and if you haven't been candid about them to begin with, it will look as if you were hiding something (which you were).

Now, obviously you need to be able to explain why you didn't get an offer. My advice, as always, is to be brief and never be defensive. It's history, and you have been gainfully employed ever since and hopefully with great references. Whatever happened to you back then is now, with any luck, a great lesson learned, never to be repeated.

So, get back on your computer, add your 2L summer employer to your resume, prepare your answer to the inevitable question as to why you didn't get an offer at the end of that summer, and hold your head up high. Best wishes!

Sincerely,
Ann M. Israel

City: Washington, DC

I can't find an attorney job, *any* attorney job, even after over a year of try-ing. I live in the Washington, DC, area, got better-than-average grades in law school, at a worse-than-average law school (if you believe the rank-ings) half a country away. Every week or so, I see and apply for a position advertised for which I feel qualified, but I rarely hear anything back from the employer. My resume was professionally prepared, and during law school I attended mock interviews and was told I present myself fairly well (although I have only had three or four interviews in the past year). Starting my own practice is out of the question—I am married and have children, and cannot go without a paycheck for any appreciable amount of time (I am currently working as a nonattorney). And yes, I have spoken to a few prominent lawyers (attempting to network) asking if they knew anyone, asking for advice, anything. They have been sympathetic but not helpful. At this rate, it could be *years* before I get an attorney job. HELP!!

Networked

Dear Networked:

I have read your question over and over and over again and I can't find any way to answer except in the following manner, and I am afraid it is not going to be what you wanted to hear.

First of all, take that professionally prepared resume, rip it up, and start all over again. Did it ever occur to you that the professionally prepared resumes all look exactly the same? I don't understand why people go to those resume houses and believe that their resumes have been tailored to them individually. It is actually insulting to me when I receive e-mails from potential candidates I have never heard from before telling me that we had spoken months earlier and now they have updated their resume and want to make sure I have the newest version. Then I get to the resume and they are all worded in the exact same format. The insult is compounded.

So, that is step #1. Individualize your resume. Rework it so that it is writ-ten by you.

Next, I am not quite certain how it is that you feel qualified for the posi-tions advertised. Based on the little you have told us about yourself and your background, it would seem that you have never practiced law. The only legal job you are actually qualified for would be as a first-year attorney. Of course, that doesn't excuse any employer for not getting back to you, but I suspect that with the job market the way it is these days, employers must receive literally hundreds—maybe even thousands—of responses to an ad each week, and it just doesn't make economic sense to take the time to reply to every resume that comes in. I do think that with an individually prepared resume that you have done yourself, and one that is geared to the particular job to which you are responding, you might have a slightly better chance of hearing back from the employer than with a resume that is the same format as everybody else's.

The other problem you face in responding to the ads is that you have only better-than-average grades at a worse-than-average-ranked school (the employers do believe in the rankings, whether or not you do), which probably means a third- or fourth-tier law school. This puts you in a very difficult position right now as you are competing with the recent law school grads who don't have jobs and are graduating from better schools with better grades. And, after a full year in which you have been applying for jobs, and as you continue to do so, you now must add the recent grads to the pool of competition.

I can understand why you don't want to hang out your own shingle at this time, particularly without any practice experience. But with all the doom and gloom that I am preaching right now, there is some sunshine in what I have to say. You do have a job. And that's a lot more than what so many of those other job applicants have right now, even though, as you have told us, you are working as a nonattorney and what you really want is to practice law.

My advice to you is as follows: Continue to network. You are doing the right thing even though nothing has panned out from that so far. But you really haven't done much of it, and so I encourage you to step up your efforts. Don't just speak to a few prominent attorneys—speak to everyone about your situation, go to local bar events, pester your law school's career services office, and continue to respond to ads, but this time tailor your resume as I have recommended. Lastly, look for jobs that are appropriate for a first-year associate without specific and previous legal experience. Perhaps your current work experience might be pertinent, but since I don't know what you are doing, I can't advise you on how to use your current work experience on your resume.

In any event, thank goodness you have a paycheck coming in right now. Don't give up your day job, but don't give up looking for the legal job. You are right: it could take a long time, but then again, you never know. Best wishes!

Sincerely,
Ann M. Israel

CHAPTER 5

Looking for a New Job

One of life's greatest stressors is looking for a new job. I am incredibly sympathetic to anyone who is out there on the job market, no matter for what reason. It isn't easy to put yourself out there and then accept the rejection from potential employers when you are hoping to get a job offer from them. There are lots of ways to cope with the stress of job searching, but the best piece of advice I can offer—and this is how I have been able to continue in my search business that is full of no-interest and no-offer-extended responses—is to believe that these rejections happened for a reason. Perhaps we will never know what the reason is, but usually it seems that these rejections happen because something better is just around the corner. Time and time again, this has proven to be true.

Looking for a new opportunity can be exhausting, disappointing, exhilarating, fun, depressing, interesting, boring, and a big ego boost. All of this rolled up into one series of interviews! But once you make the commitment to go on a job search, you must remember that you are now focused on getting out of your current firm, so in a sense, you are mentally unemployed there. You need to continue to keep up your practice with your current employer—with a continued great attitude—because your references from this employer will be critical. But you must also find the time to go on the interviews without feeling the pressure of getting back to the office. Nothing is more of an interview killer than when a candidate looks at his/her Blackberry or allows his/her phone to ring during the meeting or says after 20 minutes, "I need to end this now as I have to get back to the office." Leave your phone in your overcoat's pocket—do not bring it into a meeting with you. During an interview, you should be thinking about nothing else than the firm where you are interviewing. Don't even think about scheduling an interview when you only have a small window of time to meet. A job search is a job in and of itself, and you must be prepared to commit yourself to all that is required to find that new—and better—opportunity!

* * *

City: New York

I am a fifth-year associate at a large NYC law firm. I graduated second in my class from a less-than-top-tier NYC law school. I clerked for two years with a federal district judge in a southern/midwestern state. I have received numerous calls from headhunters. I am interested in white collar practice—an area in which my firm does very little work. I am generally happy at my firm, but I do not really know my chances of making partner. My question: How do I know when it is time to make a move? Everyone I talk to tells me that now is that time to make a move; however, having been at my firm for just over two years, I'm not sure whether I should be looking at this point. Any insight would be useful.

Thanks.
Everyone's Talking

Dear Everyone's Talking:

If absolutely everyone you speak with is telling you that now is the time to make a move, maybe you should start listening. But before you jump, let's take a look at what you are telling everyone.

The first thing that I really focused in on was the fact that you expressed an interest in a white-collar practice, but clearly there is not much of a chance for you to get any work in this area at the firm you are currently associated with. Next, I noted that you are "generally happy" but unclear as to your partnership track. I then wondered about your job history. You explained that you had a federal clerkship for two years and that you have been with your current firm for two-plus years now. Your academic credentials are stellar. Graduating number two from your law school class is a great accomplishment, and so, of course, you are receiving numerous calls from headhunters.

As a fifth-year associate, generally this is a prime time to make a lateral move, and that is probably why everyone you are speaking with is telling you to make a move now. This is going to be a critical move for you since it will be your third job. This employer is one where you are going to have to stay put for quite a while. This is the move where down the road—hopefully—you are going to make partner or else move on . . . an "up or out" opportunity.

If you decide to stick around your current firm for the next few years, you are going to end up being too senior to be marketed as a lateral associate to other law firms. Fifth- and sixth-year associates are really the most viable candidates, and I believe fifth-years are really the most desirable—once again, hence the reason you are getting so many phone calls from recruiters.

My suggestion to you is to figure out one or two of the recruiters that you have developed a phone relationship with over the past two years, or perhaps if you were placed at your current firm by a recruiter, reach out to him/her and ask to get together for an informational meeting. Express your interest in moving to another firm with a strong partnership at this time and perhaps also the opportunity to work in the white-collar practice area. As a fifth-year associate without any experience in this practice area, that might be a long shot, but it is always worth exploring, particularly with your excellent academic transcript.

I do think this is a good time for you to be exploring new opportunities but, as always, I caution you to do your due diligence and think long and hard before accepting an offer. Make sure that any offer you are considering is for a firm where you can see yourself for many years to come. This will be—without question—the most important move of your career. Best wishes!

Sincerely,
Ann M. Israel

City: [Omitted], CA

Hi, Ann:

I moved firms and across the country about seven months ago. I was paid a signing bonus (less than a month's pay), a recruiter was involved in the move, relocation expenses were reimbursed, and I was given three weeks' paid leave to take the bar in CA. I love the people at the new firm, but I have decided to shift practice areas from transactional to litigation. Given these circumstances, how long am I obligated to stay at the firm in good conscience before I can leave for a litigation-oriented firm? The standard one year, or longer? I have friends at litigation firms that would like me to start yesterday, but I'm guilt ridden. Also, in another vein, I'd like to ask if firms are more likely to hire a good candidate who just writes in with a resume instead of using a recruiter, because they will not have to pay the fee. Should I tier my job search, i.e., start out with a writing campaign, and then hire a recruiter to target firms that have not responded to my mailings? Or is this a big waste of time and I should just hire a recruiter off the bat? I had a great experience working with recruiters last time, but I don't like the guilt of knowing the firm has shelled out a lot of money to get you here.

Thanks for any advice you can offer.
Recruited

Dear Recruited:

I really am at a loss for words. I'm a recruiter . . . how do you want me to answer this question? Don't use a recruiter? Wouldn't that be a crazy thing for me to say?

Have I ever had a client say, "This is a lot of money we are paying for this candidate; we wish we could have found this person on our own"? Yes, over the years I have heard this—but not very often. More often what I do hear is how thankful the client is for the work we have done. It isn't uncommon for the client to take us out to lunch or send us a bottle of champagne after the placement has been finalized. They may be paying a fee for the candidate they have hired through us, but in the end, this individual is being hired in the hope that s/he is going to make a lot of money for them. It isn't unusual to expect the new hire to earn back the fee many times over within the first month of employment.

There are times when using a recruiter is the best way to go and there are times when using a recruiter is going to hurt you rather than help you. I have discussed in numerous previous columns the profile of the typical candidate that can be best served by a legal recruiter. I have also received e-mails asking me why someone with good credentials and currently employed at a top firm needs a recruiter. All they have to do is mail out their resume and they will have interviews and offers. Indeed, this may very well be true.

However, if you pick the right recruiter (an entire column in and of itself), you are getting far more than someone who is just mailing out your resume to scores of firms. A skilled and experienced headhunter will take the time to interview you and find out not only what you are looking for but also what you are all about. S/he knows the firms and corporations out there and has the ability to match you up with ones that will meet your practice needs as well as your individual personality needs. You will learn all about each firm before your background is ever discussed or resume is ever sent out to the hiring partner.

Before you go on an interview, you will go over interviewing techniques as well as learning all about the individuals you will meet on each interview. After the interview, not only will you be debriefed but you will learn what each interviewer thought about you. If this firm seems to fit the bill of what you are seeking, your level of interest will immediately be relayed to the firm. Conversely, if you are not interested, you will not have to withdraw your candidacy, as your headhunter will take care of these uncomfortable matters for you. If you are rejected from the firm, your recruiter is there to help you take the blow. If the firm is interested in you, the recruiter will work with your schedule to set up advanced interviews.

When an offer is about to be extended, your headhunter will field it for you and help to negotiate the terms. If there are multiple offers, the recruiter will help to hold on to all of the offers for you and arrange post-offer interviews, luncheons, dinners, etc. to help you make this important decision. S/he will have all kinds of facts and figures to help you come to a successful job search conclusion.

A job search is long and difficult. If you are working, it certainly is nice to let someone else do all the legwork for you and all you have to do is show up for the interviews and meetings. A good recruiter will take care of everything for you.

However, in your particular situation, I don't think you need a recruiter; in fact, a recruiter will hurt you on a search. There are a number of reasons why

I say this. First of all, from what you have told us, this is at least your third job and you have only been at this firm for seven months. You don't want a recruiter calling firms for you when you might have more success with a write-in campaign and without a fee attached to your candidacy. Secondly, you are planning on changing practice areas from transactional to litigation. This is not really something that a recruiter does because essentially you are going to be starting all over again, and legal recruiters don't place first-year attorneys.

Occasionally a recruiter can "retool" a candidate. For example, if you were a corporate associate thinking about becoming a real estate associate, and you had top credentials and were working in a BigLaw firm, a recruiter would more than likely be able to help you in this current market since there is such a shortage of real estate associates and the two practice areas have some commonality. But you are talking about going into a completely different area of the law, and in this particular situation, a recruiter is not the way to go.

Lastly, it sounds as if you already have some job offers ("I have friends at litigation firms that would like me to start yesterday"), and I would strongly suggest that you take a good look at these opportunities. Since you have already approached contacts at these firms (or they have approached you), a recruiter cannot be of assistance to you there.

As far as how long you have to stay at your current firm so that your conscience is clear? No matter how long you stay, you are going to burn some bridges when you leave, so I would suggest that you think about yourself and your career, decide what you want to do, and then do it now. Why do you want to be a litigator? Have you really given this the thought that is necessary to make this career-changing decision? I know your current firm has spent some serious money on you, but if you know where you want your future practice to head, you need to start making those changes now. In the final analysis, you have to think about yourself.

In answer to your question as to whether firms are more likely to hire a good candidate who writes in instead of using a recruiter, I know with an absolute certainty that this is not the case. It has been my experience that firms want to hire the best candidate, not the best candidate who answers their ad or by happenstance sends in a resume. The firms that do pay fees (the firms that work with recruiters) are budgeted to pay those fees. Sure, they are pleased when they find a great candidate without paying a headhunter's fee. But paying a fee does not enter into the equation when deciding which candidate they are going to hire. They hire the best candidate, not the cheapest hire.

By the way, don't feel so guilty about the firm shelling out so much money for you to the recruiting firm. Depending on the terms of the recruiter's search firm agreement/contract, when you leave before a year of employment there, the headhunter firm is probably going to have to refund a prorated part (or even all) of the fee that was paid to them.

Sincerely,
Ann M. Israel

▮▓▮

City: New York

I'm just finishing my first year at a top-tier NY firm. I'm generally perfectly happy here. I have recently (and quite unexpectedly) been offered the opportunity to lateral to the London office of another firm to get involved in a practice in that office that is not available at my current firm and which I would like to get into. As an alternative, I could transfer to my current firm's London office, but that would represent a departure from my chosen field. Obviously, the fact that I want to go to London is a consideration. Will moving as a 1L harm my career going forward? Can I do this without burning any bridges at my current firm? Your thoughts on this would be greatly appreciated.

London Bridges

Dear London Bridges:

First of all, you are not moving as a 1L. Law school is history for you. You are a first-year associate. I know that was just a typo in your question to me, but I actually thought about it for a minute. It was an interesting slip simply because I think the situation you are in right now has put you in a position where you are feeling not quite so much in control and more like a student than an adult. Incidentally, typos are not acceptable, whether the letter is to a headhunter, a friend, or a potential employer. As I have emphasized so many times before, check your e-mails or letters several times before you send them out.

But here's some good news. What a lovely position to be in, and especially so early in your career. Take a look at all of these wonderful options. You are at one of the best firms in the country and, as you have told us, you are basically quite happy. Now, out of the blue, so to speak, a marvelous offer has materialized to lateral to the London office of another firm and join a practice area in which you are interested. In the meantime, because you would like to move to London, the opportunity to stay with your current top law firm but work at their London office is available for you, although you would work in a practice area that is not of the greatest interest to you.

Moving as a first-year associate is never the best thing to do because it is always smart to stay somewhere for at least three or four years. But when a great opportunity presents itself, you must consider it. And at first blush, this certainly sounds as if it is a great opportunity. Let's dig a little deeper for a moment.

How does this other firm compare to your current firm? We know you are currently working at a top-tier firm. What's the new firm like? Is it a top firm as well? How does the London office compare? Is it stable? What is the prestige factor for your resume? This is important when you are making a move after less than a year at your first job. You don't want to go from a top firm to a firm that is tiers and tiers down the ladder. That will look as if you had to find a new job even if the position is in London. It is always a good idea to consider the resume factor of a new employer.

When thinking about switching to a new practice area, you must take into consideration whether or not this is a thriving practice area as well as a stable law firm. Is this an area that is just unique to this firm, or is this a practice area that is found in many other firms and will be a safe investment for your future? Or perhaps this is a practice area that is in great demand (such as intellectual property), and so it is a wise investment in your future to move into this group now.

These are the types of questions you need to be asking yourself before considering this move. As far as moving to your current firm's London office but into a practice group that you are not really interested in being associated with, I am not sure that is a wise move at all for you. First of all, you would then have to be prepared to be pigeonholed into that type of practice, especially since you are just a first-year attorney, and who knows how long you are going to be working in this practice group once you get moved over there? Secondly, once you do move to London and start working in an area that you are not crazy about, you may find yourself to be very unhappy, and as a first-year associate it will not be so easy to find a different opportunity, especially in a foreign country.

I know you are thinking how easily this opportunity just came your way in your first year, but I must say that this is one of those "in the right place at the right time" situations. Yes, you will definitely burn some bridges at your current firm—they will be dismayed that a first-year associate is leaving—but it isn't as if someone who has been with them for years is giving notice. I have a feeling that there really aren't many partners or senior associates who even know your name—that would be normal at the large BigLaw firms.

So, the bottom line here is if this new firm is as good—or almost as good—as the one you are currently associated with, and the job they are offering you is with a group that appears to be stable in a practice area that you believe is right for your future, it really does seem to be an offer you simply can't refuse. Just do your due diligence and then do it again. You have a good thing going for you right now, and you don't want to give it up at this early point in your legal career unless it is for something even better . . . which it actually might be. Best wishes!

Sincerely,
Ann M. Israel

City: Long Island City

Ann—my question is about how the lateral process works. First a general question: How exactly does the lateral process work? An average time frame? I understand that if there is an immediate, pressing need, firms will respond more quickly, but what if a firm has had an opening posted for a few months (on their website and job sites)? Does that mean that they are waiting to check resumes once a month, once a quarter, or continuously? I submitted my resume application approximately a month ago and have had no response, so I am not sure whether they (1) are ignoring me, (2) haven't looked at my application yet, or (3) already decided they don't want to notify me for an interview but are too busy/lazy/uninterested to reject me officially?

My background includes roughly six months of practice full-time since Sept. '06 (graduated in May from a tier three), admitted to the bar in January '07, but seeking to move to another firm because the practice group I was originally hired for was closed down. My grades are not stellar, but I have good work experience, strong writing skills (senior editor for a journal, note published), and a desire to learn. I've been told that a lateral search can take anywhere from four to six months (probably longer since I have not yet reached one year yet). Could you please shed some light on the lateral procedure?

Thanks!
Confused about Firm Hiring

Dear Confused:

Don't worry—you're not the only one who is confused about lateral hiring! The truth is, it can be a confusing process, not only for the candidate but for the hiring entity as well. What is important to remember is that the process is not exactly the same for each and every firm, and so there is not a set answer to each of your questions.

Some say the rule of thumb for the length of a job search is one month for every $10,000 in salary. Therefore, if you earn $100,000, your job search will take ten months on average. I don't subscribe to this theory, particularly now with associate salaries at the BigLaw firms going up into the stratosphere.

I have found that the length of a job search simply depends on the state of the job market, the candidate's practice area and credentials, timing, and luck.

The state of the job market is critical for trying to determine how long a search might take. As an example, you have told us that your practice group closed down—that would suggest to me that you are probably not a corporate or real estate attorney since those two practice areas are unlikely to be without business at this time. I really can't take a guess as to your practice area, but for the sake of trying to answer your question, we have to assume that whatever department you were in, it obviously is not a booming practice area if it folded.

Before we discuss how long the job search process might go on, I want to know if you have explored the option of going into a different department at your current firm. As a first-year attorney with "roughly six months of practice," your best bet would be to stay where you are and simply move into a new practice group. Even if you were enjoying the practice group you landed in initially, I would suggest you think about a different practice area because I am concerned about a department that folds at this time when so many other practice areas are booming.

Additionally, your competition out there is going to be tough. Coming from a tier-three school with grades that are "not stellar" does not give you an edge over a very competitive candidate pool. Lastly, I don't know how to say this any other way than just to get to the point—your legal experience is not going to be considered as "good work experience." You have described it yourself as "roughly six months of practice" in a department that has "closed down." Indeed, you may have very good work experience prior to becoming an attorney, but in an interview for a lateral associate position, the interviewer is looking at your experience as a lawyer, not your experiences prior to working as an attorney.

Whatever your good work experience might be, the best way for you to showcase and use it would be for you to market yourself as a new attorney. That would be a very good way for you to go if you do plan to start over in a new practice. If that is what you choose to do, you would no longer be involved in a lateral search process; instead, you would be looking for a job as a new first-year attorney.

As far as lateral searches go, it might very well take four to six months or longer for someone in your situation. However, I mentioned timing and luck, and if you happen to be in the right place at the right time, you could end up with a job next week.

The ads you see on job sites might represent different things: Perhaps the firm is in need of a number of associates in that specific practice area, so they just keep that ad running continuously. Or maybe their webmaster doesn't check the website frequently and the position isn't even available any longer. Or perhaps the firm simply hasn't found the right candidate and so they don't stop running the ad. There could be any number of reasons why a job stays up on a job board.

As to why you haven't received any responses after submitting your resume to a number of firms a month ago, I really can't give you an answer. Again, there could be any number of reasons why you have not heard from these firms. One reason could be that they are collecting resumes to determine the candidates they want to contact. Another reason could be that they have already hired someone. And yet one more reason could be that they are not interested in meeting with you. The list goes on. No matter what the reason, it would appear that these firms are not going to contact you to explain why you haven't heard from them; you will only hear from them if they want to meet with you. And, after a month, the chances lessen. Most firms receive so many resumes that they simply do not respond unless they want to bring the person in for an interview. Unfortunately, that's the way things work these days. Is it right? Is it fair? That's an entirely different issue. But no response after this length of time means you should move on and continue to send out your resume to other firms. If you do hear from any of these firms down the road, then that's great!

As I always suggest, you need to contact your law school's career services office along with networking at every bar event and with everyone you know.

Be prepared to run an aggressive search. I wish I could tell you how long your job search was going to take, but each search is different and dependent on, as I said before, your practice area and credentials, the job market, timing, and luck. If there isn't a place for you at your current firm, get out there, start your job search, and . . . best wishes and good luck!

Sincerely,
Ann M. Israel

City: New York

I work at a top NYC firm. I am paid very well and the quality of work I get is outstanding. My problem is there is not enough of it! My department has had little work for the past 12 months (enough to keep things "ticking over" but little enough that it is seriously boring). I am concerned that my skills are not developing and, as I become more senior, I will not be equipped with the required skills. I have raised this with the partners, who simply say that it has been a below-average year but that hopefully something will come along by the end of the year. Should I leave now before a bloodbath? Even if I survive that—ought not my professional development dictate that I move to another firm?

Survivor

Dear Survivor:

You are not wrong to be concerned, if only for the fact that you are "seriously" bored. I do wish that you had told us how many years of experience you have at this point in time. Are you a first- or second-year attorney, or are you far more experienced that that? Have you been practicing for at least three or four years?

Based on the little you have told us, I suspect you are somewhere around two, possibly three, years into your career (of course, this is just speculation). These years, as you morph from a junior into a midlevel associate, are critical years in terms of development. You are correct to be concerned that your skills are not developing and that as you become more senior, you will be ill equipped to take on the practice skills expected of your class year.

I must say that being "seriously" bored is a terrible way to face the workday. That, in and of itself, would be a reason for recommending you start a job search in order to find a firm that will be stimulating and rewarding. But I also must say that in this difficult job market where work is slow for many associates, sometimes it is better to be gainfully and securely employed rather than having a grand old time in a firm that is about to implode.

And so, that leads me to tell you this—being bored is a result of not having anything much to do, as you seem to know. You have told us that you don't get enough work to really keep you all that busy even though you are at a top BigLaw firm. It's great that you enjoy the work that you do get, but let's look at the bigger picture here. Recognizing that your department has been slow for at least the past year, you have done all the right things by speaking with the partners. However, they basically shrugged off your concerns and said that this has been a below-average year but *hopefully* things will pick up. That's not good enough.

First you should take a look around and make sure that the other associates in your department have also been very slow. If they weren't, then that would say the partners are doling out the assignments to associates other than you, and your job is definitely in jeopardy. Start a job search immediately!

But should you discover that the entire department really has had a below-average year and all the rest of the associates are sitting around hoping for a better year, then this is something you need to examine closely. The department is definitely in trouble, and if this pattern of a lack of business continues, surely there will be some cuts in the department. As a junior associate, you may be one of the first to be asked to leave.

In either case, I do think that you should start a job search as soon as possible rather than waiting around and hoping that things will pick up at your current firm, because . . . *what if they don't?* Just remember to keep your job search confidential because you want to stay with your current employer until you have a new place to practice. Best wishes!

Sincerely,
Ann M. Israel

City: Birmingham, AL

Ann, I am currently serving a one-year term as a law clerk to a federal district court judge. When I started law school, I knew I wanted to clerk. After quite a bit of hard work, I managed to graduate from one of the top ten law schools in the country, served on law review and another legal journal, and walked away from my 2L summer with an offer in hand to join one of the country's better-known and well-respected law firms. I recently learned that I passed the bar exam. With that as my introduction, I am absolutely miserable in my clerkship. The reasons for this are many, but most are purely personal. My judge is wonderful, I am learning a lot, and overall it is a good experience professionally. My nonprofessional life, however, has just fallen apart. (My marriage is suffering due to the stress of the isolation; my young son is acting out, etc.) Given my sensibilities, I think it would be irresponsible for me to quit mid-clerkship; I've worked hard to get to this point, and I would think negatively of someone who walked away from such a long-sought-after goal . . . but I would prefer to keep my marriage intact and my son healthy. My law firm position would be in a city where we have ties, family, and a support network. What are the professional ramifications to walking away from a federal clerkship?

Sincerely,
Unhappy Clerk

Dear Unhappy Clerk:

I think you are about to apply for a name change . . . soon to be a happy law firm associate!

I had some mixed feelings about how walking away from a prestigious clerkship would play out, so I decided to go directly to the source, a federal judge, to ask his opinion. When I asked the question, he looked at me as if I had just asked the most ridiculous question ever because the answer was so simple.

Although there would be some initial disruption to the judge, it would probably take another nanosecond to find a replacement (obviously I am exaggerating just a bit here!). However, as an example, this particular judge received over 850 applications this year from potential clerks. If one of his current clerks decided to leave mid-clerkship, he would pick up the phone, call his old law firm, and probably have at least half a dozen potential candidates by midafternoon. So, again, although there would be some minor disruption to the judge if a clerk should suddenly leave, it wouldn't take long to fill the vacancy and smooth out any perceived interruptions in the judge's chambers.

But of greater interest to me was how the judge reacted to your dilemma. He was incredibly sympathetic to your plight and didn't believe that going back to your law firm midterm would reflect poorly on your resume at all. Family and health are so important; they really need to take a front seat to everything else in the world.

Your e-mail made me very sad. I know this is a difficult situation for someone who is working in an ideal position, one that is, in your words, a long-sought-after goal. But I do not think of you as irresponsible by any stretch of the imagination should you decide suddenly to leave such a prestigious position. You need to take care of your marriage and your son and yourself. Since you have told us in your e-mail that your law firm position will take you to a city where you will have ties, family, and a support network, I would suggest that you start the new year with a great New Year's resolution: sooner rather than later, resolve to leave your clerkship and begin your new life at the law firm. Hopefully, friends, family, a support network, and a better state of mind will help to bring on the start of a turnaround in your marriage and an opportunity to devote more time to whatever is troubling your son.

I know everyone is rooting for you, including your judge.

Sincerely,
Ann M. Israel

▌▌▌

City: Los Angeles

I went to a top-5 law school, not Harvard or Yale. Can you tell me candidly, am I missing out on any opportunities? Am I getting fewer calls from headhunters than my Harvard- and Yale-educated colleagues? Are there firms that have a special Harvard and Yale track for partnership? At the time I chose law schools, I never even applied to those schools, and it never occurred to me that there would be any differences in opportunities between my choice and those schools. However, since I started working I've heard lots of rumors to the contrary. I've also read some of your columns, which seem to reinforce the idea that Harvardites and Yalies have more opportunities than the rest of us? What's the real story? I'm thinking about changing jobs and I want to get an idea of where I stand and how picky I can afford to be.

Thanks a lot,
Curious Law Grad

Dear Curious:

As a legal recruiter, I am always looking for several specific things if I am cold-calling for candidates. First, I look for the school, and I am always just as pleased with number five as I am with number one. As far as I am concerned, the rankings go back and forth with these top-5 schools, and since my office is in New York, all five of the top law schools have basically equal standing in my mind and to my clients.

Quite honestly, over the years my firm has successfully represented candidates from the lowest tiers of law schools, although it is clear that the bulk of our placements do come from the first-tier law schools, as is the case with all of the legal search firms.

What makes the difference? Here is what I write about in most of my columns—not whether you have graduated from Harvard or Yale, but what is on your transcript. You might very well have a JD from Harvard, but if you have Cs on your transcript and another candidate has a JD from a lower-ranked law school but straight As on his/her transcript along with law review and other honors, then all other things being equal, that candidate is going to get the job offer.

There is no question that the law firms are inclined to take a strong look at graduates from Harvard and Yale law schools, but I suspect these firms are inclined to be equally interested in Columbia and Penn and NYU, particularly the firms in New York. In Los Angeles, where you are based, the firms have a particular affinity for Boalt Hall and Stanford.

All you have to do is take a look at a large law firm's Martindale in any specific geographic area and you will see that along with the top five law schools—and notice that I refer to the top five schools, not just Harvard and Yale—you will see lawyers from other law schools from the top 20 or so that fall into that specific geographic area.

You will also see lawyers at any BigLaw firm from just about every major law school in the country, but you can be sure that their transcript has a big story to tell (or their relative is either a justice of SCOTUS or perhaps a CEO of a Fortune 10 company!).

I really don't think you are missing out on any calls from recruiters because you went to one of the three schools in the top five other than Harvard of Yale. Nor do I think that you are missing out on any great job opportunities because you chose your law school over applying to Harvard or Yale.

Here's what will cause a Harvard grad or a Yalie lawyer to get a call from a recruiter or a job offer before you do: if s/he has better grades or happens to be in a more desirable practice area at the time. That's the bottom line. By the way, you weren't really serious, were you? Best wishes.

Sincerely,
Ann M. Israel

City: New York

Dear Ann,

I graduated from a prestigious undergrad university and an Ivy League law school. I had mediocre law school grades (A to C, but mostly in the Bs). Since then, I have had a very responsible position in a small company, mostly drafting and reviewing documents for complex financial transactions. I have about a year and half on the job here. I am admitted to the bar but do not have any law firm experience. (My summers and internships were for state and federal governments and a corporation). I am anxious to work for a law firm and start practicing law.

Headhunters have nothing for me, and for three months I have been sending out resumes with targeted cover letters to any firm in the area advertising for associates in a field related to my experience. I don't send my transcript with my cover letter and resume, and I have only applied for entry-level or first-year jobs, so why have the interview requests been so few? Should I be doing things differently? Please advise.

Far and Few

Dear Far and Few:

The Grateful Dead said it best:

> Keep your day job
> Don't give it away
> Keep your day job
> Whatever they say
> Keep your day job
> Till your night job pays

For the past year and a half, you have had a very responsible position in a small company working on complex transactions. You are employed and collecting a paycheck. Consider yourself very fortunate, because I can promise you that there are many unemployed recent law school graduates who would do anything to trade places with you.

On top of the good fortune of being gainfully employed, you also have had some responses to your interview requests. That raises the question, what happened on those interviews? Maybe that is where your question about whether or not you should be doing things differently should be addressed. But since we don't know what transpired on those interviews, there is no way we can discuss what you should or should not have done while you were in the midst of your meeting with a potential employer.

As far as what you should be doing differently in terms of looking for a position with a law firm—and I certainly can understand why you now want to work for a law firm and start to practice law—I think you are doing the right things. Quite frankly, I agree with your strategy of not sending out your transcript with your inquiry and resume. Even though you have graduated from a top undergraduate school and an Ivy League law school (which generally means a top-10 law school), your grades are going to be the main issue at any firm that requires a transcript. Bs are not great, but even one C is a killer, and it sounds as if you have more than one.

Therefore, your strategy of trying to get in front of an interviewer and getting employers to want you before you have to present your transcript is the right way to go. In the BigLaw firms, the transcript is going to be a deal breaker, no matter what, but in some of the midsize and smaller firms, you do stand a chance.

Forget the headhunters. The combination of being a first-year associate and having Cs on your transcript make you a dead-end candidate for recruiters no matter where you went to law school. Be realistic about this. Anyway, clients don't pay fees for first-year lawyers. Don't bother with search firms—you are wasting your time and theirs.

As far as sending out cover letters and your resume to targeted ads for people working in a field "related to your experience," I would suggest that you broaden your area to as wide a field as possible. Since you are not working as an attorney, your experience is not really being considered as applicable to legal work by potential employers and therefore not counted as work-related. I know this doesn't seem fair, but it is the way attorneys look at nonlegal experience (I have discussed this at length in past columns). Therefore, don't limit yourself to just one specific practice area; you are really hurting your chances by doing so.

Have you contacted your career services office at your law school? If so, are you contacting them on a frequent basis? Are you networking with everyone you know? Are you attending bar events?

As I have said over and over again lately, it is tough out there for up-and-coming first-year associates, and your situation is no different from that of anyone else who is out there pounding the pavement for that first legal job. Except . . . you have an income coming in right now, from what sounds like a fairly decent position. Hold on to that job as you continue your search for an associate opportunity. Things do seem to be starting to turn around a bit, and you do have an Ivy League JD, which certainly does work in your favor when applying to smaller law firms. Just don't paint yourself into a corner in terms of a practice area. Be flexible and open to all opportunities and you may find yourself with many more interviews than before. Best wishes!

Sincerely,
Ann M. Israel

City: New York

Ann—any insights on what to do if you think the people at your current firm might sabotage you by giving bad references solely because they are angry that you want to leave (or might want to limit your options and

make you stay a bit longer). No wonder someone in this circumstance would want to leave, but as a practical matter, what do you do?

Saboteur

Dear Saboteur:

Oh dear, something like this has never entered my mind. What an awful thought. But I suppose if you have written this to me, then you must know of some situation where this has occurred or at least you suspect this has happened. All I can say is that I certainly agree with you when you say that someone in this type of circumstance would want to leave, and as soon as possible.

Unfortunately, if this is true and you believe that you are about to receive bad references simply because the people you work for are angry that you are leaving, you are in a bad situation. Telling your future employer that your references are going to be bad because you are so good and they simply can't exist without you just isn't going to fly.

Here's the only thing that I can think of that is going to help. Legally speaking, the only information that a reference is allowed to give verbally is to offer up your dates of employment and verify your salary. Other than that, references supposedly must be in writing.

Now, we all know that employers are very busy and are only too happy to give a good reference over the telephone. And why not? No one is going to commence a law suit over a good reference because it wasn't in writing. But I can assure you that there is ample precedent for a lawsuit when an employer gives a bad reference over the phone and it prevents someone from getting a job. Therefore, I would really question the sanity of your current firm thinking they could get away with talking to any future employers about you and saying anything negative to prevent you from getting a job offer just to keep you from leaving your current employ.

By the way, I would hope that you are not asking for any references from your present law firm until an offer of employment from a new law firm has been extended and accepted.

So, let's assume you have received an offer of employment from a new law firm and you have accepted this offer pending references. But, let's also assume that your current firm decides to stay within the limits of the law and writes up a bad reference on you to send to a future employer. Here's the problem: If what the firm writes up is true, and assuming they have documentation on these matters, there isn't much you can do about this. However, what if these claims are false, and it is what you suspect—the firm simply wants to sabotage any offers of employment because they want you to stay?

I find it hard to believe that any firm would be this stupid to put themselves in such a ridiculous position because I think the publicity alone from the lawsuit that you would bring against them would be outrageous. But would you really want to do this? What a nightmare. Suing a law firm is a long and difficult process, and in the meantime you are going to be unemployed.

I think what you really need to do is find out where you stand with your firm right now. Surely there must be one partner or one senior associate that you have a close relationship with—someone you can speak with honestly. If so, I would sit down and have a heart-to-heart conversation with this individual and let him/her know that you have been interviewing but are concerned that your references won't be good because the firm might be angry with you for leaving. You need to know this now before you get too far into your interviewing.

If your greatest fears are confirmed, you need to discuss this with your headhunter or with the hiring partner at the firm where you believe you are about to receive an offer. Perhaps you are only going to be able to offer up one reference from your current employer and you are going to have to come up with other references from other sources that will back up your abilities. Think of clients with whom you have developed relationships; this may be your saving grace.

I am hoping this is a situation that does not really exist for you, but I do believe you need to find out if it is a reality or not. Surely if it is real, you do not want to stay at this firm much longer, and you need to figure out how you can get away successfully from a firm threatening to give references that damage your reputation. Best wishes!

Sincerely,
Ann M. Israel

City: New York

I am a fourth-year litigator with good grades from a top law school and work at a reputable law firm. The partners in my department are great to work for and I feel trusted by them. My relationship with partners outside

the department, however, are not as good, to the point that I am not sure if I will ever make partner at this firm. Should I start looking for another job at a place where the prospects of making partner may be better? If so, when should I start my search?

Wondering When

Dear Wondering When:

The short answer to your question is that you should get out your resume, update it now, and start your search today.

My question to you is, what are you waiting for? Let's take a look at your situation. You are a fourth-year associate with everything going for you in terms of credentials. And the good news is that you have a great relationship with the people you will need for references if and when you do decide to accept a position with a new firm.

The reality of your situation is that for one reason or another your relationships with the partners of your firm outside of those within your immediate practice group are not very good; in fact, based on what you have told us, it would seem that they are not very good at all since you believe that you will not have any support from them for a partnership vote.

Sadly, what this really boils down to is that the partners in your department might not even try to fight for you if they know it is politically a lost cause to begin with. And even if they do go to battle for you, it probably isn't going to matter if you do not have any other support throughout the rest of the firm, which is basically what you have written to us. Therefore, why are you even thinking about staying there now?

I understand that it is easy for me to tell you to get up and go and that in the real world it isn't quite that simple to just quit your job and find another, especially when you like where you work and the partners you work with. However, you really do need to think long-term right now and focus on your future. And if you are doing just that, then you understand that building up to partnership at a new firm is going to take a while to establish yourself. You are at a perfect class year right now to lateral over to a firm and work on a strong partnership track.

What is critical to any job search for you is to be certain that any firm you are thinking about joining definitely is looking at you for a partnership track position. Be sure to find out how many years you need to be with the firm before you are eligible for partnership. Some firms require seven or eight years.

Now perhaps you are beginning to understand why you should be thinking about changing over to a new firm as soon as possible.

I know it is difficult to think about leaving your firm when you are not particularly unhappy, but you really do need to consider the reality that more than likely you are not going to make partner at your current firm. Facing this and accepting it (which it seems you have) should allow you to dust off your resume and start that job search. You are in a very fortunate position, as I mentioned above, in that you have wonderful credentials, are gainfully employed at a well-regarded law firm, and have a sound relationship with the partners in your practice group—the people you need for references when it comes time to make a job change. So, don't hesitate—start networking, call your favorite legal recruiter, and cull the legal pages' classified ads. Best wishes!

Sincerely,
Ann M. Israel

▐▒▌

City: New York

Dear Ann,

I am a recent law school grad and have been applying for months and finally got a job offer today. Not only was this great news because I liked the office and felt it would be a good opportunity, but it was a relief to finally have something lined up. However, there was a little problem. I walked out of the first interview for a different (perfect) job just hours before receiving the aforementioned offer for a good job. I knew the offering office was on a short time frame and I didn't want to lose the offer. I called them and asked for a few days to make a decision. They didn't sound happy that I didn't accept on the spot but told me, "That's fine, and we'll let you know if the delay imperils the offer." I really would like to get an offer for this other job, but I only have had a first interview with them and now I only have a couple of days (maybe less) to give an answer to the offer I do have. What can I do?

Can Do

Dear Can Do:

First and foremost, congratulations on your job offer! The days of sweating and worrying are over for you. After months of applying, you now are about to join the ranks of the employed. I can only imagine what a tremendous relief this must be for you.

But of course, wouldn't you know it? You finally get an offer and then suddenly the most perfect job comes along at the very last minute. Nothing like the worst timing in the world, right? And as we all know, the interviewing process can be extremely drawn-out at times. What you don't want to have happen is losing your job offer. And it sounds as if your prospective employer wasn't overjoyed that you didn't accept on the spot.

In fact, they were probably surprised that you didn't accept immediately. After all, it is December, and as a recent law school graduate who has been applying for months, we are talking about seven months or so. That's a long time to be looking for employment, and this employer probably imagined that you would jump at their offer. Being an employer's market, their attitude is *almost* understandable. But not completely. I wish they could have been a bit more compassionate in understanding that professionals generally need a couple of days to think over an offer. In fact, they should have been generous and offered you the rest of the week, along with any help they could give you in making your decision because they want you so very much.

Okay, so they aren't the warmest people in the world. Don't worry about it—it's a job, and you need it at this point in your budding career. Let's think about how you can move the interviewing process along quickly at the other opportunity—the one you have deemed to be "perfect."

Immediately get on the phone and call the person you met with and let him/her know how excited you are about the opportunity. Do not leave a voice mail message if this person is not available; keep calling back until you reach him/her. After you have expressed your enthusiasm for the job, then let him/her know that you have just received an offer for a position that is certainly a great job but not as great as this one. Tell this individual that you only have a few days to let this other employer know if you are going to accept their offer, but if given the choice, you would much rather work with him/her.

Explain that you fully understand you have only had an initial interview today, but if there is any possible way that you could return tomorrow for a full round and if a decision could be made as to whether or not you are the right candidate for this opportunity, then you would want to turn down this other job and accept their position on the spot (only say this if it is absolutely true). Then put your hand over your mouth and say nothing else and wait to hear what s/he has to say to you.

Here is what you need to be prepared for: If you are a viable candidate (based on today's first round of interviews), they aren't going to want to lose you. Perhaps this person may tell you that s/he has to speak to a few people and will need to get right back to you but they will bring you back in ASAP for a full round of interviews and make a quick determination as to whether or not you are the right candidate for them.

However, if things were just so-so today during your interview or if there are other candidates who are as good as you, more than likely they are going to tell you that it is impossible for them to move that fast and they recommend that you accept the other position.

If that's the response you hear, be happy you have that other offer and don't wait the two days—call that potential employer back immediately and accept that offer right away! No matter what happens, you are in a win-win situation. Please let us know what happens—fingers crossed for you. Best wishes!

Sincerely,
Ann M. Israel

▮▮▮

City: New York

Dear Ann,

I appreciate your answer to my question last week. It was a great boost to my morale in some ways, but at the same time . . . I should mention that your advice to apply to as many postings as you can and get as many interviews as possible is a bit like telling someone to just go to Yale Law School to jump-start their career. Um, yeah, but the question is, is it feasible I say this because few postings are even available now, and the ones that are seem to be in response to a very small minority of the population, which I don't fit. Still, I do appreciate your response. I'm sorry to sound so negative, but, well, it's hard to stay upbeat nowadays.

Regards,
Cycled

Dear Cycled:

Yes, I know. It is hard to stay upbeat nowadays—for so many people. But here's the thing: you have to figure out a way to not just not sound negative but also to not feel negative. You have got to somehow continue to believe in yourself and to try to think in a positive way.

I understand that I sound like some idiotic Pollyanna who isn't paying any attention to the real world out there. That's not the case at all. I really think it is important, especially in these times, to try to make lemonade out of the lemons we are all being handed. The more you look at the down side of the situation, the worse off things are going to seem.

I must say that I don't agree with you that the postings seem to be few and far between right now. It does seem to me that there are more ads out there than there were last fall. The corporate transactional practice area has not picked up as quickly as we had hoped, but litigation does seem to be hopping. And definitely there are some advertised needs in corporate, even though not as many as in litigation.

You write that the postings you do see appear to be geared to a very small minority of the population, which you don't fit. I am assuming that you are referring to academic credentials or specific law schools. My best advice to you is to ignore those specific specs in the ads and apply to the jobs no matter what as long as you have the right experience. What's the worst thing that can happen? You don't get any response to your application, right? Or you are rejected. Those are the two worst things that can happen. It's a numbers game, and there is no getting around that. But that's the good news.

You just keep sending out your resume to anything that seems to be remotely applicable to your experience, and the numbers game will eventually work in your favor. The more interviews you go on, the better your chances will get on all levels. Your interviewing skills will get better with each and every interview, and the more interviews you have, the better chances you will have for getting job offers.

But the most important thing for you to keep remembering is that you must have a positive outlook, no matter how tough and fruitless this all seems. So, here's your old friend Pollyanna telling you that you *must* stay upbeat, because as soon as you take a defeatist attitude, everything really will fall apart for you. Keep whistling that happy tune and sending out those resumes. And anytime you feel you just can't send out one more resume, shoot another e-mail to me and I will continue to give you those virtual morale boosts! Best wishes!

Sincerely,
Ann M. Israel

I▓I

City: Los Angeles

Dear Ann,

I've enjoyed reading and gained tremendous help from your advice and wisdom to others. Thank you, truly. Now, I hope you don't mind, but I'd like to please ask you a question. I'm a devoutly religious person who's interested in working for a national law firm. I'm wondering, can a person of faith have a career as a BigLaw attorney as well as freely practice his/her religion? Obviously, in this day and age no one would be overtly intolerant of any religion, but I realize there may be more subtle situations that might crop up and I'd have to confront whereas others might not be as concerned, or that simply might affect me differently. For example, if I needed one day per week off for religious observance, would that be a problem (not necessarily so much regarding whether or not I would complete my work—I definitely would be more than willing to put in as much time as necessary and work during the other six days—but as far as "face time")? I'd appreciate your thoughts regarding the issue of religion in the workplace/law firms.

Many thanks,
Moses Was a Lawyer

Dear Moses:

First of all, I believe that the First Amendment establishes your right to freely practice your religion while at the same time taking on a career. It would be difficult—although I am sure that it goes on—for any employer to find reasons to hold you back in your career because you need to observe certain religious bylaws and guidelines that cause you to take time off from work . . . as long as your work is done in a satisfactory manner and in the appropriate time frame.

Your question tells us that you are in Los Angeles, and I am going to tell you right away that working in a BigLaw firm—particularly in big cities such as Los Angeles, Chicago, New York—you are not going to run into any problems with taking off one day per week for a religious observance, especially when you are willing to work as much as necessary the other six days of the week to make up for that one day. The "face time" that you are going to miss for that one day is not going to hurt your career.

Here is the problem, and I have to tell you that I have run into it a number of times: Be honest and up front about your situation, and don't wait until after you have been hired and start working to discuss this with your employer, because I believe that is when it becomes an issue. When the interviewing process is well on its way and you are confident that you are a strong contender for a job offer, sit down with one of the interviewers that you feel is part of the decision-making process. Let him/her know that you are very interested in this position and that you are committed to making this a career choice. However, you need to let him/her know that due to your religious affiliation, it will be necessary for you to take one day off every week. However, you are also willing to work six days a week to make up for this day off, and you can guarantee that your work product will not suffer.

I believe that waiting until after you are hired to tell an employer about this is duplicitous; you should want this to be a condition of your employment rather than something that you keep hidden until after you are employed. I am interested in hearing from the readers of this column as to their opinions on this matter, and I will print those opinions in a column later on. All I know is that I once hired someone who didn't tell me about his religious needs and that he was going to have to take a number of different days off and on some days would need to leave the office in the early afternoon. I wasn't upset about his religious needs; I was upset that he didn't tell me prior to receiving an offer of employment. I didn't care that he had to take a lot of time off as long as he could do the job satisfactorily; I cared that he didn't tell me before he was hired. What else was he hiding from me?

As you become more senior in your practice, these kinds of situations become more and more trivial. The larger your practice becomes, the less your "face time" will matter. And, I can assure you that, for example, in New York alone there are many religious attorneys who must leave their firms before sundown on Fridays and do not work on Saturdays, and they have made partner. Trust me when I tell you that there are far greater issues to worry about that are deal breakers in your career than this. As I always advise, just be the best you can be—*on those other six days*! Best wishes!

Sincerely,
Ann M. Israel

∎▇∎

City: White Plains, NY

I recently graduated from law school and I am having absolutely no luck whatsoever finding employment. And, I am far from being alone. A number of fellow graduates who did not apply to clerkships or did have offers from firms they already worked for after second-year summer are in the same boat. I keep hearing that the economy is to blame for the lack of jobs for first-year associates. Some say it will be better after NY bar results come out. Any advice for the recent law school grads?

Thank you,
Unemployed and Going Crazy

Dear Readers:

The question above truly broke my heart. And I fear that this is just the beginning. Given the state of the legal employment market right now, I thought I might take this opportunity to attempt to answer the question to the best of my ability, and perhaps in this attempt, find some way to help out those young lawyers who are trying to start their career in this noble profession.

So where do I start? I just finished a phone conversation with a midlevel tax associate who wanted me to tell him that this will all be better after the New Year begins. I said to him, "Okay, everything is going to be great as soon as Obama swears into office." And then I said, "You don't really believe me, do you?"

Do you just want me to tell you that this is all going to go away after January 20? I can do that if you want me to say something like that.

I could lie to all of you and tell you not to worry and that this is just a temporary blip. I'd like to believe that myself. But we have to behave like grown-ups now in this very grown-up world. The truth of the matter is that we don't know when this mess is going to end or how it is going to end. So let's face the facts and recognize that things are not as they were a year or two ago.

For those of you who have a few years of practice experience under your belts, you are in a much better position than those recent grads that can't find their first employer. What can those unemployed recent graduates do with those law degrees? First and foremost, change your attitude! Be aware of what is going on in the world, but then take a moment to do some positive thinking and *know in your mind* that you are going to get a job practicing law no matter what!

Okay, I know I sound like Pollyanna, but what's the alternative? Sitting in your basement and saying to yourself, "What's the use even looking?" Get off your butt and do whatever it takes.

Sincerely,
Ann M. Israel

City: New York

I am a midlevel associate that just joined a small firm. I left my former employer on good terms. When interviewing with the new firm, I was given a detailed description of my intended role and what my responsibilities would be at the new firm. I was also informed of the firm's practice area. I have been here under a month and have learned that my role and responsibilities are not and will not be as described. Also, the practice area is very different. I am beginning to look for new employment as this new job is a huge step back for me. What do I tell potential employers about my present situation?

Stranded Associate

Dear Stranded:

The first thing to tell potential employers is that all is not what it appears to be. As quickly as possible, if what you tell us is true, you need to find a new employer and get out of this terrible new firm.

The good news is that you were very wise and left your former employer on good terms. I suppose the first question to ask is whether or not there is any point in thinking about going back to that firm. Perhaps you might want to get yourself back there for at least another year or two to regroup and figure out what went wrong with this current job change.

Absent that idea, I am afraid that this is one instance where the old adage, "Thou shall not speak badly about one's current employer," simply does not apply in your case. There is no other way out but to tell the truth. But how did it all come to this?

It is hard to imagine that everything can be so very different from when you interviewed with this firm. Not only are your responsibilities and your role in the firm completely different from the detailed description you were given, but the practice area is not the same. How is this possible? This is actually quite bizarre.

It is necessary for me to ask if you did your due diligence prior to accepting an offer from this firm. If you did and this is what happened, you have every reason to sit down with the managing partner and ask what has happened to the job you thought you had accepted. If you didn't do your due diligence on this firm, then shame on you. It is going to be very difficult to explain to future employers what happened because it is simply going to boil down to a case of accepting a job due to poor judgment on your part.

In the final analysis, though, this firm certainly burned you, and as long as you are short and sweet when discussing this with potential employers, and not angry or defensive, the interviewer should believe you and then move on to the rest of the interview. Fortunately, you have only been there a very short while and your references from your original employer should still be strong (be sure to call them and let them know what is going on).

The most important thing for you to do is make the move as soon as possible and not stick around at this crazy firm any longer than is necessary. And don't forget to do some major due diligence prior to accepting any offers! Best wishes!

Sincerely,
Ann M. Israel

▮▮▮

City: Beaver, OR

Ann, can you shed light on how firms make hiring decisions? What if a firm does a soft search for candidates for a potential opening, interviews several candidates, and likes one or two. If there is no listed opening, how long can the process to getting an offer take? What exactly goes on behind closed doors? Must a firm post an opening under the labor laws (or Oregon law)? You read about all these partners and associates joining firms, yet there wasn't a "posted" opening. Thanks.

Oregon Beaver

Dear O.B.,

I wish I had the ability to shed light on how firms make hiring decisions! After all these years, I certainly haven't a clue.

Well, that isn't exactly true. Of course I understand to a certain degree how a hiring decision is made. But no one can really tell you what goes on behind closed doors unless they are present there at the time. Let me take your questions one by one and try to answer them to the best of my ability, having not been behind those closed doors.

A soft search is exactly that. The firm, corporation, or other entity is not really in a big rush to fill the position, but if the right person should come along—and "right" means an individual who really hits the ball out of the park—then an offer might be extended. So, based on your hypothetical situation where the firm has a soft search going on and occasionally interviews a couple of people that are likeable enough, the process could go on indefinitely. Unless one of those candidates is an absolute star, more than likely the firm is going to be willing to continue on with the interviewing process when they are conducting a soft search. There is no reason to hire an average, likeable candidate when undergoing this type of search since there is no urgent need to fill the position.

I am not familiar with Oregon law, so I really cannot tell you if an opening has to be posted first before someone can be hired. However, just to be sure that I am giving you the right advice, I contacted one of the top labor and employment attorneys practicing in New York, Al Feliu, a partner at the law firm of Vandenberg & Feliu LLP.

In speaking with Mr. Feliu, I asked him if he had ever heard of any law regarding the posting of positions for attorneys. His response:

> There are no pre-established deadlines for completing a search except as dictated by the needs of the business; if there is no listed opening as appears to be the case here, perhaps the employer is looking at succession planning or bench strength in anticipation of personnel changes on the horizon in which case there really is not an opening (yet) and therefore no prescribed timeframe for the search; there is no legal requirement for posting per se but is a good practice in many settings, e.g. to avoid internal perception of unfairness or incestuous hiring, to help ensure a diverse slate of candidates, etc.

I have worked with some corporations over the years with corporate guidelines that insisted on openings being posted internally for a certain amount of time before an offer could be extended to my candidates. However, I have never heard of an internal posting for a lawyer being necessary within a law firm. Who would respond to the posting?

It is true that there are notices every day telling us about partners—and sometimes associates—joining new firms where there never was an opening, posted or not. Mr. Feliu noted, "A lawyer changing firms is not necessarily tied to an 'opening' but rather may be tied to expansion of the business base, etc."

Indeed, a headhunter might be representing a partner with a large book of portable business and market him/her to several different firms simply by cold-calling the hiring or managing partner. If the partner's book of business makes sense to the firm, the candidate may very well end up becoming a member of a firm that never had an opening but rather recognized a great business opportunity.

The same might happen with a star associate even though an actual opening does not exist.

I will close this column with a final observation from Al Feliu:

> The questioner may be coming at the issue from the employment discrimination context. There is case law authority for the proposition that employers may be subject to claims of discrimination in hiring in the absence of a posting for a position. The context is usually a candidate in a protected category argues that hiring was "word of mouth"

and closed to individuals not of the favored category. For example, I am an African-American secretary and wake up one day with a new white head of secretaries taken from the secretarial pool. I was never asked or invited to apply nor was there a general search complete with a posting. The hiring was arguably with "a wink and a nod" with the purpose or result of perpetuating the status quo, e.g. whites in authority hiring their friends or candidates who look like them. The failure to post would be cited as evidence for the proposition that the hiring was closed to all but those of the race of the selected candidate, white. [However,] I do not recall such a claim arising in the context of the recruiting of legal professionals.

I hope this answers your questions. I am not really clear on where you are coming from or what your situation may be, but I suspect you are trying to figure out why it is taking so long to hear anything after you had a good set of interviews with a particular firm. If they do have a soft search for this position and you are not being called back for advanced interviews, I would assume they are not ready to hire at this time; you should probably continue interviewing elsewhere and forget about this opportunity for the time being. Best wishes!

Sincerely,
Ann M. Israel

Looking for a new job at any level of one's career is a daunting and difficult task. But it can be especially challenging for those of you who are looking to change jobs/firms midcareer or when you are already at the top of your game. Expectations are higher and competition is often fiercer in a much more specialized field. There are some valuable lessons to be learned from the experiences of senior associates and more seasoned legal veterans who have written to me over the years. Here are just a few of the best.

City: New York

As a senior associate, I am considering joining one of the several virtual law firms that lack their own offices and send lawyers to work on-site with clients. I am thinking that the law firm life just isn't for me, and I like variety and would be fine working on short-term projects with different clients. Would working at one of these firms kill any chance of returning to a large firm or in-house if I reconsider?

Thank you.
Virtual

Dear Virtual:

If this were any other time, then I would be writing a completely different response to your question. But things being what they are right now, I have to look at things differently, as do you.

In ordinary times, whatever/whenever those are, I would tell you that leaving your law firm and going to a virtual firm would not be the best choice for you if there is any chance at all that you are thinking you might reconsider going back to a large firm or want to work for a legal department at a major corporation.

But that was then and this is now and oh, how times have changed. As a senior associate who I am going to assume is not about to be voted into the partnership, you need to look to your future and figure out what your next move is about to be. Since jobs for senior associates (as well as midlevel and junior associates) are not plentiful these days, all we have been hearing and reading about the future is temp opportunities.

Taking a position with the virtual firms right now is a great idea, as far as I am concerned. The top virtual firms hire the cream of the crop and offer a good benefits package as well as a steady income. Placements into the top law firms and corporations with interesting assignments seem to be plentiful at this time since temp attorney hiring appears to be the hiring alternative of the moment.

Down the road, should you decide that you want to go back to a full-time, permanent position, I don't see that working for one of the prestigious virtual firms is going to do harm to your resume. It's not as if you have decided to be unemployed or are taking temp jobs here and there; you will actually be employed by a firm, albeit a virtual law firm that is simply loaning you out to major law firms and corporations.

In light of the state of the job market at this time, I don't think anyone would question your motive in joining this type of firm at this point in your career. I will say that if you have not been asked to leave your firm, and if you can stand to stick around for another year or two, it would be my first choice to stay where you are (or try to find another opportunity in another law firm or an in-house legal department) if you think you are going to want to eventually continue in the law firm or in-house environment. Failing to find that type of opportunity, and if you are forced to leave your law firm, going to the virtual law firm environment is certainly a million times better than being unemployed or registering at myriad temp agencies and sitting at home waiting for an assignment.

The virtual law firms seem to be placing their attorneys into long-term assignments that replicate permanent positions in major law firms. These assignments are not so very different from the job you are currently holding; this is something you need to keep in mind. You certainly do not want to take on an assignment and then resign from it—do this once or twice and you will find that you are on a "do not call" list from your virtual firm. I am not certain that these assignments are so very "short term" as you have described. Some of them last over a year; this is something you really need to investigate before signing on.

Additionally, getting hired by the top virtual firms is similar to getting hired by a BigLaw firm—they look for the best and brightest. Assuming your credentials are top ranked, you shouldn't have any trouble becoming part of one of these firms.

The bottom line here is just as in any job search: you need to do your due diligence before quitting your current job. Best wishes!

Sincerely,
Ann M. Israel

City: New York

I am an associate at a BigLaw firm considering my career. I have heard rumors that the height of an associate's marketability for in-house and

other post-BigLaw positions is when he is a midlevel. By the time he is a senior associate, and especially by the time he is in the "up for partnership" years, his marketability decreases. An explanation I have heard for this is that it is assumed by prospective employers that senior associates looking for jobs are those who weren't good enough to make the cut for partnership. Is there any truth to this?

Rumor Has It

Dear Rumor Has It:

I suppose many years ago, long before lateral moves were the norm, it may have been true that a senior associate out on the job market was branded as one who could not make partner and was asked to leave his/her firm. However, more and more these days we find senior associates looking to make a lateral move long before that "up or out" decision is made.

Incidentally, in recent years some firms have relaxed their "up or out" rule and have created counsel slots where once none existed.

Firms no longer look upon senior associates as cast-offs from other firms. In fact, since fewer and fewer associates make partner at BigLaw firms, there is no shame in a senior associate deciding to take a look at the job market, either before or after the partnership cut has been determined. Based on this, I would say there is no truth to the explanation you have heard explaining the decrease in a senior associate's marketability.

First, let's clear up one misconception. Most general counsels believe a senior associate is far more marketable for their in-house opportunities than is a junior associate. In-house legal departments by and large require skilled attorneys, those who do not need to be trained or mentored but rather can operate on their own. True, there are junior positions for in-house legal departments, but the really exciting and defining opportunities generally require a minimum of seven years of practice.

Smaller boutique-type law firms also lean toward the more senior-level associates since they do not tend to hire large groups of junior attorneys for many of the same reasons that exist in the in-house departments.

Where the "shelf-life" (for lack of a better descriptive expression) rumors become reality is when an associate decides to lateral within another BigLaw or into a midsized law firm. In those situations, the partners are trying to keep a balance within each class year, particularly among the more senior associates—those on the partnership track. Bringing in a senior associate, one who will present more competition for the elusive and highly valued partnership opportunities, will deflate morale and injure a firm's reputation for future hiring.

Thus, when a recruiter calls a fifth- or sixth-year associate and suggests that this may be one of the last years to look at prime law firm opportunities, that headhunter is not just giving a sales pitch. The more senior you become, the fewer available lateral law firm opportunities for associates there are.

Typically, we see associates making lateral moves in their third, fourth, and fifth years as the most common years. This allows the associate ample time to get to know the firm and determine if this is where s/he would like to become a partner. It also gives the partners of the firm the required "look-see" time to determine if the associate is partnership material and if they should vote this person into their partnership.

A senior associate not making partner no longer carries the stigma it once did. Unless some horrible error in judgment or an inability to keep up with your practice causes the firm to tell you that you have no future with them and you had better start looking, I can't imagine anyone thinking you are a loser because you are senior and looking for a new position.

On the other hand, it never hurts to keep your options open and to think about your future. If you don't feel your partnership track is rolling along the right track, and you want to spend some more time being mentored and trained in a law firm, why not make that move before you are senior and your options are not as plentiful? Best wishes!

Sincerely,
Ann M. Israel

❙❚❙

City: New York

I am a graduate of Columbia Law School, law review, top academics, who has worked at several different types of litigation, including government work for the city of New York. Although I've had several different types of jobs, they were all in litigation and I have several successful federal court trials under my belt. Because of life changes—greater emotional maturity and having a family to help support—I am more suited to a big firm job than I was when I was younger, although I did previously work at Debevoise for about four years. But I've found that big firms will not consider me for any position, even though I would work for midlevel associate pay at big-firm scale. Why do law firms systematically favor less experienced candidates when there are more experienced lawyers with the same credentials who would do the same job and do it better for the same money? Why is this anything but age discrimination? Thanks for any thoughts.

Frustrated in NY

Dear Frustrated:

I can understand your frustration. On the surface it would certainly seem to be age discrimination. But if you thought about it and if it truly turned out to be age discrimination, don't you think someone, somehow, would have eventually broken through and successfully sued one of these firms that refused to hire an attorney with 17 years of experience who was willing to work as a fourth or fifth year?

It has been very frustrating for me, as well, to try to explain why I cannot present someone such as you to my clients for their junior or midlevel associate needs. And equally frustrating over the years to try to convince my clients that my senior candidates will reclassify themselves and will honestly be satisfied doing the same level of work that an associate ten years their junior will be doing.

Although I do not believe age discrimination is the main factor that prevents the firms from hiring the experienced attorneys over the junior lawyers, it may play a very small part. The small part may be due to the need for junior attorneys to stay up all night photocopying or drafting or doing whatever grunt work is typically assigned to more junior attorneys. As we age, it becomes more and more difficult to pull all-nighters. Perhaps the firms are concerned that more mature attorneys will not be able to withstand the work hours that junior attorneys are required to maintain. And perhaps this concern is unfounded. But this is a very small part of why the firms do not hire more senior attorneys for the junior positions, and in fact, I have only read about this occasionally in blogs and columns and have never actually heard anyone tell me that this is why they won't hire someone.

The real reasons are due to some very understandable factors. First and foremost, it has to do with past bad experiences. Firms that have hired senior attorneys for more junior positions have found that these individuals are easily bored and unchallenged by these jobs (understandable, don't you agree?). They are doing work that they did years ago and probably never thought they would ever be doing again. Eventually, and because they do it so well and so quickly, they go to their supervisor (who generally turns out to be an associate who is quite junior to them) and ask for work that is more challenging and stimulating. Unfortunately, the position they have been hired for does not allow them to be billed out to the client at a rate that allows them to take on the more sophisticated work. That work goes to the more senior associates who want—and deserve—those assignments. So inevitably, someone is unhappy.

Or let's say that the firm decides to take matters in a different direction: They recognize that this person who has been hired in at a lesser rate is a real find, and they decide to move him/her up the ladder to a higher classification, maybe even to a counsel or partnership opportunity. What do you think happens to the morale of the rest of the associate base—all of those home-growns who have been loyal and toiling away for years, waiting to move on up themselves?

There is a place for bright, experienced, talented individuals who have so much to offer. Unfortunately, it is not in the BigLaw community based on the way it is now currently set up. And especially now, when the BigLaw firms are hemorrhaging associates, I wouldn't think they would dare bring in someone out of the system. But there are so many other places besides BigLaw where someone with your experience can be put to great use. Particularly in this economy, where smaller firms are placing a greater emphasis on maturity and experience, I would think someone with your background would be in greater demand than ever before.

In these rough economic times, we all need to start rethinking what we want. I understand that ideally you would like to be working in a BigLaw firm. Good times or bad, that is going to be difficult for you (no matter what the reason may be), and particularly difficult right now. So instead of being frustrated, start thinking of different types of places to work. Perhaps some of those smaller law firms might provide the stimulation and challenge that you never thought possible. Give it a chance—you never know unless you look. Best wishes!

Sincerely,
Ann M. Israel

City: Chicago

I'm 36 and am seriously considering attending law school. I just received notice that I've been accepted to a top-25 school, but I want to do my due diligence. What's a first-year associate's life like? Is that the only way I can afford to pay off law loans? In general I'm concerned I'm turning in my 45-hour-a-week job at $60K a year for an 80-hour-a-week job and not much more compensation. I want to practice law, but I'm trying to weigh the costs and benefits. Thank you.

Diligent

Dear Diligent:

If you are truly doing your due diligence, you might have learned that right now a first-year associate's life is fairly unstable. Large numbers of first-year attorneys have been asked to leave their firms and are without employment at this time. Others have been asked to take a year off at a greatly reduced salary. Still others are quaking in their figurative boots, waiting to see if the ax is about to fall on their employment.

The situation is even scarier for those 2L and 3L law students who entered law school dreaming of BigLaw paychecks and long billable hours. Many 3Ls have been told that the start date for their new jobs as associates at law firms has been deferred for as long as a year. And 2Ls looking forward to cushy summer jobs with beer-infused parties are now happy if the law firms are having summer programs, and if they are, for the most part, they have been shortened by several weeks—and my guess is that those fancy parties, Broadway plays, and forays out to the new ball parks' private boxes probably are not going to happen.

Having said all of that, I saw Jim Cramer announce to the world (well, whatever portion of the world happened to be watching MSNBC at that moment) the other day that the depression was over! Oh yes, he said, watch for better times. Of course, he reminded us that the recession is still here but the depression is definitely over.

So, what does that mean for you? I suspect (*I hope!*) that this might be a very good time to attend law school and wait out the next two to three years for the economy to heat back up again. However, I can't make you any promises that law firm life is going to be waiting for you with open arms upon your graduation. In an editorial in the *New York Times* on April 1, Adam Cohen predicted a different world in the future (http://www.nytimes.com/2009/04/02

/opinion/02thu4.html?_r=1&em), with salaries at the BigLaw firms for first-year associates falling from $160K to as low as $100K. I don't know if the firms will do that across the board, but it has already started to happen, and only you can decide if it is financially worth it to you, because I doubt that the workload will become any lighter. And I doubt that your law school tuition is going to drop down percentage-wise by the same amount, certainly not this coming school year, even if you are going to Northwestern, which is changing to a two-year law school.

Can you keep your job and attend law school part-time? That is really a difficult thing to do, but perhaps in your situation, until you determine that you really do want to continue on with law school, this might be the best solution. It will give you a chance to see what going back to school is all about without having to give up a job you have had as a career thus far in your life. Just a thought . . .

The only advice I can give is for you to really think about one of the last sentences you wrote to me: "I want to practice law." If that is a burning desire, if you truly love the law, then you will find a way to work through the financial worries and the difficulties of law school and the uncertainties of the future. You are not a 21-year-old kid trying to figure out what to do with your life; instead, you are a mature adult who has some life experience. I think you probably do know what you want to do at this point in time. It won't be easy, but if this is really what you want, go for it before it really does get too late. Just be aware of what is going on with the BigLaw firms and hiring and firing, and understand that no one can predict what the legal community will be all about three years from now when you emerge from law school. Please let us know what you decide to do. Best wishes!

Sincerely,
Ann M. Israel

City: Hong Kong

Dear Ann,

I would like to ask some questions of the individual who is a later-in-life lawyer. I also have similar concerns as the qualified LLM who wrote to you. I am comfortably ensconced within a hedge fund as a credit analyst, so at the moment the opportunity cost of quitting and pursuing a full-time law degree is high. However, I am interested in pursuing a law degree because (1) I am becoming the de facto firm lawyer, (2) I may make a lateral career move to law/corporate in the future, and (3) I enjoy the subject matter. So, given the need for part-time study and the fact I am based outside the United States, does it make sense to study LLB/LLM, or will I be wasting my time? Nonpracticing lawyers have told me LLB/LLM is fine; law firm partners have wrinkled their noses and said to go for the full JD. Your thoughts appreciated. Kind regards.

De Facto

Dear De Facto:

Our friend who volunteered his time to speak to people regarding life as a more mature law student probably did not intend to counsel people on whether or not they should go to law school or advise them as to what degrees they should pursue. I believe his intent was simply to let people know about the pros and cons of going back to school as an older student and then starting out at a BigLaw firm as an older associate. However, I am happy to address your concerns to the best of my ability.

First, though, I would like to comment on the fact that I am interested in your statement that your hedge fund has been treating you as the "de facto firm lawyer." These are some dangerous waters you are swimming around in if you are passing out legal advice (and they are accepting it) since you are not an attorney. Please do be wary and careful here. Malpractice suits abound these days.

Nevertheless, it seems that this has tweaked your interest in the legal profession, and in the near future you would like to move over from being a credit analyst to becoming a transactional attorney.

I do understand the economics of quitting and entering law school full-time. Obviously this does not seem to be a reasonable choice for you at this juncture. However, if you have read any of my archived columns on this subject, then you probably know that I disagree with the nonpracticing attorneys advising you to simply get your LLM and not worry about a JD.

In reading the June 1 posting, you must know that this individual has had nothing but heartbreaking problems in trying to find his dream job, in spite of the fact that he has marvelous credentials and experience. Now, after all of these years, he basically is starting all over again by going back to law school in the United States and earning a U.S. JD, just so he can be employed in a BigLaw firm here in the United States.

If that is your goal, then you must know that an LLM from a foreign law school is really not going to do much for you without a JD from a U.S. law school. Quite frankly, I don't know how you can get an LLM without having a JD or equivalent since the LLM is a master degree of law.

As for the joint LLB/LLM program, that is something I am not qualified to address, but as far as I know, the program is for individuals intending to become British barristers and solicitors. That is not the same program as an American JD, and the law is quite different. If you are planning to practice in England, for example, yes—this would be exactly what you should do.

It would seem to me that the full-time partners who have wrinkled their noses at the idea of an LLB/LLM program are most likely affiliated with American law firms and that is why they are advising you to go after your JD. If you are interested in ultimately working for an American law firm, corporation, bank, or hedge fund, your money and time are best spent and invested attending an American law school where you will receive a JD upon graduation.

Ultimately, everything really depends on where you plan on practicing law. If you are going to live under British rule, you should go after the LLB/LLM degrees. However, if you plan to work for an American law firm or company, you will want to have a JD. I think if you go by this simple rule of thumb, then you will be able to determine which degree to go after. Now the big questions will be when to go to law school, whether to be a full- or part-time student, and how to pay for it! Best wishes!

Sincerely,
Ann M. Israel

▮▮▮

City: New York

I am a senior associate at a top BigLaw firm. During my last review, I was told that I would not make partner and that I should start looking for a job. I intend to interview at boutique firms. How should I handle the question of why I'm leaving?

Passed Over

Dear Passed Over:

First of all, I am sorry to hear your sad news. I know this must have been very difficult for you to hear. Your firm did you no favors by holding on to you and not letting you know that you were not going to make partner until you were a senior associate. I suspect you must have thought you had a decent shot at partnership since they apparently didn't say anything to you until now.

One would hope that a firm would tell an associate earlier in his/her career that the chances of making partner are not good and the firm recommends looking for a new employer. Of course, as is sometimes the case, associates on a strong partnership track go the distance and at the final hour find out that they are not going to be voted into the partnership. But this is not what happened to you. Clearly your reviews were good all along and you saw no reason to suspect what was eventually going to happen, or else I would hope that you would have changed jobs long ago.

I know it is maddening to many associates when the headhunters call them during their third, fourth, and fifth years and suggest that they take a look at the job opportunities out there before they become too senior to take advantage of their most marketable time. But the reality—and especially these days when a partnership in a BigLaw firm has become less and less of a certainty than it ever was before—is that there is no such thing as a sure thing, and if you think that you have a secure shot at making partner, take a look around you and accept the fact that fewer and fewer associates are being voted in the partnership nowadays.

Does that mean a lateral has a better shot at making partner? Well, perhaps it does because a lateral is being hired on a partnership track (unless you are told specifically that the position is not a partnership track job) and the hire is based on, among other attributes, experience, not just law school grades and potential.

So, that's my pitch to not hang up on your friendly headhunter when they call with an opportunity!

But, let's get back to your query on how to handle the inevitable question of why you are leaving your current employer at this point in your career. The good news is you have survived all of the firings that have occurred at the BigLaw firms, so clearly you are able to point out that your reviews have always been good. However, there is no reason to think that any of the partners at the boutique firms are naïve and don't understand how things work at the major law firms. They certainly understand that sometimes even the best associates are asked to move on, particularly in times such as these.

I suggest that you speak with your partners before you go on your interviews and make sure that your references are going to be as good as you hope they will be. Then you will be able to say on your interviews that even though your firm was not going to make you a partner, this had been a tough decision for them, as evidenced by your continued good reviews and excellent references; this decision had just been told to you, and it was now time for you to find a firm where you could continue to have a home for the rest of your career (all true).

The partnership track in boutique law firms may be just as tough right now as it is in any other law firm; I don't recommend pushing the fact that you only want a firm where you can become a partner—please note that I am suggesting that you say you are looking for a firm where you can find a home for the rest of your career. Of course, if they ask if you want to become a partner, you should tell them that if it is possible down the road, it is something that you hold out as a goal. However, more important is to find a firm where there is not an "up or out" policy and where you can continue to practice at the same top level that you have done in the past. Best wishes!

Sincerely,
Ann M. Israel

▌▐▌

City: North of Newark, NJ

I am the managing partner of a small boutique firm [north of Newark]. I have been admitted to practice for ten years and have been in my own firm for five years. I am not challenged by my real estate practice, and certainly not compensated nearly at comparative colleagues' salaries. Is it advisable to consider joining a larger firm hoping to attract a more interesting and lucrative commercial real estate practice indigenous to larger firms?

Unchallenged

Dear Unchallenged:

In a word, yes.

On the surface, of course it makes perfect sense to join a larger, perhaps national, firm that would enable you to grow a larger and, as you put it, more lucrative real estate practice. In such an environment you would set yourself up to attract national and international developers and commercial real estate clients rather than residential clients, which are often the typical clients of small real estate boutiques. By the way, there is not anything wrong with that kind of client, but obviously you are looking for something bigger and, in your mind, better.

However, moving on to that larger firm is easier said than done, particularly in the real estate practice area. There are many factors that are required by the BigLaw firms and specifically in certain departments. I wonder if you have thought about what you would need in order to satisfy these requirements.

As I have written too many times of late, these are difficult times. Granted, you clearly have management skills as well as practice skills, but I am afraid that the larger firms are not interested in hiring attorneys for these reasons. Although you may believe you are not being compensated fairly within your current firm, you will find that the BigLaw firms compensate under the theory of "you eat what you kill." In other words, do not expect to be hired as a service partner in a real estate department thinking that you will be given a chance to build up a practice. The BigLaw firms are interested in attracting real estate partners with existing lucrative practices.

If your practice currently is a lucrative commercial practice that has the ability to be even bigger and better given the right environment, and you can support this with a real business plan, your chances of moving on to a BigLaw firm and earning a better income are very good.

However, if you are thinking that a move will be the right stepping stone to grow your practice—and that practice right now is around $100K—it is going to be very difficult to sell yourself to the larger real estate departments.

If in fact this does describe your practice, then I would suggest you focus more on building up your book of business rather than spending time managing the firm in order to make it possible to move on to a larger firm down the road. If it is at all reasonable or possible for you to hand over the role of MP to someone else at the firm, I recommend you do it and concentrate on the practice of law. This will not only help you to grow your practice but will also allow you to increase your current compensation.

On the other hand, if your current book of portable business is significant, there is no time like the present to pick up the phone, call your favorite headhunter, and get a confidential search started on your behalf. The large firms are all very excited about finding real estate partners with strong portable books to bring over to their departments. Working with a reputable, experienced recruiter should result in a number of excellent meetings set up on your behalf.

Sincerely,
Ann M. Israel

I█I

City: Long Island

Dear Ann,

I am a recent graduate of a second-tier law school. The practice of law is my second career after a successful career in law enforcement, which I finished as a police commander. I am 45 years old. I have been fully employed in the legal field since graduating for two small/midsized firms, one located in Nassau and one in Suffolk. I have worked in general practice firms mostly in the areas of litigation, trusts and estates, and intellectual property/entertainment law. I am happy at the firm I currently work for, but due to their size, my income has stagnated over the past couple of years, even with my own small book of business. Recently, within the past six months, I have been searching for a new position. I see job postings that I believe my qualifications fit perfectly—the areas of practice, the experience, etc.—and I have submitted numerous resumes. The problem I am having is that even though I fit the qualifications requested in the job postings, I do not receive a call for an interview. My resume reflects that I have the necessary experience and background, yet I cannot get the initial interview. My current salary is in the mid-70s and my salary requests are in line with my current salary and level of experience. The only thing I can think of is a possible age issue, but obviously, it is only an assumption. I am fairly confident that I could sell myself if given the opportunity. I present myself well and have the necessary confidence that is needed in the areas that I practice. My question is how do I defeat what I believe to be an age issue when I cannot even get the first interview?

Looking for Direction

Dear Looking:

Unless you are putting your date of birth on the resume, the fact that the practice of law is a second career for you, or the number of years that you were in law enforcement, there is no reason at all for potential employers to know that you are 45 years old.

If you are putting this information on your resume, get it off. The way to indicate your prior life in the police force is to list it after all of your legal experience under the heading of "Other Experience." You might want to put it in a brief sentence and write exactly what you wrote to me—enrolled in law school after a successful career in law enforcement. That's it.

Frequent readers of this column know that I am an advocate of not telling too much in a resume. Use it as a tool for getting an interview—just telling enough to pique someone's interest. If you really believe that there is an age issue at play here, make sure that issue doesn't exist on the resume.

However, I don't believe that is the problem. Here I go . . . the broken record again. This is a very difficult job market, and quite frankly, I don't think you have the necessary experience and background to compete with the probable candidates responding to those ads. Although you didn't tell us how you did in law school, I suspect if you graduated with honors or if you were part of the law review, you would have mentioned those facts. Coming from a second-tier school without any honors or special achievements puts you at a distinct disadvantage in this particular job market. You are competing for those jobs with all of the top-tier law school graduates who were let go from the BigLaw firms over the past year or two and who have had major law firm training.

Your training at two small/midsized firms since law school graduation doesn't compare in a potential employer's eyes when s/he is looking at resumes from associates who have gone through the trials and tribulations of the summer associate programs and then the major law firm associate game.

Additionally, you have spread yourself very thin by practicing in three very distinct and separate practice areas. Litigation, T&E, and intellectual property/entertainment law require knowledge and training in very different areas of the law. Although working in these three practice groups allows you to apply to many different ads, I would think it makes you less qualified in an employer's mind.

Lastly, and this is not an ageist issue, you are quite senior in terms of an associate hire now. Your class year is heading toward the title of senior associate. I have written so many columns over the years as to why law firms hesitate when it comes to hiring senior level associates. It has nothing to do with your age but rather with the seniority of their associates and the sense of loyalty the firm has to them at this point in their tenure. With partnership becoming less and less available to senior associates, the partners are—hopefully—becoming more and more sensitive to this issue.

One more thing—you mention that you have your own small book of business. Most firms are not looking for their associates to bring in business. They need the associates to service the business of the partners. However, when there is a book of business, it needs to be significant in order for a firm to be truly interested or impressed. I would not suggest you mention your book of business on your resume. This is something that you certainly can bring up to see if there is any interest from a potential employer once you are far down the road with advanced interviews.

The bottom line here is that you need to revise your resume and then keep responding to the ads with the fact in mind that this is a tough time to be looking for a job. Fortunately for you, you are gainfully employed at a firm where you are *happy*. As the expression goes, don't give up your day job. Keep searching but stay happy until that new job comes around. Eventually it will, but in the meantime, you've got a steady paycheck to collect. Best wishes!

Sincerely,
Ann M. Israel

City: Paramus, NJ

Dear Ann,

I graduated law school in 1996, and I worked on the corporate side of employee benefits for a very large, high-profile Wall Street financial institution right out of law school for three years. I then practiced employee benefits law for the largest law firm in New Jersey for three more years. I left that position in 2002 to help my husband start his own law firm, which I office-managed until this past month, when our divorce was final. I am licensed to practice in New Jersey only. How can I market myself to get back to the practice of law? My legal skills are a little rusty, but I know all the aspects and the economics of running a law firm, and I can be added value to a firm. Please help.

Rusty

Dear Rusty:

I wish I could help you. From what you have told us, I am sure you could add tremendous value to all aspects of running a law firm, including the economic end. Those are valuable skills in addition to your legal training.

However, there are so many other issues at hand here, and you do need to face them. First of all, even though you worked for a large Wall Street financial institution when you first graduated from law school, if we do some simple math it would seem that you graduated at least 15 years ago and the last time you practiced law was in 2002. The employee benefits practice area has changed dramatically over the past nine-plus years. To say that you are a *little* rusty is an understatement, and one that is going to be very hard to defend in an interview.

You stated that you are licensed to practice in New Jersey; does that mean you have kept up with all that is required of New Jersey attorneys over the past nine years while you were not practicing law? Specifically, were you paying your state bar association fees and licensing fees and taking all those many hours of very expensive CLE classes that are required every year? If not, then I would suggest you first start looking into getting your license to practice law reinstated before you do anything else.

When a law firm is looking for an employee benefits/ERISA attorney, it is due to the fact that they have more work than they can handle in that particular practice area and need to add an additional person to the department. Generally speaking, they do not need an administrative person as well. In my experience, I have never seen a situation where a firm wants to hire an attorney (an associate, as it would be in your case) who would also run the administrative and economic aspects of the firm.

If there isn't already an administrative department (or person, as it would be in a small firm) handling this function in the firm, then there would be a job description out there to hire someone to fill this spot. And that job opening would be for an administrative/associate attorney. Attorney and administrator are two very different and distinct positions. I'm sure you recognize this from working with your husband at his firm. I suspect it would have been impossible for you, working on the administrative side of things, to find the time to practice law, and that is why you administered the workings of the firm rather than continuing to practice employee benefits law.

Here's some good news: the employee benefits practice area is one of the busy practice areas at this time. There are actually openings in employee benefits and firms are hiring. However, you need to recognize that the law in this area is very different than it was back in 2002, and you will need to bring your skills up-to-date very fast if you expect to be a viable candidate.

If your license to practice in the state of New Jersey is current and you are up-to-date on the practice of employee benefits law, you only have the hurdle of explaining why you haven't practiced since 2002. However, there is not an abundance of employee benefits attorneys, so you may be given a pass on this matter by some employers if there are a number of openings out there in the New Jersey firms.

My main suggestion to you is to drop the "added value" you can bring to a firm unless an interviewer seems to think that this is something his/her firm wants. This is not what interviewers want to hear from you; they want to hear that you are committed to being an employee benefits attorney and you want to practice law, not be an administrator. Best wishes!

Sincerely,
Ann M. Israel

City: New York

I was laid off from a large law firm after almost five years. Now that I have over ten years' experience I find that most law firms don't want attorneys who don't have business or who have more than three to six years' experience. What does a lawyer do in this situation?

P.S. The continuous mergers that are eliminating midsized law firms are hurting my job search because midsized firms are more open than large firms when it comes to hiring attorneys with ten or more years of experience.

What to Do

Dear What To Do:

There is no question that merger mania has changed the number of law firms that are available for associates to apply to. As if it isn't hard enough to find a new opportunity, it seems that all of a sudden there are so many fewer places to look.

Sadly, it isn't just due to the many mergers that have happened over the past ten years or so. I am afraid that in the past three years or so, not only have there been scores of layoffs and firings on the associate, partner, and in-house levels from law firms and corporations, but there have also been firms that have just disappeared into the night, so to speak. One day they claim they are thriving and the next day—boom, they are gone. Howrey closed their doors last week. Remember Thacher Proffitt? Heller Ehrman? Wolf Block? Thelen?

And these are the large national firms that have gone away over the past few years. There are scores of those midsized and boutique law firms all over the country that you would like to interview with that no longer exist; they were unable to garner enough business during the down economic times to be a viable merger candidate. Or perhaps they thought they could weather the tough times on their own and turned down those merger offers, and when it was finally too late, they were forced to close their books and consequently their doors.

Of course, there are still plenty of law firms out there, and they have picked up the business that was left hanging by the dearly departed firms. So why are you still having a tough time finding a job?

Sadly, the hiring mentality doesn't change just because a firm may have picked up another firm's business. Law firms still do not want to hire senior associates for the same exact reason that they have not wanted to hire them over the years. One: senior associates are very expensive and the clients are more cost-conscious now than they ever were before. Two: partnership opportunities within law firms are now few and far between. Fewer and fewer associates will make partner than ever before. Bringing on a senior associate is a morale buster for those less-senior associates who have been loyal to the firm, working off their rear ends and hoping against hope that they might make counsel or even some kind of partner status. Three: firms generally need more junior and midlevel associates, period.

So, what does a senior-level associate do in this situation? Everything possible. Let me say it again: *everything possible*. Go visit several of the headhunters that used to call you all the time (even though you haven't heard from them in the past few years since you became a senior-level associate). You never know. They might just have something, even if it is only an idea. Or they might have a great in-house opportunity because you are definitely at the right level for in-house positions.

Also go to visit recruiters who offer contract opportunities. First of all, you want to be bringing in a paycheck at this time instead of hanging out at home worrying. Secondly, you never know when a contract position *might* turn into something full-time. It can happen. At the very least, you will be getting paid.

Call your law school's career services office. I know, they do nothing. Stop telling me this. Obviously they do help someone or else they wouldn't exist. Pester them. Remember what I said—do everything possible. This is one of those possibilities. Don't leave it out.

Network, network, and then network some more. Call everyone you know. Everyone. Send letters. Good ones. Proofread them.

It's a lot of work, but you want a job, right?

I wish I had more to give to you right now. It's tough out there, especially in your situation, but I do think you are not in the most untenable position. You have a very stable job history and hopefully employers will take this into consideration. It is no longer a black mark on a resume to have been laid off— it appears you are in a great majority these days. Just be prepared to face a bit of a challenge, and remember, do everything possible. Please let us know how things turn out for you. Best wishes!

Sincerely,
Ann M. Israel

City: New York

My question concerns getting a job with one of the top, top-paying firms. I am [an eighth-year associate] who graduated from [a law school that is approximately ranked around #25]. I am currently trying to get a job at one of the high-paying firms in Manhattan. I am frustrated because I have friends working at these firms who either (a) went to schools that are not of [my school's] caliber or (b) had grades equal to or worse than mine. (I have over a 3.0.) I have excellent credentials as a writer and was published in one of [my law school's] journals. (Incidentally, I called your recruiting office and they would not even accept my resume.) What can I do to increase my chances of getting into a good firm, and how do other, less-qualified people manage it?

Thanks, Ann.
Qualified

Dear Qualified:

In ordinary times and in an ordinary profession, you wouldn't be writing to me. You would be sought after by many employers and would be fending off multiple job offers. However, you are not living in ordinary times and you certainly are not working in an ordinary profession.

About four and a half years ago, you would have been offered jobs at all of those "top, top-paying" firms where your friends are currently working. As I have written previously, I was placing people in those firms at that time whom I couldn't believe were being hired. You would have been snapped up by any firm that asked you in for an interview.

But, that was then and this is now.

I suspect that your friends who are working at these firms and who had grades equal to or worse than yours or went to schools that are ranked lower than yours have been working at their firms for a number of years already. More than likely they were hired before September of 2008.

Aside from the tough job market that exists today, I need to point out some of the tough reality that also is standing in your way from getting a job with those firms where you want to work. First of all, as I have explained many times, coming from a law school ranked around number 25 means that you need to have more than a 3.0 GPA. That just isn't going to cut it in today's job market with the New York BigLaw firms.

But what is really standing in your way is that you are an eighth-year associate now. The firms simply are not going to bring on someone who is going to be competing for a partnership slot with other senior associates who have been with the firm for a significant period of time already. It would be a devastating blow to the morale of their own senior associates who have no idea if they are going to make partner or be asked to leave the firm. Unless you can bring a significant book of portable business along with you, these firms are not interested in hiring yet another senior associate. They are concerned enough about the ones they already have.

As far as my firm not even accepting your resume when you called, I hope the recruiter you spoke with explained why h/she was taking this position. Quite frankly, we don't want to give you false hope that we are able to do something for you. We honestly believe that someone in your position—an eighth-year associate from a number 25–ranked law school with a 3.0 grade point average—in today's job market most likely would be hurt rather than helped by a search firm. It would be so very unfair—and dishonest—for us to tell you that we could place you in a BigLaw firm when we know that our clients are not going to pay us a fee for you. Our recruiters are expected to explain this to you and to tell you that you would be better off conducting your job search on your own without a fee attached to your candidacy.

We are not in the business to take on the resumes of people when we know we cannot help them. We do not tell people we will see what we can do for them when we know that our clients are going to reject their candidacy. We are in the business of being honest and suggesting other methods of job searching if we are unable to be of assistance to you. I hope you understand our position, and I certainly hope that the recruiter you spoke with in our office explained all of this to you thoroughly and professionally.

I suggest at this time that you set your sights on midsize and smaller boutiques that might be able to take some senior-level associates as well as looking at in-house opportunities where, as an eighth-year attorney, you are now a prime candidate. Of course, if you do have friends in these BigLaw firms, it can't hurt for them to pass your resume on to their partners. Again, as I always advise, network, network, network. Best wishes!

Sincerely,
Ann M. Israel

CHAPTER 6

Interview Questions and Behavior

There are so many books and videos out there on how to interview, but as far as I am concerned, there are only a few critical rules that must be followed. First—and of most importance in my mind—do your due diligence prior to going into an interview. Research as much as you can about the firm, its practice area, the partner(s) you are about to meet, and why you would want to work for this firm and this particular department. Nothing could be worse than telling an interviewer that you are interested in their M&A department when the firm is a litigation boutique! Have solid reasons why you want to join this firm. Dress properly for an interview. Keep good eye contact with the interviewer. Don't wear cologne or perfume. Bring extra copies of your resume and transcript. Have questions to ask (that are appropriate for that specific firm). Sit up straight. And lastly—and a real job killer if you don't do it—express an interest in the opportunity at the end of the interview.

My favorite story on this subject is about the candidate I was representing who was going for an interview with a firm he really wanted to join. I prepared him for the interview and reminded him over and over again to express an interest in the opportunity. He called me after the interview and told me how great it went, that he really wanted an offer for the job, and if he did receive one that he would accept it on the spot. I had never heard anyone so excited about a job prospect! After doing my follow-up with this candidate, I then called the client. To my surprise, the client told me that he really liked the candidate but was going to pass on him because he didn't think my candidate was interested in the job. I was ready to murder my candidate because even though he thought he had expressed an interest in the job, he had not said it in those words! Fortunately for all concerned, my client trusted me, and when I told him how excited my candidate was about the opportunity, he agreed to interview him one more time. And this time, the candidate followed my advice (under threat of death!), told the partner that he wanted the job (he expressed more than just an interest in the firm—good for him!), and he did receive an offer, which he immediately accepted.

Expressing an interest in the opportunity won't guarantee that you will get the job, but believe me, it can make a difference. Bottom line—it can't hurt!

City: Toronto, Ontario

Hello. I have three upcoming interviews with large NYC law firms for second-year summer positions. They will be coming to Toronto to interview me and other students. Do you have any advice on how I may best be able to stand out from the other students being interviewed so that I am asked back for a second interview in their NYC offices? Thank you.

Stand-Out

Dear Stand-Out:

You have your work cut out for you, no question about it. I say this simply because not only are you facing competition from other students at your own school, but you are also facing the fact that you are trying to get a job in another country, where there are scores and scores of rising 2Ls who are also interviewing with these same large NYC law firms. Not only do you have to stand out from the other students in your class so that you are asked back for the callback round, but you also have to be so good that you overcome the hassles that the firms must deal with in terms of immigration issues.

So, let's remember the first and most important thing about this first round of interviews—what they are really all about: selling yourself to the firm. That's it—the bottom line.

First impressions are critical. Somewhere, someone once said that a hiring person makes a decision to *not* hire someone in the first 60 seconds of an interview. If that is true—and from years of hiring people, I believe it is—keep in mind how important that first impression will be. What should you wear? There is no question in my mind that you should be dressed in business attire—suits for men and women. You may receive notices that certain firms allow students to attend their interviews dressed in "business casual." Forget it! You have no idea who is going to show up to interview you. It might be a third-year associate from that firm who is casually dressed, or it might be a senior partner who only wears bespoke suits. Keep in mind those first 60 seconds. Better to be dressed professionally than take a risk.

Although the firms already have your resume, it never hurts to be prepared in case somehow the interviewer lost it or never received it or whatever. Make lots of extra copies of your resume; put one in a folder, portfolio, or briefcase; and bring it with you to the interview. You never know. Be prepared!

And speaking of being prepared, readers of this column know what I always advise: do your due diligence before your interviews! Know everything about the firm before you walk into the interview. Understand what the firm does and especially what it doesn't do. You won't score points when you start telling the interviewer about your great interest in a practice area that his/her firm doesn't have! However, when you know what practice areas the firm does specialize in and you talk about those areas and let the interviewer know that is why you are interested in his/her firm, you will get his/her ear.

If possible, find out who will be interviewing you. Frequently the interviewer's name is listed prior to your interview, and you will be well advised to go to the firm's website and study this person's bio and background.

I mentioned at the beginning that the most important thing you can do in these brief on-campus interviews is to sell yourself. That doesn't mean to walk in and go over your resume and your transcript. The interviewer can do that on his/her own. It means that after you have done your due diligence, you are able to convincingly discuss why you want to come back to this specific firm and meet more people and have an opportunity to work there during your 2L summer. It means discussing more than just the law. It means being able to find some common ground between you and the interviewer and establish some kind of relationship where s/he sees you as more than just another 20-minute meeting.

None of this is easy. These on-campus very brief interviews are tough. But if you put some time and effort into learning about the firms and interviewers prior to stepping into the interviewing room, you might just find that you are able to click with that person sitting across from you, and that's what it takes to get that magic invitation known as the callback. In doing your homework prior to these interviews, you might even come across some people at these firms that you know; give them a call and ask them for some information about their firms for some extra hints. Search through the NALP books; there is a tremendous amount of information about law firms in their books. Speak with the people at your law school's career center. Leave no stones unturned. And please write us back after your first round of interviews and let us know how things went. Best wishes!

Sincerely,
Ann M. Israel

▌▊▐

City: Unknown

I didn't get an offer. I think it has been haunting me, and the only reason I can think of is not something I can say in an interview. I graduated from a top-20 law school, with honors, and was on law review. My work product was excellent, and my midterm and final reviews were excellent. The managing partner at the final review told me to be optimistic. When the hiring partner came to my school during OCIs to recruit the next year's class, he told me, "The word on the street is good." A senior partner wrote on my reviews that I was the best summer associate there. In all honesty, and I'm not searching for a whiny reason, I suspect I didn't get an offer because I am a minority female. I felt very out of place and unwelcome. I honestly felt that I was filling a quota of some sort. To top it off, I was working in a city that is considered to be one of the most liberal cities in the United States, so this came as rather a shock.

I didn't go to law school in the same region as the firm, so it wasn't until later that I found out from attorneys at other firms (both big and small) that the firm had a lot of question marks surrounding it regarding its treatment of minorities and females. Nobody was surprised about how I felt; some were even the first to ask me how I liked the firm, being a minority female. On top of it, my supervising attorney left in the middle of my summer with less than graceful good-byes (she hated the place), and my second supervising attorney left the same month my summer ended (with even less graces than the first). Needless to say, I didn't want to work there, but I was willing to stay for one to three years to gain experience before moving.

After graduating, I found a job with a solo practitioner who called up a senior partner at the firm I summered as a reference. The senior partner said that I was an excellent summer associate and had no idea why I did not receive an offer. The solo practitioner, who has practiced in the area for over 30 years, also made a remark that I didn't get an offer because of "internal problems" with the firm. I've had lunch with another junior partner and a senior partner that I worked with, and they both said that work product was spot-on. The firm gave me some excuse about overestimating how many people they could hire and something about an LLM student coming back to work and a senior associate coming back from maternity leave, even though the next year, they hired more summers than they did for my year.

The problem is, I would like to find a job at a BigLaw firm. I don't have much work experience and my resume just screams "I didn't get an offer." I have three partners and one associate from the old firm as references as well as the solo plaintiff attorney and a professor. However, I haven't received one phone call. In fact, rejection letters come in as early as two days after I send my resume.

So, in a nutshell, my questions are: (1) What's going on?! (2) Am I ever going to get my foot in the door at a BigLaw firm? (3) If and when I do finally get an interview, what should I say when asked why I didn't get an offer? Needless to say, I can't say that the firm was conservative and an unfriendly place to work if you are a minority female. Should I just say they over-hired and leave it at that? (4) Also, wouldn't staying at a small plaintiffs' firm hurt me the longer I stay?

Offerless

Dear Offerless:

This should not be. I am having a very difficult time trying to answer your question #1: "What's going on?!" In my wildest imagination, and if everything you are telling us is exactly as it happened, it just doesn't make any sense. Top-20 school, graduated with honors, law review, a diversity candidate, and the firms aren't knocking down your door to meet with you? Just what is going on?

What is really confusing is the fact that it seems any time a reference is checked or you happen to speak with a partner from your summer firm, no one has anything to say about you except that you were a terrific summer associate. You received rave reviews and yet they didn't hire you. This doesn't make sense.

I do agree with you that staying at a small plaintiffs' firm is not the best place to be if you want to end up in a BigLaw firm; you are doing the right thing by getting your resume out there sooner rather than later.

Your resume right up to your current employment is beautiful. I don't think the reason you are not getting any interviews is because you didn't get an offer from your summer firm, especially since you are now living in a different city. I think what is really hurting you at this time is that you are working for a solo practitioner in a plaintiffs' firm while at the same time trying to get a job in a BigLaw defense firm. I suspect this is the biggest problem.

So, what to do? First thing, get yourself over to your law school's career services office and pound on the door. I can't believe they don't have some connections with a number of the top BigLaw firms seeking highly credentialed first-year associates. And all of the major law firms have a strong commitment to diversity hiring—this should work in your favor, not against you!

Next, get out there and start networking . . . go to bar association events, talk to everyone you know, network in every possible way and let everyone know that you want to work in a BigLaw firm.

Although you probably are too junior to work with recruiters, you might want to speak with several of the top headhunters in your region to see if they have any suggestions or even if they know of any opportunities that might be appropriate for you. You never know . . .

When you do get an interview (or interviews) at the BigLaw firms and they ask the inevitable question as to why you didn't get an offer at your summer employer, the only way to answer is with the truth: "I really don't know." I wouldn't go into too much detail, but I would let the interviewer know your reviews were stellar and you absolutely felt confident that you were going to receive an offer. You have tried to find out why you didn't get an offer, and in fact, several partners from that firm now stand as your references, and you invite anyone to call them. But the bottom line is that you are baffled as to why you did not get an offer after the summer because you were told by one senior partner that you were "the best summer associate there."

That's all. Don't be defensive; don't make a big deal out of it. Just tell the truth, simply and to the point.

I remain confused. You have so many people saying such great things about you from that firm. What happened? Someone cast a vote against you, that's for sure. But why? Can you think of anything at all that happened during the summer that might have turned off one of the partners? Could it be, as you suspect, because you are a minority female? That just leaves me speechless, and I simply cannot buy it. There are all kinds of avenues for you to follow if you really believe that to be the case, but in the final analysis, aren't you glad that you don't work there? After all the wonderful things they said to you, and then they didn't give you an offer, why would you want to work there? Good riddance to them! Move on! Be tenacious! You can do it! And best wishes to you!

Sincerely,
Ann M. Israel

City: Madison, WI

How do you answer the question, "Why did you leave your last employer?" if you did not leave on amicable terms or you were fired? If you do not leave on amicable terms with your supervisor, can your supervisor prevent others in the office from giving you references?

Mad

Dear Mad:

I'm afraid you are in a tough position if this is your situation. If you have been fired from your last job or have left on terms that are not exactly amicable, there really is not much you can do but answer truthfully when asked why you left your last employer.

If you have read any of my past columns then you know I always advocate telling the truth. No matter how you slice it, if you don't tell the truth, you will eventually be caught, and then what will happen? More than likely you will be asked to leave your job, or, at the very least, you will never get a good assignment again and your future with this employer will be trashed.

If you were fired, you need to go over the facts of what led up to this final event and try to put them into a succinct and nondefensive narrative because you certainly will be asked why you left your last employer. Make your answer simple and don't put the blame on anyone. You might want to shed light on what you learned from the situation and why whatever happened will never happen again.

You might want to go over the cause of the termination with your boss on the day that you leave and discuss what will happen in the event s/he is ever called as a reference. Ask him/her to discuss this with you candidly so that you can be prepared to know what your prospective employers will hear when they check your references.

Your past supervisor cannot prevent others in the office from giving references for you. You are free to give out whatever names you choose as your references. However, there may be a rule in any particular firm that on a reference check of a departed employee only dates of employment may be discussed. The law on this matter says that a past employer may only verify dates of employment and salary during a telephone reference check. By the way, that's about the same as a bad reference. And since you don't want that on a phone check reference, try to use either people who have already left that firm or people you worked with at other firms as your references.

However, there is no doubt in my mind that a prospective employer will want to check references at the firm where you last worked. In this situation, you need to find someone there who is willing to offer up good things about you when you ask him/her if s/he will be your reference—and emphasize that what they say will determine your future.

I believe the most important thing you can do in this situation is to be aware of what your past employer is going to say about you when s/he is called as a reference. Being prepared for this eventuality is your best defense. Good luck!

Sincerely,
Ann M. Israel

City: New York

HOW DO YOU ANSWER A QUESTION LIKE, "WHERE DO YOU SEE YOURSELF IN FIVE YEARS?"

Looking to the Future

Dear Future:

Whoa, are you really angry or something? Shouting, whether in person or online, hurts my ears and/or my eyes. I hope that question about where you see yourself in five years doesn't make you so angry when it is asked in an interview that you start screaming!

Actually, it is one of those interviewing 101 questions that could make me scream. I often think that an interviewer resorts to a question such as this when s/he cannot think of anything else to ask or when there is an interviewing form s/he is supposed to follow. I'm not sure what someone expects to learn from the answer to this question because rarely is it a truthful answer; instead it is an answer that the candidate thinks the interviewer wants to hear.

Unfortunately, it is a question that one generally cannot avoid, particularly during in-house interviews. Therefore, it is best to be prepared to have appropriate answers in case you are asked this question—answers that are appropriate for the firm or company where you are interviewing.

If you are clever during the interview, and long before this question appears, you have found out what promotional, growth, or partnership opportunities exist short-term and long-term at the firm or company where you are interviewing. Then, when you are asked where you see yourself in five years, you can gear your answer to fit that particular growth or partnership track.

What is important when answering this question is discussing how you intend to get to that five-year mark. That is the real key to your answer and what I believe should be the substance to the discussion. A one-sentence answer to the question doesn't deliver the same punch that will come with a well-thought-out explanation of your goals and how to attain them.

If you are quite junior in your practice and you are unclear as to how to answer the question, then it is fair to let the interviewer know you are not quite certain where you see yourself five years from now, but you know that with the mentoring, knowledge, and experience you will receive from this firm, you expect to be a strong midlevel associate by that time.

The main thing to understand about the question is that it is a time-filler, but it possibly gives you a chance to distinguish yourself in an interview that may have been lackluster. If the question does come up, take advantage of it by showing that you are a professional and someone who truly wants to be a part of this firm or company for now and into the future (or at least for the next five years!). Good luck!

Sincerely,
Ann M. Israel

⊪

City: **New York**

Dear Ann:

When is it appropriate during the interview process to ask the questions I really want to know about a firm? I.e., what are the hours like, what is the face time like, what is the bonus structure, what is the maternity leave policy, etc.? Are these questions best left until after the offer? To whom should I address these questions?

Practical

Dear Practical:

These are very important questions, and clearly the answers will make a difference as to whether or not you want to accept a job offer at a specific firm or corporation. However, *when* you ask these questions might very well make a difference as to whether or not you receive a job offer!

If you are working with a recruiter, you certainly can ask these questions in the very beginning of the interviewing process when you meet with the recruiter to discuss specific job opportunities. If s/he does not know the answers, s/he will be more than happy to find out for you sooner rather than later. In fact, if your headhunter doesn't know the answer to a few of the questions right away (what are the hours like? what is the bonus structure?), you might want to hold off giving permission to present your background to this firm or corporation until s/he does have the answers.

However, other questions that relate to issues such as vacation, maternity leave, face time, etc., are matters that are not substantive to your practice area and should either be left to your headhunter to ask for you or else for you to ask the recruiting coordinator at the firm (or human resources at the corporation) after you have received an offer (but before you have accepted it).

What's important for you to remember here is that your goal is to get the potential employer to be interested enough in you and your legal skills first and foremost—interested enough that you receive an offer of employment. Then, and only then, are you in a position to ask all of the questions you want about benefits and hours and perks without looking as if that is all you are interested in with this particular employer. Good luck!

Sincerely,
Ann M. Israel

I▦I

City: New York

Dear Ann,

About three weeks ago, I went to a final-round interview at a firm that I am very interested in. Unfortunately, on the day of the interview, a big deal I had been working on blew up and I got a number of e-mails and phone calls on my Blackberry during the interview. While I did not answer the phone calls or respond to the e-mails during the interview, I did pull out my Blackberry and take a quick look at them because my handheld had been vibrating off the hook. Although the interviewer did not say anything to me about this during the interview, I have not heard a thing from the firm since then and am very concerned that they are no longer interested in me. Do you think my looking at the Blackberry during the interview could have derailed my chances with this firm?

Derailed

Dear Derailed:

Yes, I do think looking at your Blackberry during an interview might have ended your chances with the firm of your dreams. But don't be too upset— they certainly have acted poorly by not getting back to you over the past three weeks, especially in light of the fact that you were on a final interview. Even as just a courtesy, one would expect that they would give you some sort of feedback or at least a phone call to say they weren't interested.

Now, why am I so certain that pulling out your Blackberry during a meeting might have ended your chances with this firm? Well, first I can tell you from personal experience that when I am interviewing a candidate, I am always surprised to see someone pull out his/her Blackberry in the middle of our meeting. It seems incredibly rude to me to stop a conversation to read a text message. I wouldn't think of walking into a meeting without turning off my phone or Blackberry, and it surprises me when someone doesn't do the same with me. Clearly the person does not respect me in the same way that I respect him/her. It also makes me realize that the individual has no idea that their interview with the headhunter is really the first interview with the client.

That's right. If the candidate doesn't pass muster with the recruiter, s/he doesn't get passed on to the client for an interview. The headhunter truly is the first interview for the client firm or company.

But don't go by my opinion alone. It's a coincidence that this question should come to me this week because last month I had lunch with the hiring partner of a BigLaw firm at a place where we were required to turn off our phones and Blackberries when we entered. This nicety led to a conversation about Blackberries in interviews, and the HP told me about a recent incident that was quite upsetting both to him and to the firm. It is so similar to your situation—I wonder if he actually could have been referring to you!

A candidate had been brought back to the firm for a final round of interviews. This individual was someone liked by everyone in the firm, and in fact, they had hoped to extend an offer soon after this round of meetings if all went as expected. However . . .

During the interview with a senior partner, the candidate's Blackberry started to vibrate, and he pulled it out of his pocket to read the message while the partner was discussing some of the firm's policies. The partner didn't blink an eye but certainly was well aware of what had just happened. When it came time for the partners to decide whether or not to make an offer to this candidate, they all gathered together, eager to discuss this exceptional candidate. Unfortunately, when they heard from their beloved senior partner that he had taken out his Blackberry during their interview, they weren't so enamored of him any longer. They were all very surprised that he would show such a lack of respect and judgment during a meeting. Could anything be that important to interrupt a conversation with a senior partner of the firm?

The partners of the firm were all very sad about their conclusion on this candidate, but the decision was unanimous—they voted to pass on this candidate.

I know many of you will think it was petty of the firm to pass on a candidate simply because he looked at his Blackberry during an interview, but if you do feel that way, you had better think twice. It was simply out-and-out rude. When you walk into an interview, turn off your phone and/or Blackberry. You know you can't respond to a call or message while you are in an interview, so why even be distracted by the ring or vibration to begin with? The candidate showed very poor judgment and exceptionally poor manners. The partners were thinking that if he behaved this way in an interview with a senior partner of the firm, how would he act with clients?

Now, in your case, this certainly doesn't excuse the firm from not getting back to you with some kind of answer as to whether or not they are still interested in you. However, I suspect their silence—after such enthusiasm initially—is an indication that you are no longer on their short list of viable candidates. Next time keep your Blackberry in the front hall closet when you go in for an interview. Best wishes!

Sincerely,
Ann M. Israel

▮▮▮

City: Los Angeles

Ann—I have been on a few interviews with some big firms that I really want to work at. The problem is, whether it be the preliminary interview or the callback interview, there are always those interviewers who act as if you have no place in the firm and don't know why s/he needs to be interviewing you. They make it pretty obvious because they will ask you a simple question and look off in the distance while you answer or be incredibly condescending. For example, I once had a hiring partner during a second round of interviews ask me if I thought my work experience looked terrible. I once had an associate on the recruiting committee come get me for my interview 20 minutes late, and while I was interviewing with her, she was sending out e-mails and had her side turned to me the whole time. What can one do to deflect this? Or how can I save the situation the best I can? Notwithstanding the glaring question of whether I want to work at a place or not after such treatment, what I'm really after is how to save an interview when you have odds stacked against you or when the interviewer doesn't seem to like you from the start. What can one do to change the situation in the 20 to 30 minutes you are allotted?

Need to Change a First Impression

Dear Need to Change,

"Need to change"—a bad attitude of an interviewer is what needs to be changed. You had an interview with someone who, after arriving 20 minutes late for you, then proceeded to turn away from you and send out e-mails during the entire interview? Where was this individual raised? Apparently in a barn, based on her behavior during her interview with you.

Listen, I don't know how an interview can possibly be saved when an interviewer is this uninterested in a candidate. The good news is that this has nothing to do personally with you. The interviewer obviously has problems that have nothing to do you with you whatsoever. However, she never should have taken on this meeting with you and, if she could not get out of it, even at the last minute, common courtesy would dictate that she explain why she kept you sitting there for 20 minutes and why you were going to be spending the next 30 minutes in an interview talking to her backside as she sent out these very important e-mails.

I have tried to put myself in your situation, and the only thing I could come up with was to say, "It seems as if this is a very bad time for us to be meeting. Why don't I step outside and ask your assistant to reschedule a meeting for another time that might work for you?"

My first thought when I read your question was that perhaps you were not creating a good first impression and the interviewer was turned off by you. But after rereading your question, I realized that probably was not the case because you indicated that you were having this same problem both on initial and callback interviews. If the first impression you created was off-putting, more than likely you would not be getting callback interviews. Therefore, I had to look a bit deeper to figure out what might be happening.

Quite frankly, I didn't have to look very far. In BigLaw firms, it isn't unusual to find one very difficult partner or one cranky associate who has been thrown (for some unknown reason) into the interviewing schedule. It wouldn't matter who you are, they simply aren't in a mood to like you. Or so it seems.

I say this because I can't begin to tell you how many times I have had candidates return from an interviewing session completely devastated because one of the interviewers behaved in exactly the same way as you have described. It would seem that s/he was totally uninterested in my candidate, even to the point of absolute disdain. And then I do a follow-up call and find out that this interviewer thought my candidate was absolutely fabulous. Go figure.

The best advice I can give to you is to hang in there during those horrid interviews. Some people are just jerks, plain and simple. If someone asks you if you think your work experience is terrible, and you know damn well that it isn't, tell him/her exactly why you are the right person for the job and why your experience is right on target. On the other hand, if it appears that they don't have time for you, let them know that you recognize this fact and will come back at another mutually agreeable time. Don't let the interviewer do this crap to you! If you bust them on their bad behavior, maybe—just maybe— this will get them to stop it right away and start behaving properly.

The bottom line is that if these are firms where you would like to work, or at least continue to interview, you need to accept the interviewing system for what it is. Best wishes!

Sincerely,
Ann M. Israel

City: Charlotte, NC

Dear Ann,

I am an associate in a small, family-run law firm where I have worked for several years. I have been wanting to head to another firm for several years. People in my firm regularly tell minor lies to clients, and recently one supervisor of mine told a major lie to an outside party and is very open about having lied and about the need not to let the lie be known to others. I am very uncomfortable working in such at atmosphere, and the lack of honesty among people at my firm is, I think, a sufficient reason to leave. Should I bring this reason for leaving up during interviews, and if so, how should I phrase it?

Thank you.
Phrased

Dear Phrased:

The very worst thing you could do on an interview is talk negatively about your current employer. In fact, it is commonly known in interviewing circles as the 11th commandment: *Thou shalt not speak badly about one's current employer.*

Sitting in an interview and bad-mouthing your current employer only reflects poorly on you—it makes you look like a complainer, and we all know that no one wants to hire a complainer. From personal experience, I know that I have interviewed potential recruiters from competing search firms and listened to their tales of woe. It's fun for a moment to hear the gossip, and then it isn't fun at all. I really don't want to hear it. It only makes the person telling the tales look bad.

There is, of course, a way for you to get your point across to potential employers without being a complete open book. In your particular situation, when you are asked the inevitable question about why you are thinking about leaving your current firm, you might simply answer that you have heard that the interviewer's firm would be a better fit for you, that you think it is a better firm than the one you are currently practicing at, and that it offers better legal skills and a chance to learn more than where you currently work.

If you are smart, you will have done a good deal of due diligence prior to going on an interview and at this point will be able to talk about the firm's expertise and reputation in your particular practice area. The interviewer will be impressed and instead of looking at you as a malcontent will see you as someone who is trying to better him/herself.

Of course you are uncomfortable working in such a dishonest atmosphere as the one where you are currently associated; I hope you are able to find a new home as soon as possible. Just make sure that you are positive and enthusiastic in your interviews; no one wants to hire someone who appears to be chronically discontented. Make your glass half full instead of half empty when asked why you want to leave; it always is the best way to look at things. Good luck!

Sincerely,
Ann M. Israel

⬛

Dear Readers:

I am answering this week's question not so much for the benefit of the individual who wrote to me but rather for law school students and for those of you in a similar situation.

Best,
Ann M. Israel

City: New York

Although I attended a top-10 law school, my grades suffered when I made the choice to stay in school while nursing a close family member through [an illness]. Now, I am left to explain the bad grades. Since the grades do not reflect my true abilities, as demonstrated by my post–law school success, what can I say to employers without making them uncomfortable when I am asked for my transcript?

Reflection

Dear Reflection:

I am about to give you a rather harsh answer. I am sorry to do so, but I know of no other way to answer your inquiry.

What is your post–law school success? I am very confused by this statement since you do not even begin to explain what you mean. In fact, we know absolutely nothing about you except that you went to a top-10 law school and you decided to stay in law school at the same time that you also decided to nurse a critically ill family member.

Why don't your grades reflect your true abilities? Apparently they do. What else do they reflect—perhaps a bad judgment call that you were unable to go to class or do any studying during a time of personal crisis? Why didn't you take a leave of absence? Did you speak with your professors about what was going on in your life at the time?

Personally, I don't think employers would be uncomfortable when you are asked to show your transcript and you must explain the bad grades. They have heard this song before. And unfortunately, it doesn't make employers feel uncomfortable, nor does it make them feel sorry for you.

The reason for this is that many people endure difficult hardships and family ordeals during law school, and they either take a leave of absence or drop out or else they figure out a way to still maintain their grades.

The sad news is that your transcript with those bad grades is going to follow you for the rest of your career, and that is why I wrote above that the grades do reflect your true abilities. The only way to explain your grades to prospective employers is to be honest about what happened. Sadly, I don't know that you are going to receive much more than a sympathetic, "I'm sorry for your loss." Your transcript is definitely an indicator of abilities when you are interviewing with strangers since there really is not much else to go on. It truly is the only benchmark in the beginning of a relationship with an interviewer or a firm. Of course, if you have a large book of portable business, we are talking about a different situation. But I did not get the feeling that you are at a partner level in a law firm.

Interestingly enough, and I have written about this before, I have represented partners with significant books of portable business who have transcripts that have been scrutinized. The bottom line, and I keep writing this over and over again: your law school transcript follows you for the rest of your career.

Again, I know you have written that your grades do not reflect your post–law school successes, but unless you have tangible evidence of these successes—and they are unique and important to the interviewer's practice—I suspect that your claims are going to fall on deaf ears.

Am I saying that you will never get hired again? No, that is not my position. What I am trying to tell you is that you have to stop blaming your poor grades on something other than the fact that you didn't study or you didn't go to class or you screwed up or you weren't focused or whatever. I truly am sorry for you that you were involved in a difficult family illness—I really do know exactly the trauma you went through and it is a horrible, painful experience. However, you need to be ready to explain your situation without being defensive and without the excuse of your grades not really reflecting your true abilities. Certainly you want to discuss the highlights and successes of your legal career since law school, but for some reason, I suspect that expression of yours is not going to convince potential employers of your abilities.

Simply and briefly explain the unfortunate circumstances that caused the drop in your grades (I am assuming your grades were not bad during all three years of law school). Then go on to discuss your achievements since you have started to practice and why you want to join this particular law firm or legal department (be sure to do your due diligence prior to the interview).

Sadly, as I have written many times previously (including today), a law school transcript does follow you during your legal career. Some employers, particularly during your associate law firm years, place an enormous emphasis on the transcript. The transcript is always a factor. If your transcript reflects poor grades, then you must live with that. Keep this in mind if you are currently in law school. If you are out of law school with this type of transcript and thinking about interviewing for a new position, you need to be prepared for questions about why your grades are so low. Don't be defensive, and don't bring out the world's tiniest violin on your shoulder. Just briefly explain what was going on in your life—and be honest—and then move on with the rest of the interview. Best wishes.

Sincerely,
Ann M. Israel

I█I

City: Philadelphia

I graduated last year with dual degrees. I am licensed to practice in New York, but I also want to use my other degree. The problem is that public interest work pays poorly, and I have a family and massive loans. How can I find out how much a prospective employer is willing to pay? I do not want to waste time going to interviews where I cannot possibly take the job and make ends meet. If I do go to an interview blindly, how can I delicately ask about salary?

Delicate

Dear Delicate:

Over the years I have noticed a common trait among lawyers: they are filled with bravado. That's why they make great litigators and why the transactional attorneys make such great deals. And it's what I love about lawyers, among many things.

So . . . what's with you, my shy friend? You certainly seem to know what you want and don't want and you make no bones about not having your time wasted. Good for you. No one wants to have their time wasted, and that goes for the employers as well. Think about that.

So, don't be afraid to ask what the going salary is for the job.

If an employer has a certain salary range—or if a position is lockstep and pays a specified and locked-in wage—and your requirements are far above what the potential employer can or is willing to pay, why waste everyone's time sitting in an interview? Unless . . .

There are several differing opinions on this issue. Some experts believe that you should ask up front about the salary, and if it is not to your liking or your requirements, forget about the opportunity. However, I really do not subscribe to this way of thinking.

I think it is just fine to ask about the salary before going to the interview, but I do believe that sometimes the initial salary changes once the employer gets to know you. For example, if a position is lockstep, there may also be signing bonuses and year-end bonuses to consider that help to bring the total package up to exactly what you are looking for. And of course there is the benefit package, which is never something you should discount. A good benefit package can increase the value of your salary anywhere from 30 percent to 150 percent of the base salary, depending on what is included.

Now let's talk about non-lockstep opportunities. If you find out the salary is not what you are looking for prior to going in for the interview, don't despair, and don't give up just yet *if* the job description seems to fit your background. Think about it—what do you really have to lose? An hour of your time, and you never know who you might meet and what might come of those contacts in the future.

My opinion is not to worry about the salary initially. Get the employer to want you so much that s/he can't live without you.

I have known of far too many situations where the employer intended to pay a certain salary but the candidate was so fabulous that, after the interview process, allowances were made and the salary was raised. I also have known of situations where candidates went into interviews and the job turned out to be so amazingly terrific, with such a great future (and the chance to make so much money down the road), that cutting back and figuring out a way to make ends meet on less money for the short-term was not going to be a problem.

The bottom line is that you just never know. Granted, you might be wasting your time going on that interview, but again, you might be walking away from the opportunity of a lifetime if you don't check it out. It's only an hour out of your life. Is it worth it? Best wishes!

Sincerely,
Ann M. Israel

City: New York

Hi, Ann, I have a couple of questions for you about interviews: Firstly, how can a midlevel lawyer (four years) ask questions at an interview (or otherwise investigate) a firm's financial viability? As a partner, I imagine you would have a lot of reasons to ask financial questions (and indeed the partner interview would include a discussion about the firm's financial health). But I'm not sure how this can be done at my level without looking nosy or perhaps like I'm asking the wrong questions. The reason I want to ask is even though I'm looking at the top-100 firms (which you might expect would have good financial health), I'm conscious about what's been happening at Dewey.

Conscious

Dear Conscious:

Oh, good for you! When I write about doing your due diligence before joining a new firm, this is exactly part of what I am talking about. You are one sharp cookie, and I am so proud of you for wanting to know about this.

It is so true that one would expect a firm in the big AmLaw 100 to be financially healthy and a safe place to join. And yet, without doing some investigating prior to joining a firm, you really don't know what you are getting into, do you? In the case of Dewey LeBoeuf, all it really takes is a tour of the latest articles on Google to find out that the financial health of the firm does not seem to be stable. With all of the current articles discussing the firm's bleeding of partners with their business and a problem with paying compensation out to the partners, one would certainly question the sanity of joining that firm at this time. Of course, I doubt that they are hiring right now!

Once you have passed the formal interviewing stages and you have received—or are about to receive—an offer of employment, there is practically nothing you can ask that will make you look nosy or could be interpreted as a wrong question. In fact, in this day and age, you would look less than intelligent to accept an offer without asking certain questions.

Just remember that other associates at the firm where you are interviewing are basically as much in the dark as you are. Only shareholder/equity partners know the true story of the firm's financial health. So, it would be best to determine which partner during your interviewing process you feel you have developed some type of a relationship with—more than likely, it will be the partner you will be reporting to or else it will be the hiring partner. Ask this individual if s/he is available for lunch or drinks with you and hope that you will have an opportunity to meet with him/her out of the office for an hour or so. Worst case is you will meet with him/her in the office.

At this time you will have the chance to discuss all the questions you might have about the position and your role at the firm. And now will be the time that you can bring up your questions about the financial health and future of the firm. Make sure that you do this in a very positive manner. In other words, you might want to say that you are asking because until very recently, statistics were all that mattered when looking at the financial health of a potential employer. However, in light of what has been happening in the legal community, and because you want this move to be your last move in your career lifetime, you just want to discuss whatever this partner is free to tell you about the future of the firm in terms of growth, finances, planning, etc.

This meeting should only be held if you are very excited about this particular opportunity and are truly considering accepting their offer based on the outcome of the meeting. In fact, during the meeting and before asking questions that might require confidential fiduciary responses, you should absolutely express your excitement about the offer and the fact that your intentions are honorable.

This is a tricky subject—no question about it. Googling the firm and looking to see if there has been a parade of recent defections should certainly raise a giant red flag about the finances of the firm, as should a recent merger with a firm that was about to blow up.

It would appear that the safest firms right now have had careful and measured growth and continue to operate with somewhat leanly staffed teams.

The offices have state-of-the-art technology and resources and do not skimp on providing these resources to both partners and associates (and support staff as well). But even with this type of careful management, one cannot guarantee the financial well-being of the firm forever.

It's a scary world out there for the AmLaw 100—even the AmLaw 250—right now. In fact, the entire law firm world is changing. I wish I could give you some specific ways to judge the financial health of a firm before you join it, but in 2012 I am afraid no one really knows. Any ideas or tips from readers of this column would be greatly appreciated!

All I can urge you to do is as much due diligence as possible, talk to anyone and everyone who might know anything about the firm in question, and don't be afraid to ask those questions you want to know (once you know the firm wants you!). Best of luck!

Sincerely,
Ann M. Israel

City: Stamford, CT

I am a senior associate (ten years) who got asked to leave the firm. I have a confidentiality agreement, so I am not supposed to let anyone know they let me go or, of course, bad-mouth the firm. Now in interviews for a new position, how do I answer the question, "Why did you leave your old firm?"

Confidential

Dear Confidential:

Although you have left out a number of really important facts (clearly due to your confidentiality agreement), you have told us the most critical issue we need to know. Thanks to what I suspect was some terrific negotiating on your part, you have secured this confidentiality agreement and so, whatever the reason was that caused the firm to let you go, no one is ever going to know that this was not of your own doing.

Now, first and foremost, confidentiality agreement or not, of course you would not bad-mouth the firm, right? We all know about the 11th command- ment that I have pounded into the minds of all interviewees: Thou shall not speak badly about one's former employer.

There are so many reasons for this that I don't even know where to begin. Just put yourself in the shoes of the interviewer. You are interviewing someone and the candidate starts bad-mouthing his/her last employer. It just so hap- pens that this is where your spouse works, and you have heard nothing but great reports about this firm over the years. Or, you start thinking—wow, if this person has so many negative things to say about his/her last employer, what will s/he say about me someday? The last thing anyone should be doing is ranting on about his/her previous employer and portraying him- or herself as a victim.

Since we don't know why you were asked to leave your firm, I am at a loss to give you a specific answer to your question. But the good news is that since you don't have to ever tell anyone that you were asked to leave, it would seem that your old firm is allowing you to portray your exit as being your decision that it was time to move on.

You just need to hope that everyone at your old firm is either aware of the confidentiality agreement or believes that your departure was indeed at your request, because clearly references will be checked at some point. I am assuming you have covered this issue with your past employer? How does this firm plan to cover the matter of references? This is something that you need to address prior to going on any interviews, and make certain that your stories are the same. In other words, let's say you are going to tell potential employers that you realized, as a senior associate with this firm, there clearly was not a future for partnership and that has always been your goal. Then you had better be certain that your last employer is willing to say that the reason for your departure had to do with the fact that currently associates are not being elected into the partnership, or whatever the case may be at this time.

Whatever you do decide to say—and remember, the question as to why you decided to leave your job will definitely be asked—be sure to practice in advance and know the answer to this question backwards and forwards.

Your answer needs to be short and to the point. This is not the question on which to spend a lot of time on and deliberate. Besides, the more you talk, the more you are liable to get into some areas that will lead to some issues in that confidentiality agreement. Focus more on the achievements you have accomplished and why this potential new employer offers what you are seek- ing. If your confidentiality agreement allows you to say that you have left on good terms—and if you really have—make sure you offer up this information.

One question you probably will encounter will be why you left your job before finding a new one. Again, make your answer short and sweet, however I would suggest you acknowledge that this might not be the traditional route, and that in this difficult job market you wanted to focus all of your time on your job search and did not want to short-change your employer on your work schedule.

The most important issue for you to deal with here is to work on what you are going to say as to why you left the firm. It might be the nonexistent partnership track, a lack of challenges, a desire to face new challenges, etc. All of these reasons do not reflect poorly on the old firm, and, remembering that 11th commandment, make sure you speak well of your past employer. Just be sure, as I have suggested, to practice your answer, keep it short, and then move on to what you have to offer to this new employer. Best wishes!

Sincerely,
Ann M. Israel

CHAPTER 7

Thank-You Notes

I guess I am incredibly old-fashioned about this because I can't believe the number of people that no longer write thank-you notes. Not only do they not write them, they don't e-mail them, either. It seems that an entire generation of people does not believe in thank-you notes. Now, the truth of the matter is that a thank-you note alone will not get you the job, but in the final analysis, it might make the difference when a potential employer is deciding between you and an equally strong other candidate. I know that when I am interviewing candidates for opportunities within my firm, I am always impressed with someone who takes the time to write a thank-you note to me. And as for an e-mailed thank you, well . . . sometimes I receive them and sometimes I don't because it is caught in our firm's spam filter, and sometimes I don't open them because I don't know who they are from and I am concerned about viruses. I don't think I am alone in this. I always write a thank-you note after a client has been generous with their time and met with me, or when someone takes me out for a meal or invites me to their home or gives me a gift. It is how I was brought up (I always had the threat of being grounded hanging over my head if I didn't get those thank-you notes out in time!), and it is how I continue to live my life. It is just plain old good etiquette with a dollop of thoughtfulness. Take the time to write a thank-you note. And, before you mail it out, make sure that you have proofread it about a million times!

City: New York

What is the current etiquette on post-interview thank-you notes? Is e-mail acceptable? Does it matter if the firm requested that you send your resume via e-mail?

Etiquette

Dear Etiquette:

Although I have addressed this topic previously, I believe it deserves another look.

First of all, I am a firm believer in post-interview thank-you notes. I'm a believer in thank-you notes altogether. It's how I was brought up, and I believe it is the appropriate and proper thing to do.

I love receiving a handwritten note after I have met a candidate who has interviewed for a job at my firm. It doesn't necessarily mean that s/he will get a job offer, but it certainly helps to keep that candidate in my memory.

These days I receive fewer and fewer handwritten thank-you notes. More than likely the thank-you messages come by e-mail. Several years ago I wrote in a column that you should never send a note by e-mail. The truth is that I really feel the same way now, but I suppose I need to be a bit more flexible. Although times have changed, my opinion hasn't really changed all that much, but for specific reasons.

I worry about unsolicited e-mail messages getting caught in a spam filter or being immediately deleted without ever being read. I know you've deleted e-mail messages from names you don't recognize or have not examined every message sitting in your spam filter! Now think about the spam filter of a very busy partner who simply doesn't have the time to go through all those messages sitting there. Do you really believe that your e-mailed thank-you message is going to be read? I think the chances are probably 50/50 if the message gets dumped into a spam filter.

So now, what happens if the firm has requested that you send your resume via e-mail? Well, I don't think that makes a difference in terms of your e-mailed thank-you note. Your resume is going to the recruitment department and then will be entered into the database. I don't think that is where you want your thank-you note to go, is it? Wait, let me clarify that statement. You might very well want to send a thank-you note to someone you have met during the interviewing process from the recruitment department. That e-mail probably will find its way to the right person.

So, let's get to the bottom line here. For what it is worth, my opinion on all of this is that I like thank-you notes sent after an interview, and I prefer handwritten notes sent by snail-mail. I worry about thank-you notes sent by e-mail being caught up in spam filters or being deleted because they have come from an unknown source. However, an e-mailed thank-you message is better than no thank-you message at all. And last but not least, sending a resume by e-mail to a firm doesn't mean that a thank-you e-mail will get to the right source. Happy New Year and best wishes to all!

Sincerely,
Ann M. Israel

City: New York

I've recently had a callback interview, and when I asked a career coun-selor at school about writing thank-you notes to the people that I meet with, he told me that they were not necessary because the meetings were brief (20–25 minutes). I always thought that writing a thank-you note was proper etiquette, but maybe I am wrong. What do you think?

Proper

Dear Proper:

Sometimes we do something just because we think it is the right thing to do . . . even though it may not be *necessary*.

If you have read my past columns in which I have discussed the topic of writing thank-you notes, then you know I believe it is always in good form to send a thank-you note after meeting with an interviewer. I am not clear what the length of an interview has to do with whether or not you send a thank-you note. A 20- to 25-minute meeting is not considered so very brief; in fact, it is more than likely the average length of a typical callback interview.

In my opinion, you are not wrong; it is indeed proper etiquette to send a thank-you note after an interview. But much more than proper etiquette, it is smart thinking.

Whether it is sent by e-mail or by snail mail and written out on a piece of personal stationery, a thank-you note lets the interviewer know that you appreciated the time s/he took to meet with you. It gives you an opportunity once again to express your interest in the firm and the specific position and to say why. And if for some reason you didn't cover this during your interview, it gives you a chance to make up for that mistake.

A thank-you note gives you the opportunity to keep your name on the mind of the interviewer and remind him/her about you long after the interviews are over and other candidates are forgotten.

I know that for me personally, whenever I interview someone for an opportunity with my firm and receive a thank-you note within one to three days later, a very positive impression is left in my mind regarding that individual. It doesn't always mean that I am going to hire that person, but I will tell you if it comes down to making a decision between two people and all other things are equal, the one who stands out in my mind is the one who took the time to follow up with a thank-you note.

The only time a thank-you note can hurt you is if it is filled with grammatical/spelling errors, so be sure to proof it carefully. Other than that, I can see no reason in the world why you shouldn't send interviewers a nice note after you meet with them. It certainly can't hurt you, it can only help you, and as far as I am concerned, it is necessary and the right thing to do. Best wishes!

Sincerely,
Ann M. Israel

❚▓❚

City: New York

The thing about thank-you notes is that they may not get you the job, but they can definitely lose it for you. Lawyers are extremely anal. Maybe

it's an urban legend, but I have heard that some people have lost offers because of typos or other sloppiness in their thank-you notes.

Some People

Dear Some People:

Well, I hope you are not included in that group of "some people" because that is a tough lesson to learn. I have discussed the danger of typos and, as you put it, other sloppiness in thank-you notes, resumes, cover letters, etc., many times before. And yes, you are correct—I do know of a number of specific examples where people have lost offers, or at least the opportunity to return for callback interviews, because of an oversight in a thank-you note.

This could be attributed to lawyers being extremely anal, as you have pointed out, or perhaps this is simply a case of the recipient of the note realizing that the mistake indicates some serious flaws that are not acceptable in a potential candidate.

Whether the thank-you note is handwritten or computer generated, a mistake or typo should not happen. You should proofread a thank-you note once, twice, and then a third time before sending it out. You might even want to read it out loud just to be certain that there are no mistakes. This is serious stuff (and by stuff I don't mean malarkey, as defined by Vice President Biden!).

I know that this column has had typos from time to time, and I have an editor who proofs and edits it after I have gone over it numerous times. There is no good excuse for the typos that slip through, although we try our best to not allow this to happen. But in a brief thank-you note, there is no excuse whatsoever. And that thank-you note is the only thing at that moment standing between you and a job offer or a callback for an advanced interview.

You have described lawyers as being extremely anal, but let's think about what lawyers do for a living. Don't they really have to be incredibly thorough, meticulous, and excruciatingly precise in their work or else risk losing everything for their clients? I suppose you might describe those characteristics as anal, but I think you might also describe them as the characteristics of the top attorneys.

If thorough, meticulous, and precise become descriptive characteristics of successful attorneys, then it would make sense that a thank-you note filled with typos would raise a red flag. It might suggest to the recipient that the author was careless or rushed—exactly the qualities that could jeopardize a client and his/her business to the firm.

I will tell you my personal experiences with thank-you notes when I have been interviewing candidates for positions with my firm. You are correct when you state that the thank-you note doesn't always get you the job, but I will say that it does leave a positive impression. I always remember the candidates who take the time to sit down and write a note to me, thanking me for taking time to meet with them. It's a thoughtful, polite gesture that speaks volumes to me. However, you are also correct that a poorly written thank-you note might suddenly eliminate a top-ranked candidate.

When I receive one of those notes in which either my first or last name (or both!) is spelled incorrectly, other words throughout the note are misspelled, perhaps grammar is completely ignored, or there are other obvious mistakes throughout, it is hard for me to think about the thoughtful gesture instead of the careless tone. This is someone trying to impress me enough that I will bring him/her back for a second interview. Is this really someone I want to represent my candidates to my clients? I don't think so.

So now take it a step further. Is this someone that a partner in a law firm trusts to work on assignments for his clients? I don't think so.

Instead of thinking of lawyers as being anal, start thinking of yourself as being careful when representing yourself for your career. Take the time to ask yourself how you would judge yourself if you sat in the interviewer's chair. Proof your resume, your cover letters, and your thank-you notes, and then once you have done that, proof them again . . . and again. Best wishes!

Sincerely,
Ann M. Israel

CHAPTER 8

Getting the Offer/ Checking References

What feels better than someone saying, "I love you"? And that is exactly what an employer is saying when an offer is extended. What a feeling! But how does one get that offer? What is the best way to get an offer extended? Through all these years of placing attorneys, I have found the best way to get an offer extended to you is simply by expressing an interest. But I don't mean mildly expressing that interest or sort of expressing an interest in the opportunity. I mean actually saying the words. I know I have previously discussed the situation where I told my candidate to express an interest in the opportunity at the end of the interview by saying the following words—by the way, only if he really meant them—"Based on what I have seen here today and on earlier interviews, there is no doubt in my mind that this is exactly the kind of opportunity I am looking to find." And, if he honestly wanted an offer and planned to accept it, then he should add, "Should an offer be extended, I will accept!"

Well, he went on that advanced interview and was very positive about everything and everyone and told the senior partner how great everything was at the firm, *but* . . . he forget to expressly state that he was interested in the opportunity! When he had finished his interview, he called me and was very excited—oh yes, he had followed my instructions to the word and absolutely had told the senior partner that he wanted the job. But when I did my follow-up with this partner, he told me they were going to pass on this candidate—even though he was everything they were looking for—because he didn't seem interested in the job. Fortunately for all concerned, I had a great relationship with this partner and he was willing to listen to me as I explained that I knew this candidate was more than interested and, in fact, would accept an offer on the spot. The partner agreed to bring the candidate back for another meeting. In the meantime, I got back to the candidate and told him, under threat of bodily injury, exactly what he was supposed to say to that partner. He followed my instructions and an offer was extended. By the way, this firm hired my candidate as a very junior associate in their very prominent real estate department. Today he is one of the top rainmakers in the real estate practice area.

The bottom line here is that you have to be willing to say "I love you" first if you want that offer. But in the case of getting an offer of a job, that "I love you" is simply "I want the job."

It is important to remember that when an offer is extended, it is always contingent on references. And you can be sure that your references will be checked. Only twice in my entire career have I seen a situation where an offer was rescinded because of a bad reference. This is devastating as well as just plain stupid. How could a candidate give out a reference that ended up being negative? Stupid, stupid, stupid. You really need to know if a reference is going to be willing to say good things about you. The best way to do this is to be open and honest about what you want. Think carefully about the people you want to choose as your references and then approach them by saying, "I would like to use you as a reference for a new opportunity I have been offered. I hope you will accept this request knowing that what you say will determine my future."

If certain people are not able to provide positive remarks about you and your work product, they will tell you that it would be best to not use them as references. What is critical here is that you tell the potential references how important what they say will be for your future.

Be sure that you do not provide these references prior to receiving and accepting your offer, because if you do, you can be sure that these references will be contacted early on and any confidentiality surrounding your search will no longer exist. It is always best to write a one-line sentence at the bottom of your resume such as this: "References provided upon request."

City: New York

Dear Ann,

Can you shed some light on the lateral process? In particular the conflict checking that is done, how long it typically takes, what they are checking for, the background and reference checks.

Thanks,
Lateral

Dear Lateral:

The conflicts check is something I have never discussed in any of my columns, and it is a good question since it is done with every lateral hire. There really isn't any great mystery behind it; it is exactly what it says it is—a check to find out if you have ever worked on anything that would conflict with the clients and/or work your new employer currently represents.

Why is it done? Well, it could be a terrible situation, if not in some instances grounds for malpractice, if you had represented, for example, a client at your last firm who is now suing a client of your new firm. I say it could be a terrible situation because during the conflicts check, the firm might discover that they are able to "screen" you from ever working with this particular client, or perhaps the client might feel that having you as part of the legal team would not present any conflicts for them. But this all has to be checked out prior to you coming on board.

There are many other scenarios for conflicts, but hopefully you get the picture here. Generally the conflicts are flushed out long before an offer is ever made, but a formal conflicts check generally is made after an offer is extended and accepted. I have been in situations where an offer has been made when all of a sudden a conflict appears that cannot be screened or resolved. When this happens, nothing can be done and the firm is forced to pass on the candidate, no matter how much they want to hire him/her (unless they want to get rid of the client causing the conflict, which rarely happens). Fortunately, conflicts usually are identified early in the interviewing process, and it is a rare situation when the conflict doesn't show up until after an offer has been accepted.

You asked how long the conflicts check takes . . . generally not more than a week, but then again, you can't count on that time frame. If people are not available or don't return messages, it can take longer. There is no set time frame, but I can tell you that the firm wants it done as soon as possible.

In the background checks, the firms are verifying the information on your resume. They are checking to make certain that your degrees and the dates you attended and graduated from the schools are all accurate, along with your grade points and honors, if any. They are also checking your bar status. Believe it or not, there were a number of situations in the 1980s where background checks were not as thorough as they are today, and there were some attorneys who were practicing without being admitted to the bar; there were even some who had not graduated from law school even though they claimed on their resume to have graduated with honors! Fool me once, said the firms. . . . Background checks are very thorough these days.

Reference checks have become very complete pretty much for the same reason that background checks needed to be more thorough. I knew of an attorney back in the early 1990s who had an amazing-looking resume that claimed he worked at one of the best firms in Boston after graduating with all of the honors from one of the top law schools. He came to New York and wanted to interview at all of the major BigLaw firms, and they all wanted to see him. Fortunately for the firms, one of the associates on the hiring committee of a firm where he was interviewing saw his resume prior to meeting him. She had worked at the Boston firm at the same time when he supposedly was working there in the very same department. Except she had never met him, and in fact, she had never heard of him. It didn't take more than a phone call to the firm to find out that this man was a complete phony, even down to his law school honors. Since then, reference checks have become more and more stringent.

There are all sorts of stories about lawyers practicing without bar admission, without law school degrees, without having worked at the firms on their resumes, etc. All of this puts a firm in terrible jeopardy should a client decide malpractice has been committed. This makes reference checks much more critical than just being a tool for finding out if an individual will be a good hire for a specific practice group.

I hope this helps you understand a bit more that the conflicts, background, and reference checks are not a waste of anyone's time. They are important pieces of the interviewing process, and we all need to remember that a job offer is not really final until all of these pieces of the puzzle are put together. Best wishes.

Sincerely,
Ann M. Israel

City: Los Angeles

I am currently interviewing, and a prospective employer has asked for references. However, I have only worked for one firm and I do not want them to find out I am looking. How should I address this issue with the prospective employer?

One Firm

Dear One Firm:

You are not alone! This is what happens to just about everyone when they are about to make their first job change. But not to worry—every problem has a solution.

Are you working with a recruiter? If so, the recruiter should explain to the prospective employer that you will be more than happy to give references as soon as an offer has been extended and accepted and you have given notice. That is normal procedure and how 99.9 percent of the law firms operate.

If you are not working with a recruiter, then you are going to have to speak with someone at the firm yourself to relay this message. If it is a firm with a recruiting coordinator or manager, s/he would be the best person to call. Surely s/he will be sympathetic to your situation and the need to keep your job search confidential.

I have come across one or two firms over the years that claim they can't extend an offer until they check references. Of course, this is utter nonsense, and I would question why you would want to work at a firm that insists on such an unreasonable request. However, there are always alternatives to references from your current employer.

Were there any professors at your law school with whom you had a close and positive relationship? They certainly can provide a good reference for you. If by any chance you spent your 2L summer at a different law firm, you certainly can find some references from that firm. Perhaps you have confided in an associate or two at your current firm? I suppose you could provide those names for references as well.

Again, I would not be thrilled with any prospective employer who is insisting on references prior to extending an offer. You don't want to put yourself in a position of letting your current employer know that you have been inter-viewing and then this potential employer decides not to hire you after all. By the way, I wouldn't give out references unless you are positive you are going to accept the offer. Again, there is no reason to announce to your current firm that you are on a job search unless you plan on giving notice at the same time. Best wishes!

Sincerely,
Ann M. Israel

City: Long Island City

I read your advice column on a regular basis and I don't understand why you seem to believe that a prospective employer would contact a can-didate's current employer for reference checks. Please explain this in a future response because it makes absolutely no sense that a prospective employer would contact a candidate's current employer. If that doesn't sound the alarm, I don't know what would. Think about it—it could put the candidate in a precarious position if the prospective firm decides not to hire the candidate and the current firm decides to retaliate and fire the candidate, leaving the candidate jobless.

Alarmed

Dear Alarmed:

I don't think a prospective employer would contact a candidate's current employer for reference checks without the candidate's permission. I don't know where you picked up the idea that I am concerned this is something that frequently happens. Quite to the contrary, I generally tell my candidates—and write in my columns—that partners have fiduciary responsibilities to their firms and really cannot discuss these matters with attorneys at other firms.

That doesn't mean it doesn't happen from time to time, and when it does, it can bring on disastrous consequences. Therefore it is critical for anyone who is commencing a job search to be prepared to make it very clear to all concerned that your job search is confidential and until you give the say-so, no one at your current employer is to be contacted regarding your references or, for that matter, anything to do with your current job search.

It never hurts to put a disclaimer at the bottom of a resume that reads: "References to be provided." Or "References available upon request." Or "Please do not contact my current employer." Or "Resume submitted in confidence." All of these basically are saying the same exact thing, which is, "You really should know this already, but I have a great job and they don't know that I am looking around at other opportunities, so please don't screw things up for me by speaking to my current employer and letting them know that I have been out interviewing or else I will hold you personally responsible for getting me fired."

I can tell you that when you are working with a headhunter s/he will always make this crystal clear to the potential employer even though it is obvious. Your recruiter will tell the interviewer many times that you are gainfully employed (as long as this is the truth), that your employer has no idea that you are looking (again, as long as this is true), and that it is critical that the confidentiality of this job search be maintained.

Although I always assure my candidates that the confidentiality of their job search will be meticulously maintained, I also want to make certain that all job seekers are as careful as I am about this matter. It doesn't hurt to be careful and make sure that everyone concerned is aware that your job search is confidential and that your current employer has no idea that you are looking.

So, the next time you decide to start searching, take that extra step and follow a simple word to the wise by making sure that all involved know the confidential nature of your search, even though the chances of a prospective employer turning around and reporting your moves to your current employer are quite slim. Best wishes!

Sincerely,
Ann M. Israel

City: New York

Hi Ann, I'm a fourth-year associate at a big law firm and I'm currently looking to make the move to another firm that has more expertise in

the area I'm interested in. I was writing to ask if you have any advice about asking for references from my current employer. Given that my next employer would want two current references, how should I approach the senior people in my team for a reference? I wouldn't be asking the partners I report directly to (as our team is big enough that I don't have to), but I would be asking two senior colleagues who have been practicing about ten years. To clarify, I'm confident I'd get good references from them, so that's not an issue. I guess as I haven't done this before, I'm concerned it might get back to my direct partners. I'm also concerned about whether the senior colleagues would mind giving the reference, given that I work quite closely for them. Also, given that the job market is *very* slow, I don't want to foreshadow this with them until I'm near the offer stage. Is this what you would recommend? Thanks!

Foreshadowed

Dear Foreshadowed:

You have a good sense about how to go about all of this. I always believe in following my gut sense and you should do exactly the same.

In other words, you absolutely do not want your references or anyone else at work to know that you are even thinking about looking for another job until you have that job offer, have accepted it, and have given notice at your current position. Any sooner and you are in jeopardy of committing career suicide.

You are correct that the job market is slow. Given this unfortunate variable, it is a fact that no one knows how long it might take to find that perfect opportunity you are seeking that will offer more expertise in your practice area. Because your job search is so specific, it might take weeks, months, or even a year or more. Therefore, it is critical that you keep it highly confidential to protect your current employment. No matter how close you might be with your colleagues at the office, keep your plans to yourself.

As you start to interview, various prospective employers will ask for references. Your resume should state at the bottom, "References provided upon request." And when they are requested, you need to explain that your search is confidential and no one at your current employment knows you are interviewing. Because of this, you would be happy to provide references from other resources, but you cannot give any references from your current employer until an offer has been extended and accepted. This is a common practice. Any employer who doesn't accept this explanation is someone you really don't want to work for—that red flag is waving and you should take that warning as a real sign that something is amiss here.

An offer from a new employer is generally extended "pending references." This means that it is given to you in good faith but it is not official until the references have been checked and you have been cleared. At this point you will give the potential employer the names and contact information of the people at your current employment who will determine whether or not that offer is going to stick. For that reason, you need to be sure that you are giving the names of people whom you truly believe will be giving you a good reference.

Consequently, I urge you to notify these references prior to giving their names over to the new employer. You might want to say something along these lines (assuming this is true), "I have truly enjoyed working for/with you these past several years. You have been an incredible mentor. However, recently I have been offered an opportunity that I cannot pass up, as difficult as it is to leave here. I would like to use you as one of my references, knowing that what you say will certainly determine my future. May I use you as a reference?"

If the answer is affirmative, let the individual know the name of the firm or corporation where you will be going and who will be calling. And now, and only now, you may give your new employer the names of your references! Best wishes!!

Sincerely,
Ann M. Israel

||||

City: Unknown

Dear Ann,

I am a fifth-year associate at a midsize firm. Last week, I interviewed at another, larger firm and it seemed to go very well. Since the interview, I have been receiving e-mails from the prospective firm's head of administration asking for additional information. Among the questions she posed is whether they can contact someone at my current firm, who presumably will serve as a reference. I don't want to do anything to jeopardize my current position by tipping them off as to my job search. Am

I justified in saying absolutely not, or will this put off the new firm and cause them to pull the offer?

Thanks.
colLATERAL damage

Dear colLATERAL (loved this!):

Not to worry, my clever friend. You are absolutely justified in saying no—that is, if you don't have an offer from this firm. And that is where I am confused.

In your question, you indicate that all that has happened thus far is a first interview at this firm, albeit in your opinion it went quite well. Now this firm has been e-mailing you (and I hope those e-mails are not coming to your e-mail address at the office—more on this in a moment) asking questions, one of which is asking to speak with someone at your current firm. You don't want to tell them no because you are concerned that this response will cause them to pull the offer. Is there an offer?

I suspect not and that you are just assuming that if you say no, this will just end the process. For the sake of this column, let us go by the assumption that after your first round of interviews, there is not an offer of employment just yet.

First and foremost, *no, no, no* they are not allowed to contact anyone at your current firm to check references. You don't have to worry about insulting them or turning them off or jeopardizing your chances with them. In fact, should this happen, would you really want to work for them?

All you have to do is simply tell them that you are currently employed at your firm and well respected there and that your job search is highly confidential. Your current employer is unaware that you are interviewing, and it is very important that you continue to keep your job search very quiet and confidential.

However, do let them know that when an offer is *extended* (pending references, of course, as is always the case) *and* you have *accepted* the offer, then you will be more than delighted to give them the names and phone numbers and/ or addresses of anyone they need at your current law firm.

Now, about those e-mails that they have been sending to you. Please do not have them send them to your office e-mail address; those e-mails are the property of your employer. Please have any e-mail of a personal nature (such as a confidential job search) sent to your personal e-mail address. I know that is what you're doing, right?

And what other reasons could there be that a firm is asking for references besides getting ready to make an offer to you? Well, they could be on the fence about you or deciding between you and another candidate and just want to check out your references before continuing on with the interviewing process. So why would you jeopardize your position with your current law firm before receiving *and* accepting an offer of employment? The minute your current employer finds out you are interviewing for another job, your position with them is mighty tenuous. The last thing you want in this tough job market is to be fired from your firm and then to be unemployed and looking for a new job.

Just be sure to stay very quiet about your job search, and don't worry about having to say no to anyone asking for references before they hand out an offer that you want to accept. Best wishes!

Sincerely,
Ann M. Israel

City: New York

Employment History Form

Hi, can you tell me what the purpose of the employment history form is? The form that highlights all your previous employers, the dates of employment, and the reason for leaving? I was recently given this form during my second interview with a Big Law firm in NY. I have been working in law now for three years and left my previous employer after one year due to failing the bar exam twice. I passed it now on my third try and have worked for two years since then. However, now I filled out this form and I put the only answer I could put on the form that was the truth, that I left due to firm policy of letting associates go if they did not pass the bar twice. My question is this—do you think this will affect a potential offer? During the first interview, one of the partners told me he wanted to give me the offer right then and there and thought they were the perfect firm for me. But this issue never came up, and quite frankly I have put it in the past and do not consider it a major issue anymore. However, now I have had to put this on my employment history form and I am not sure how this will affect any potential employment with the firm. Please tell me if there is a way I can salvage this offer if it becomes a potential issue for the firm.

Very Worried!

Dear VW:

First of all, stop worrying. There's no value in it; there is nothing you can do to change whatever will happen, so just try to stop worrying (easy for me to say, right?).

There are many different reasons for using an employment form, and this particular firm could be asking you to fill one out for multiple reasons. My experience has been that when an potential employer asks you to fill out an employment form or application when you come back for an advanced interview round, it means that they are very interested in you, and in many cases it means that they are getting ready to make you an offer and want to have all the human resources paperwork in order.

I will commend you for doing the right thing, which is answering truthfully on the employment form regarding why you left your first legal employer. The truth would have come out one way or another eventually and you would really be in a bad position had you not told the truth. If having failed the bar exam twice is what prevents this firm from hiring you, better it happens now then having them fire you when they find out down the road. And they would have found out. If you think you are worrying now, just think how you would be worrying if you had not been honest. You did the right thing.

Not all firms have formal employment applications on file, but somewhere there is an employee file on every hire at every firm. So, just because you haven't filled out an official-looking form prior to this one doesn't mean that there hasn't been something similar to this at the other places where you have worked. In some instances it is filled out for you by a personnel employee who is putting together your employment file. At this particular firm where you are interviewing, you are filling out information they need to have, such as your personal information (address, phone number, who to reach in an emergency), educational background, work history, references, etc. Some employers have candidates fill out forms when they arrive for their first interview, and I have some clients that have potential employees fill out book-like applications before they even have an interview scheduled.

Companies that are subcontractors for the government have very specific employment applications to be filled out. And as surprising as it may be to many candidates, there are companies that have nothing to do with the military but since they are owned by larger entities working with government contracts, the smaller firm is required to enforce the same employment application rules as the parent company.

It may very well be that the firm where you are interviewing will be concerned about your bar exam situation. However, you are now in your third year of practice and applying for your third job. This obviously didn't seem to bother the partner interviewing you on your first interviewing round, and so I suspect that the bar exam issue is not going to be a huge concern either. Besides, surely he noticed on your resume that your date of admission to the bar was a few years later than your year of graduation from law school. Don't you think this firm is already thinking that you may have had some trouble with the bar exam?

By the way, luck may be on your side, and there is a slight chance that what you write on that employment application may never be seen by anyone at the firm. It may just be a formality at this particular firm that you fill out this form so that they have the information to check references, your degrees, and your bar status. Then again, this may be a sticking point with some of the partners on a next round of interviews if the application is passed around with your resume. You need to be prepared to discuss how you have overcome the problems you had during your first year with trying to pass the bar and to talk about how the next two years have been very successful for you. Remember what I always say—don't be defensive, just deal with the hesitation, overcome it, and move on.

It seems to me that this firm is excited about you. The partner wanted to make you an offer during your first meeting and then you were invited back for an advanced round and asked to fill out an application for employment. The real question here is how long will you wait to find out if an offer is forthcoming? You need to make certain that you keep your name fresh in their memories and find out sooner rather than later if they are going to make you an offer. Worrying will get you nowhere, so if you haven't heard from them within a week after your last interview, pick up the phone and call that partner from the first interview, let him know how excited you are about his firm, and ask if there is anything else he needs to help the firm make a decision about you. Please let us know what happens. Stop worrying and take action! Best of luck!

Sincerely,
Ann M. Israel

City: New York

Dear Ann,

I submitted a question two weeks ago regarding filling out the employment history form and not knowing how failing the bar twice would affect a potential offer. Thank you so much for your response. I did as you suggested last week: I called the partner who seemed to be very keen—indeed, he is the hiring partner of the office I was interviewing for. However, I was unable to reach him and left a message basically saying exactly what you told me to say. I mentioned my continued interest in the firm and how excited I was at the possibility of working with him and his colleagues. However, the second interview took place over two weeks ago, and I left the message eight business days later. It has now been just over a week since I left the message and there has been no phone call—nor any rejection letter in the mail. I am very confused. I was hoping to get a chance to speak with the partner who really liked me as I would have been able to address any concerns. However, I do not want to be a pest. I know the more time goes by, the worse my chances are. I sent thank-you letters a few days after my second interview. There is really no reason for me to keep contacting them. At what stage do you become a pest?

Still Worrying

Dear Still Worrying:

I am afraid that I have to take some blame here. I assumed you knew the cardinal rule (though we all know what happens when we assume anything)—never leave messages. I know that I have advised against leaving messages in many of my past columns. The reason for this is to avoid just exactly what is happening to you. The message has not been returned, and if you call back, you start to be a pest.

However, if you don't want to leave a message when the person is not available, you should say to the secretary or assistant, "I'm away from my desk a lot during the day, so I would prefer not to leave a message right now; I'll just try back later. When is the best time to reach him?"

Even better, if the call goes straight to voice mail, you can just hang up and try again later.

Unfortunately, your message has been left and can't be taken back at this time. After this amount of time has gone by, I would suggest that you move on. There is always a slight chance that they are still interviewing other candidates and you might hear from them in a few days from now, but realistically, I doubt it. This just doesn't feel good to me.

I know you are hanging on to the fact that the hiring partner said he wanted to make you an offer when you met him initially. You were invited back for a second round, and for all you know, the employment form may not have been the reason for you not getting an offer. As I had mentioned in the original column, that form may not have gone any further than your file. Perhaps the other partners interviewing you during the second round liked another candidate more than you. Who knows what happened? In fact, you probably will never know. But at this point, you need to stop worrying about it and move on.

I think you have done everything you could possibly do to express your interest in the firm and the position. Anything more and not only do you look like a pest but you start to look desperate. I'm sorry that this turned out the way it did, but you must know that it happened for the best. Telling the truth on the employment form was the right thing to do because the truth would have come out eventually. If that is the reason the firm decided not to hire you, then there is nothing you can do about it. And just remember, it wasn't meant to be—and perhaps someday you will find out the reason why.

Sadly, this is part of your history and you will have to deal with it. Happily, the last two years of your practice have been very successful. Focus on your successes and the right opportunity eventually will come through for you. Best wishes.

Sincerely,
Ann M. Israel

❚❚❚

. . . Speaking of reference checks, remember the reader who worried because s/he was honest on the employment form and had written that s/he had flunked the bar twice before passing on the third try? Read on . . .

❚❚❚

Dear Readers:

Frequently I will ask a reader to let us know how things turn out for him/her. Happily, this individual has gone from being "Very Worried" to "On Top of the World!" Thanks so much for sharing your story with us and congratulations to you! There is nothing better than learning that a troublesome situation has worked out in the long run.

City: New York

Dear Ann,

I want to thank you for all the hard work you put into this column and for all the help you have given to me and many others during the lifetime of their career. You responded to me a few times in the past, most recently to "Following up after an interview, at what stage do you become a pest?" and "I flunked the bar on my first try. What can I do to keep that from preempting offers?" I wanted to inform you that the firm did call me back a few days after I posted the message; they apologized for the delay in their response and explained that it was due to trying to fit me into a particular practice area. Then they offered me the position, which I accepted. I wanted the readers out there to know that you can overcome a bad past, whether it be from failing the bar twice or however many times or from any other negative mistake from your past—in the end, someone will see past that and see you for the value you can bring to a firm and judge you solely based on your successes since the bar. It feels great to be released from what seemed to be a never-ending nightmare. If I look back on all the worrying and fear and anxiety I put myself through, it was really not worth it. Everyone told me that one day this issue would be behind me for good . . . and now it is. I wish the same for all of you out there who are going through similar things. Keep praying, keep motivated, be determined, and never give up—always be truthful, and all the best to each and every one of you.

On Top of the World!

CHAPTER 9

Which Offer to Accept?

Oh, to be so fortunate as to have two offers at the same time! The gods surely are shining down on you! But how do you decide which offer to accept with all things seemingly being equal? Well, as I have written in too many columns to count, I always rely on Benjamin Franklin, one of my very favorite historical figures. As you will read, our friend Ben had a surefire way to make a decision, so why change something that works? He always used this method, and I have adopted it from him and use it for every decision I have had to make in my adult life.

The beauty of Ben's system is that it is foolproof. It spells out your answer for you so that there can be no question as to what you should do. Long before I knew this was the Ben Franklin system of making decisions, I actually used it when I had to decide whether to accept a position in the mailroom at William Morris Talent Agency and work my way up the corporate ladder or take a job as an executive search consultant in an area I knew nothing about.

I guess it is fair to say that the rest is history because I used Ben's system—without knowing back then that it had such an esteemed name—and made the decision to join the search firm. Thirty-five years later and I have never looked back and never had any regrets.

It's a tried and true system for me, and I love to share it with anyone and everyone who needs to make a decision. Read on for instructions . . . and much thanks to Ben.

City: New York

I am a former magic circle corporate associate who was made redundant last winter. I now have two job offers that are completely different: (1) an in-house position at a major bank and (2) an associate role in a local business law firm with a good but very regional reputation. This is not only a choice of career, this is also a choice of lifestyle. If I choose the bank, I will stay in the big city, while if I pick the law firm, I would have to relocate. Working at the law firm will let me learn the actual practice of law as opposed to the way it's practiced in major corporate firms, which may be interesting, with the opportunity to go solo or to become partner soon. However, I would have to take a big pay cut on my magic circle salary. Finally, the bank position would be highly specialized derivatives etc. Any advice?

Magic

Dear Magic:

I love that game where people ask who you would pick if you could meet anyone, dead or alive. Benjamin Franklin is one of my favorite answers. Yes, I would have loved to have known him. The more I read about him, the more fascinated I become with him. He certainly was a quirky kind of guy, but he had a way of doing things that makes so much sense to me.

So, why am I writing about Benjamin Franklin this week when you clearly have a big decision to make? Well, I really can't answer your question, mainly because I don't know anything about you, and your choices really depend so much on what you are all about. However, I think old Ben Franklin can provide the answer.

Whenever Benjamin Franklin was presented with a difficult decision, he never left the final answer up to chance; instead, he took a sheet of paper and divided it into two vertical columns. The left side was labeled "Cons" for the negative consequences of his action and the right side of the column was labeled "Pros" for the positive benefits of his decision. And then he started listing all the pros and cons for making the decision on each side of the vertical line. Whichever side had the longest list in the end was the winner. (I don't know if this story is apocryphal, but I love telling it, and besides, it has always worked for me when I've been faced with a tough decision.)

In your particular situation, you need to change the formula just a bit. You are going to start out in exactly the same way that Benjamin Franklin always did; that is, take a sheet of paper and make two columns by drawing a vertical line down the middle of the paper. But now you are going to make a bit of a change: at the top of the left column, write "In-House Bank Job." At the top of the right column, write "Out-of-Town Law Firm Job."

And now, really take all the time you need to think about all the reasons that the bank opportunity is right for you and the law firm job is not. Put all those reasons in that left-hand column. At the same time, start thinking about why the law firm job is the right way for you to go and the bank job would be a mistake and list all of those reasons on the right-hand side of the vertical line.

This is not an easy exercise, and you should not look at it as being one. In doing this exercise, if you are taking it seriously, you are going to be forced to think about what is really important to you in your career and in your personal life. You have to be completely honest when writing down why you should or shouldn't do something or else you're just playing a game without thinking about potential implications or prices you might have to pay in the future.

The answer to your dilemma lies in the bottom of these two columns. Whichever column is the longest is the right decision for you to make. It's that simple. You don't have to trust me; trust Benjamin Franklin.

I wish I knew about you, your family situation, your lifestyle, your background, etc. But I don't know the first thing about you; it would be so wrong for me to advise you as to which job you should choose. They are so very different, with each one leading you down a completely different career and lifestyle path. However, I hope I have given you a tool that will help you make the right choice—please let us know what you decide to do. Best wishes!

Sincerely,
Ann M. Israel

City: New York

I am a third-year law student at a top-5 school. I spent this past summer at one of the top 10 to 12 firms in the country and was happy to receive an offer. Being a prudent law student, I went ahead and did one or two interviews at OCIs just in case. Lo and behold, I was offered a position at one of the top-5 firms in New York, with a stronger practice group for what I want to do. I feel like I should go to the more prestigious firm, but I really liked my summer experience. But I am confident that I will like the environment and culture at the new firm I have been offered a position in.

What should I do?

Prudent

Dear Prudent:

Nothing like an embarrassment of riches to make for a very happy third year of law school, right?

Listen, I don't see that you have a problem at all . . . that is, as long as you have not yet accepted your offer at the firm where you summered.

If you have not yet accepted your offer, then what is the big deal? You have two offers and you believe that one is better than the other, although it would seem that both are good opportunities. If you did end up accepting the offer from the firm where you worked, I would imagine you would be happy since you did really like your summer experience and it is clear that they really like you.

However, there must have been some reason other than simply being prudent that caused you to continue interviewing after your summer ended even though you already had an offer of permanent employment. Something about the firm or the practice group must have been bothering you, or why would you have taken the time to continue with the interviewing process? Most people are so relieved when they receive an offer at the end of the summer that all they can do is party, not continue interviewing.

The only reason to continue leaning toward the firm where you summered is that it is the devil you know. You have already worked there, you know some of the ins and outs of the firm, some of the partners—or at least some of the senior associates—are already familiar with you, and you may have already forged some relationships there. At the other firm—and granted, it may very well seem to be more prestigious and have a stronger practice group for what you want to do—you are the last man (or woman, as the case may be) hired and really an unknown to all the players. And by the way, how much of a difference is there between a top-5 and a top-10 law firm for a first-year associate?

I mention all of this in case you have already accepted your offer from the firm where you spent your 2L summer. This is a tricky situation if you have already accepted their offer of employment. Although I truly believe that this is your future and your career that we are discussing and you have to ultimately do what is best for you and not for other people, you will burn bridges if you rescind your offer of acceptance and go to a different firm this late in the season.

I am not telling you that you shouldn't do it; I am simply telling you to really think it through, and then once you have figured it out, think it through again from different angles.

This is a tough situation if you have accepted that offer, but ultimately—as I have just pointed out—this is your life and your future and you need to do what is going to be the best move for you and your future. If you truly believe that the top-5 firm will be the better place for you to start your law career, then that is where you must go. But do not delay letting your summer employer know your decision. You need to be a professional about this situation and give them notice that you will not be joining them next fall as soon as you make your decision (and you need to do that immediately).

It is truly wonderful that you have these two fabulous offers, but do be fair—make your decision and then allow the firm that gets the heave-ho from you the opportunity to fill the slot that you have vacated. Just think of it this way—some third-year law student is about to be as happy as you are! Please let us know how this all works out for you. Best wishes!

Sincerely,
Ann M. Israel

City: Washington, DC

I am a Columbia grad who is in the middle of the first of two federal clerkships. My first clerkship is with a district court, my second, with a prestigious judge on a U.S. Court of Appeals.

After the completion of my clerkships, I plan to return to NYC and go to work for one of three firms. I am interested in developing a career as a firm litigator, and I am also interested in eventually leaving private practice (at least for a few years) to go to a U.S. Attorney's office.

My options are as follows (and I assume the names of the firms will be omitted):
(1) Return to [a firm that is made up of several merged firms], where I spent my 1L summer.
(2) Return to [a top-tier New York firm], where I spent my second summer.
(3) Go to [another top-tier New York firm]. I know a number of the top litigation partners at this firm through Columbia programs, informational interviewing during my 1L year, and the like. I keep in contact with [firm #3 partner], and I know the firm is eager to have me join them, with interviewing for a post-clerkship position basically just a formality.

I have outstanding offers from (1) and (2), and the offers will remain open until next summer. I enjoyed both of my summer positions, but I'm not sure whether [firm #1] is a good place to begin a career, nor am I sure if I would enjoy being an associate at [firm #2], despite its sterling reputation for litigation and the interest level of the work there. And I don't know which place would be best for me as I return to NY to begin my career as a third-year associate. I am also uncertain as to which firm would enhance my prospects of becoming a prosecutor in the future.

Enhanced

Dear Enhanced:

I could answer your question with one sentence if I so desired: two birds in the hand is worth much more than no bird in the bush, meaning you have two offers from two good firms and no offer from the third firm.

Firm #3 is a terrific firm. I have placed many partners there, and we have also placed many associates at that particular firm. They are all still there and very happy. The litigation department is extremely busy and they work very hard—probably just as hard as the associates work at Firm #2. Quite frankly, I don't think there is much of a difference in the hours billed. I will say that I have found the firm to be corporate driven, although the litigation practice is working its way up to becoming an extremely important department within the firm.

I think it is just great that you know a number of the top litigation partners at this firm through different programs and informational interviewing and that you actually keep in touch with one of the partners. However, when it comes right down to it, you don't have an offer there, and a lot can happen between now and the time you finish your clerkships. Those partners you know could have long since moved over to other firms by that time, and the partner you are in contact with could also be in contact with other junior associates, for all you know. Or maybe he doesn't have enough business to keep himself busy during the day and so he is more than happy to enjoy e-mailing back and forth with a pleasant junior attorney. And who can say if he carries the clout to bring in a junior associate? Certainly he can't just bring someone in without going through the right channels. Who knows?

There is no such thing as interviewing for an associate position being a formality. That is a very naïve statement. Indeed, from what you have told us, you have an impressive resume, but why haven't they made you an offer just like the other two firms have done? Don't assume that an offer from them is an absolute.

But let's move on to Firm #1 and Firm #2, where you actually have offers. There is no contest here. Firm #2 is the clear winner. This firm has one of the best—if not the best—litigation departments in the country. If you are looking for the top training and the most interesting cases, you will have hit the jackpot by signing on with this firm. Read the reports from the past years and check out which firms are always winning for best litigators and are considered to have the top litigation department. Wow! You really have hit the jackpot. And read some resources a bit further and see how your path to being a prosecutor might be beautifully paved after working at this firm.

Firm #1, while certainly having a good litigation department, is trying to stay afloat by merging with firm after firm after firm. Not a good sign. And so much of their work is international—not really what you are looking for, is it? Don't you think this firm is driven by their corporate department instead of by their litigation practice? Without question, Firm #2 has a great corporate practice, but their firm is driven by litigation.

Firm #2 has a reputation that is beyond sterling. There is no question that, should you decide not to stay there forever (don't be so sure you wouldn't enjoy being an associate there—the associates I know seem to be very happy working there), it is a strong resume builder. Of the three firms in question, in my opinion, this is a no-brainer. And congratulations—this is a beauty of an offer! Best wishes!

Sincerely,
Ann M. Israel

▮▮▮

City: Philadelphia

I am a rising 3L student and have received a callback interview with a well-known management consulting firm. I have received an employment offer from a law firm at which I was a summer associate. If I receive an offer from the management consulting firm and decide to work there for several years, would I encounter difficulty if I desire to return to BigLaw?

Rising

Dear Rising:

There are so many variables that make your question very difficult to answer. But let's start with the short answer: yes, you would encounter difficulty trying to get a position with a BigLaw firm.

Please note that I did not say "return" to BigLaw because that is not what you would be doing. You only did a summer associate job at a BigLaw firm; you never practiced law as an attorney there, nor would any BigLaw firm consider you to have law firm experience.

Working at a "well-known" management consulting firm such as McKinsey & Company is definitely a prestigious employment position to list on a resume. It isn't easy to get an offer from McKinsey; their interviewing process certainly eliminates everyone but the best. But working there is not necessarily a resume builder to get a job in a law firm as an associate, if that is what you are thinking. In fact, you should do your due diligence on where JDs move on from a management consulting firm such as McKinsey & Company. Very few make the decision to return to law firms.

Someone who is interested in both the law and a career in management consulting generally follows a career path where s/he works for a few years in a BigLaw firm and then attempts to interview with a firm like McKinsey & Company. These types of management consulting firms are always interested in people with JDs and some practice experience (as well as various other types of graduate degrees, although most of their employees have MBAs).

I have met candidates who have worked at McKinsey & Company. But they have also worked at BigLaw firms first and have been trained as associates prior to working in the management-consulting world. Depending on the economic state of the job market (one of those variables I referred to above) and the practice area they were trained in, they may or may not be viable candidates since they have been out of the practice of law for several years.

Quite frankly, although there is no question that an offer from a prestigious management consulting firm is difficult to turn down, if there is any thought in your mind that you do want to practice law now or at some point in the next few years at a BigLaw firm, I suggest that you accept the offer from the BigLaw firm where you summered. The state of law firms and the economy is in flux, and we don't know where things will be in the next year or two or three. Get some experience under your belt as an attorney and then the world will be open to you to do other things. It is difficult to work it the other way.

If the management firm is interested in you now, they probably will still be interested in interviewing with you in two or three or four years down the road. In fact, they might very well be more interested in you with several years of BigLaw training behind you. You have a solid offer from the law firm, but there is a time constraint in terms of accepting it or turning it down. At this time you only have a callback interview with the management consulting firm and, as I mentioned before, it is a rigorous interviewing cycle, with many candidates vying for the same opportunity. Do you have enough time to compete for this job before you have to give an answer to the law firm? That should be the first thing for you to consider in making your decision. Don't lose a sure thing!

Again, my advice at this time is to go for the training as an associate at the BigLaw firm. You can always move on to another career once you have the practice experience and training, but you can't go back to a major law firm without having any experience as an attorney. Best wishes!

Sincerely,
Ann M. Israel

CHAPTER 10

How to Work with a Recruiter

It's an interesting phenomenon when, as a recruiter, you call an associate about a really and truly great opportunity and they hang up on you. I don't understand that kind of rudeness. At least have the courtesy to say you aren't interested. But surprisingly, that very same person who has hung up on me one day is calling on the phone the next day for my help. Of course, I am always happy to speak with that person, but I never forget that they once hung up on me.

What is the best way to work with a recruiter? First you need to remember that the top recruiting firms never charge the candidate—not even a penny. The top recruiting firms also don't bribe you with offers of money if we place you or one of your friends. Be wary of those headhunters. In fact, giving or taking money from a candidate violates the Code of Ethics of the National Association of Legal Search Consultants, generally known as NALSC (see article 3, number 3 of the code: http://www.nalsc.org/about/ethics.cfm).

And speaking of the code of ethics, it is important that your headhunter abides by it. It is preferable that s/he is an active member of NALSC, but if not, just be sure that s/he and the search firm agree to abide by the code.

Many people use a number of recruiters for their search, but if you really want your headhunter to work for you, you will limit your number of firms to one or two. It takes a tremendous amount of time and effort to market a candidate properly, and if you are spreading yourself thinly among many search firms, no recruiter is going to make you a top priority.

Which leads me to the next important point: Keep careful track of which recruiter you give permission to present you to a specific firm. Write it down under the recruiter's name. Do not under any circumstances give permission to more than one recruiter to present your background to a specific firm, because if you do, I promise that the firm will not want to get involved with this kind of nightmare.

Meet with your recruiter in person if you are in the same city. Why would you want someone to represent your career without meeting you?

Do not hold back any information. The more you can tell a recruiter about you, your practice, your background, your likes, and your dislikes, the more productive your search will be.

The experienced and ethical attorney search firms are there to help you. They will be your advocate, your rabbi, your parent, your confidante, and, if you allow it, your best friend. And if you are with the right recruiter, s/he definitely will be your friend for life.

IMI

City: New York

I'm considering searching for a new job. Would you mind talking a little bit about how legal recruiting and headhunting works? Is it advisable to tell the recruiter everything—for example, that I would be interested in more of a lifestyle firm, or would eventually want to work part-time? Is there any downside to working with a headhunter? Thank you.

Considering

Dear Considering:

Would I mind? I never mind talking about my profession, particularly when someone is interested in hearing about the ways to approach a recruiter.

I do believe it is advisable to tell your recruiter as much as possible about what you are looking for. The more candid and honest you are with your recruiter, the more s/he can (a) find the right opportunity for you and (b) help you with your resume and interviewing style.

Of course, if you are having second thoughts about being honest with your headhunter and really don't want to disclose everything to him/her, perhaps you should be reevaluating the person you are dealing with. Is this really the right person to be representing you, your career, and your future?

The most important thing to keep in mind is that you are the boss here. If you don't like the person or if you are having some second thoughts about whether or not you want to disclose everything to this individual, I would suggest you interview other headhunters. After all, a job search is something that ultimately can affect not only your entire life but also the lives of everyone around you. You are putting your future in the hands of someone you really need to have good feelings about and, most of all, trust.

A good recruiter needs to know if you are looking for a firm that will offer a different type of lifestyle than you are currently experiencing. If you don't discuss these kinds of issues with your recruiter, then you are going to end up wasting your time, the recruiter's time, and the time of a lot of partners who are meeting with you for no good reason. Why would you want to do this?

The more honest and open you are with your headhunter, the happier you are going to be with the interviews you get. They are going to be on-target for what you are looking for instead of a total waste of time.

Of course there are downsides to working with recruiters, but that depends on individual situations. Headhunters have guidelines set up by the clients who pay their fees. Although we would like nothing better than to represent many of the wonderful people we meet in the course of our day, clients say they will hire only certain people through a recruiter. These people qualify for the guidelines, whether these guidelines are certain practice areas, certain years of experience in a practice area, certain amounts of portable business, specific law schools, a minimum grade point average, etc.

If you do not fall into one or more of these very specific areas that the client has demanded of the recruiter, there is nothing the recruiter can do for you. This is where a recruiter could really hurt you much more than help you. So, if you find that you have been calling around to the recruiters and most of them say they cannot help you, but all of a sudden one recruiter tells you to send in your resume and s/he is going to send it out to his/her clients, be wary. This is where there is a tremendous downside to working with a recruiter. Your resume could go out to a number of firms who would never pay a fee for you and yet, perhaps without a fee attached to your candidacy, they might have been interested in meeting with you. The recruiter has now effectively blocked you from applying to these firms on your own.

Another downside is when a candidate is working with more than one recruiter and does not have control of the situation. One of the recruiters sends out your resume without your express prior consent. The other recruiter is working ethically and never sends out your resume without discussing the opportunity with you first and getting your permission. However, after receiving your okay, the resume goes out and the headhunter finds out that the firm already has your resume from another search firm. The end result is that the law firm doesn't want to get into a legal battle with two search firms and you are no longer under consideration. Make sure you are clear with your recruiters, and in no uncertain terms let them know that your resume is not to be sent anywhere without your express prior consent.

Working with a recruiter can be a wonderfully rewarding experience if you have an open and honest relationship. I hope you find the right headhunter for your background. Best wishes!

Sincerely,
Ann M. Israel

City: Orange County

I am a fourth-year attorney working with a couple of different recruiting agencies. I'd like to know what exactly the relationship is between the recruiter and the attorney. There does not seem to be anything contractual in the sense of exclusive service, because isn't the concept essentially "you go with the recruiter who gets you the job you like best"? I ask this because I have gotten a slew of calls from different recruiters and all promise to place me here and there and then I never hear back from them. Bottom line, is there anything contractually binding between the recruiter and the attorney?

OC

Dear OC:

I found this to be such an interesting question because I think there are probably a dozen different answers. However, the only answer I can give you here is from my point of view and my experiences. I will say that I have spoken with many of my colleagues over the years and it would seem that my feelings are shared with the majority of recruiters.

I can't imagine that there are any search firms that have contracts in which you become obligated to work with only one recruiter or firm. At least, I have not heard of this. What I do know is that it makes perfect sense for a recruiter to ask for exclusivity. Why not? I know that at my firm, when we meet a candidate who is not working with any other recruiters, we ask him/ her to work with us on an exclusive basis for at least two weeks. If we have not performed up to expectations within that time frame, then s/he should definitely broaden the search to include other recruiters because clearly we are not doing a good job.

Why do we want exclusivity? Well, it would make perfect sense that if we have a candidate who is working only with us, we would give special consideration and attention to that candidate. The chances of placing that candidate are excellent since s/he has entrusted us with his/her job search. On the other hand, if we are representing a candidate who is working with two or three or four other recruiters, we know that we are going to run into potential conflicts and also narrow the field of clients with which we can work.

For example, last week we met a stellar candidate and we really clicked. We had a number of opportunities for this candidate, but he had already been submitted to all of them by several other search firms. Now, as much as we are crazy about this candidate, it is not a good business decision for us to spend a tremendous amount of time trying to find places to send him because thus far, every place we have mentioned has already been covered. Of course, as new opportunities occur, we will tell him about them, but there really isn't too much else we can do at this time.

On the other hand, it is a good business decision to spend the lion's share of our time with the many candidates who want to work with us exclusively. These candidates must be our first priority; we owe it to them, to our clients, and to ourselves. The top well-established and well-known search firms basically all have the same openings, and so the chances of finding the job a candidate "likes best" with one search firm are pretty good. Keep in mind, I am speaking about law firm jobs right now. I do think an in-house search needs to be handled in a different manner, but that is something I have discussed in past columns and will discuss again in the future.

Now, what about all those recruiters calling you with promises of placing you here and there and then you never hear from them again? What is that all about? If a recruiter calls you with a great opportunity and you are interested, go in and meet with him/her. Some recruiters will give you the name of the client over the phone; most will not simply because it is not good business sense to give out the name of a client without meeting the person first.

There must be a reason that you aren't hearing back from these recruiters. Are you telling them that you are interested in the opportunity? Are you telling them that you are already working with a number of other recruiters? Are these recruiters from search firms that you have never heard of and they are just canvassing the market without any real clients? Are they asking you a lot of questions during these phone calls in which the answers would indicate that you are not the right person for these opportunities? No matter what, I can't figure out why a recruiter would call someone and tell them they have a great job for you and then never follow up by meeting with you or at least calling you back. I would block that person's phone number.

The bottom line here is that unless you sign something, there is no contractual obligation to work with just one recruiter. But as far as I see it, it makes good business sense to start out a job search with one recruiter and see what s/he can do for you. By all means, go meet a few recruiters before deciding which one is the best one for your search. Working with a headhunter is a team effort, and if you find someone that seems to be a good teammate, stick with that person exclusively for a bit and see what s/he can do for you. It makes sense that they are going to work much harder for you if they know you are entrusting your search entirely to them for a certain period of time. Best of luck!

Sincerely,
Ann M. Israel

I█I

City: New York

I am a sixth-year IP litigation associate who was unfortunately let go because I had to drop my big client as they were not paying their bills. I have been out of work now for three months and am actively looking for work. I have had no luck with headhunters. Recently, a fairly reputable headhunter called me to ask to submit my resume to a large out-of-town firm for an associate position in New York. The headhunter asked for a reference from my previous employer, who, according to the headhunter, gave me a glowing recommendation. The headhunter then asked me to explain in an e-mail the specifics of why things did not work out at my previous firm. I replied in a succinct e-mail the reasons why I no longer worked at the firm; namely, that I lost a big client that did not pay their bills. I never heard back from the headhunter after leaving two voice mails and sending an e-mail. I feel foolish for going through the trouble of bothering my previous employer and then spending the time and effort to further explain why I no longer work at my previous firm. What is your advice for anyone in my position for the future? Should I have gone to such trouble to bother my previous employer and explain myself to the headhunter with the alleged promise that a firm was interested in me? Thank you.

Troubled

Dear Troubled:

Your entire situation confuses me, but I really want to address the headhunter issue first and foremost.

Based on what you have told us, it sounds to me that you never had a face-to-face meeting with this headhunter. Since you have been out of work for three months and are actively looking for work, I have to assume that the headhunter called you at home or on your cell phone; s/he had your number because you had submitted your resume to his/her firm. My first question to you is why are you dealing with a "fairly reputable" headhunter? What does that mean?

I certainly would not want to go to a "fairly reputable" doctor or lawyer. I would want to go to someone who is known as the best. I understand that you have had no previous luck with headhunters, but have you asked why? Perhaps the recruiter route is not the proper avenue for you. Clearly this recruiter is not doing you any favors.

Rule number one in my book is that you should not let any recruiter represent you who does not want to meet with you in person (assuming it is geographically possible). Not only is it important for him/her to sit down and interview you in person, but you really need to see who is going to be responsible for representing your future career.

This entire situation sounds very strange to me. Didn't you explain your situation to the headhunter to begin with? Why would you need to send an e-mail specifically outlining what happened at your last employer after s/he checked references and reported back that they were "glowing"? And why are your phone calls and e-mails going unreturned? Do you know where your resume was submitted? Do you know if it actually was submitted? And why was the recruiter speaking with a partner at your last place of employment? Something is not right here.

My suggestion is that you put this all behind you and move forward. It seems to me that headhunters are not the right way to conduct your job search. You need to get out there and start your own job search. Network, contact your law school's career services office, read the classified job section in the paper of record, talk to people in your practice area.

The IP practice area is sizzling hot. You should be able to get law firms interested in you. It is surprising that the recruiters are not interested in representing an IP attorney, so I suspect there is something you haven't told us. I just hope you are being honest with yourself as to why you were asked to leave your last firm. It is impressive that you had your own client base as a midlevel associate. It is a nightmare that your client was a deadbeat, but why would your firm fire you because the client didn't pay? Is there more to this story? Generally speaking, associates don't have clients, and their firms don't expect them to have any. It was a bonus for your firm to get a new client from an associate, but it shouldn't have caused your termination with the firm simply because the client was a no-pay. Something else must have happened here . . .

Whatever the case may be, don't look back. Forget that headhunter; s/he belongs in the same category as your deadbeat client. What a jerk. Move on because there is no percentage in the past. Get your resume out there. The longer you are unemployed, the more difficult it will be to get back in the swing of things. I wish you the best of luck!

Sincerely,
Ann M. Israel

◼

City: New York

Why do headhunters fail to care about the firm that they are sending a lawyer to for a job?

Caring

Dear Caring,

Your question reminds me of the response I frequently get whenever I am with a group of nonlawyers and am asked what I do for a living. As soon as I tell people that I work with lawyers, I see revulsion and/or pity on some of their faces and I have to listen to some stupid lawyer jokes or stories about how lawyers have burned someone. Now of course, all of this is simply undeserved and, as far as I am concerned, in very bad taste. Unfortunately, a few bad attorneys have spoiled it for the entire profession.

The headhunting profession is no different. A few recruiters out there who have no training and no idea what they are doing but think that this is a way to make a quick buck have come into the profession and ruined the reputations of the rest.

Think about it. Do you really believe that every recruiter out there just sends candidates to any firm without caring about the client firm or where the candidate is interviewing? If this happened to be true, how would the profession have lasted? Why would the law firms continue to use recruiters who were so callous and uncaring? How would a recruiter continue to get candidates' permission to submit their backgrounds to firms if every recruiter didn't care enough about their client firms to know all about the practice areas and the people working there? Do you really believe that every search firm out there just sends a candidate anywhere there happens to be an opening?

What kind of a candidate would give permission to go to just any and all law firms without knowing all about each firm and hearing some sort of passion and caring from the headhunter? If you are willing to work with a recruiter that doesn't care about you or the client law firms, then there is no wonder that you feel the way you do. But the big question is, why do you work with a recruiter who behaves in such a way? If you don't feel you are being treated properly, why don't you go to a different recruiter?

I really have to turn this question around and put the blame on the candidate who is willing to work with a recruiter who doesn't care about where they are sending you. As I have written many times before, you need to be in control of your job search. If you believe that your recruiter is not doing you right, speak up, move on, find a better recruiter. Just as in the legal profession, where there are good attorneys and bad attorneys, in the search profession there are good recruiters and bad recruiters. If you suspect your headhunter does not fall into the "good" category, do something about it.

If your recruiter's firm is a member of NALSC (the National Association of Legal Search Consultants), then you are in luck. This national organization abides by a strict Code of Ethics (http://www.attorneysearch.com/ethics.html), and if your recruiter does anything that you consider to be unethical, there is an avenue to use to report him/her. Non-NALSC firms are unregulated, and there is no way to do anything about them (unless they do something so egregious that you determine you want to file a lawsuit against them). However, there is always a way to police the NALSC member firms should you decide that you have encountered a problem. The NALSC member firms are listed on the NALSC website (http://www.nalsc.org/membership/directory.cfm).

If you were being treated by a doctor and felt that this doctor didn't care if you were healthy or not, would you continue to go to him/her? If you were being represented by an attorney and you believed s/he didn't care what happened to you as a client, would you continue to allow this attorney to represent you? If you answered no to either of those questions, then why would you think it should be any different in letting a recruiter represent you if s/he failed "to care about the firm that they are sending a lawyer to for a job"? Be a grown-up and take control of your life. If you don't like what is happening, do something about it.

Sincerely,
Ann M. Israel

City: New York

How do legal recruiters handle conflicts of interest? For example, if you have two or more candidates that are vying for the same position (and you obviously want to place one because that's your job), how do you present them to the firm? Do you push for one and not the other? Do you talk about one more if you think that one has a better chance? And if so, do you tell the other one frankly that s/he might not be the best candidate or that you are pushing more for another candidate you feel is better qualified, or do you say anything at all? I'd like to know so I know where I stand and also so I could find another legal recruiter who will more zealously push for me. I'm certainly not implying that I would find any yahoo who has nothing better to do than to push for me, but let's be honest, I think it would increase my chances if another good recruiter was pushing for me as hard as the first recruiter was for the other candidate.

I understand that you're running a business that's not built on just goodwill, but I'm wondering how much fiduciary duty a legal recruiter has to his/her clients and how much our legal recruiters are telling us and how much they are holding back. Certainly, we as lawyers cannot represent two clients bidding to acquire the same project, so I'm wondering how that plays out for legal recruiters.

Bidder

Dear Bidder:

You ask a valid question. I am surprised that in all the years I have been in business, no one has ever asked this question before.

You are correct that as a lawyer you cannot represent two clients bidding to acquire the same project, but your profession and my profession are very different.

The first thing you need to recognize is that if we really want to get down to the nitty-gritty, our client is defined by the entity that pays the fee. Therefore, the candidate is not really our client. On the other hand, because we work so closely with our candidates, it is difficult to separate them from the role of client. I know that I cannot represent anyone that I do not personally like and am not proud to represent. When you feel that way about your candidates, it is impossible to sell out someone.

The things I am about to write today can only apply to my firm. I cannot speak for any other legal search firm out there.

I will say that in the larger search firms, where you have many recruiters working on the same searches, there are bound to be a number of candidates vying for the same opportunity. Nevertheless, even in a smaller search firm, it is the norm for there to be several viable candidates presented to a client for a specific position. Again, speaking strictly for my firm, each candidate presented to a client has to be a stellar candidate or else that client is going to lose confidence in our ability to find the right people. Hopefully they will want to see two or three of our candidates for the same job. And if we are doing our job properly for our clients, we will find them more than one candidate for the job. If we only presented one candidate for each position, the chances that another search firm would fill the job are tremendous because they are probably going to service the client better by presenting a number of very qualified candidates.

So what do we do if the final decision comes down to two or three of our candidates? Generally the client does not ask us to make the final decision for them, although they may very well ask us which one we like the best. When faced with this question, I do not choose one candidate over the other (unless there is a specific reason to do so) but instead I give reasons to hire either one of the candidates. Since both candidates are from my firm and I am in a win-win situation, I want to be honest and candid with my client and help him/ her to make the best decision without any bias involved. I will have spent a tremendous amount of time debriefing both of these candidates and will have insight as to why this is a good fit for either candidate (or not).

On the other side of the coin, while all this is going on, hopefully these candidates are working with us on other opportunities at the same time. There is nothing wrong with this since the client has been working with our firm on a contingency basis. And just as we are honest with our candidates, we are honest with our clients about what is going on with the interviewing process. So, in the best of all possible worlds, one candidate may get an offer at the first firm while at the same time the other candidate is getting an offer at another firm. Or the candidate that one client is interested in hiring is also being sought after by another one of our clients. In this type of situation, we need to discuss with the candidate which opportunity might be better for his/her career.

Incidentally, when a candidate asks if I am representing other candidates for the same opportunity, I always answer honestly. It is my responsibility to give the clients a number of qualified candidates for each opportunity if possible. Not only is it my responsibility to my client, it is my responsibility to my company to make sure that we are the search firm that fills the opening.

You wondered how much fiduciary responsibility we have to our clients; I can tell you that if you are working with a recruiter whose firm is a member of the National Association of Legal Search Consultants (NALSC), the responsibility is spelled out in our Code of Ethics:

ARTICLE I
Relations with Employers
1. Information provided to employers shall be the most accurate information known to the search firm.
2. No search firm shall withhold candidate information which the employer would reasonably consider essential to its hiring decision.

ARTICLE II
Relations with Candidates
1. Information provided to candidates shall be the most accurate information known to the search firm.
2. No search firm shall withhold employer information which a candidate would reasonably consider essential to his/her hiring decision.

There it is: the minimum level of responsibility we have both to our clients and to our candidates. And when you are involved with both your clients and candidates, it goes much deeper than this.

If you are working with a recruiter who is not a member of NALSC, then there is no Code of Ethics and no way to monitor what they are doing.

Lastly, do we ever push for one candidate and not for another? Well, I suppose there certainly are occasions when this happens and when this action is definitely called for. If one candidate really wants the job and is ready to accept on the spot and the other candidate has no intention of taking the job, I believe it is our responsibility to let the client know that there is a candidate that will accept immediately if offered the position and the other candidate is ambivalent about the opportunity.

It is always a rough position to be in when you have two candidates whom you care about and one is going to get the job and the other is going to be passed on. The worst part about my job is telling someone that they did not get the job offer that they wanted.

In all the years I have been in this business, I have never told one candidate that I have another candidate interviewing for the same job who I believe is the better candidate. The reason for that is because I only represent people I like and who I believe are the best candidates for the job. I don't send inappropriate candidates to my clients. They are all good prospects for the job. The client can decide in the end that one is the best candidate for the job over the other. But by the time my candidates are presented to the client, they are all the best ones for the job, in my opinion.

It sounds as if you have had an unpleasant experience with a recruiter. I think it is going to be a difficult task to find a search firm willing to represent you and only you, but it shouldn't be hard to find a recruiter who promises to be honest with you, as long as you are willing to be honest with him/her. Good luck!

Sincerely,
Ann M. Israel

Ann, thanks for answering my question regarding recruiter ethics. You stated that you only work with candidates that you feel are good matches for your clients (the firms) and that you like. If you choose to work with a candidate, and then for whatever reason, you no longer like them, do you tell them so? Or what if you take on a candidate and you haven't decided if you like them or not—do you just sort of string them along because you don't want them to go somewhere else but you're not sure you like them?

I am working with a recruiter I thought was very good (or at least has a good reputation), but s/he is not very responsive and I only receive e-mails from him/her once a week or so. I also never receive a response right away to an e-mail I send to him/her. Am I being dropped without being told? Should I find another recruiter?

I realize that part of the response time is waiting for the law firm to respond, but that doesn't explain why s/he is not responsive to my e-mails (normally takes a few days). As an attorney, I cannot be nonresponsive to clients without having a detrimental effect, so what gives?

Following Up

Dear Following Up:

Yikes! Did you read my answer? I only work with people I like. I don't work with people when I haven't decided if I like them or not and then just "sort of string them along" to prevent them from going to another recruiter. What kind of people are you dealing with? Or even more important, where do you come up with these ideas? Geez, if I were dealing with someone who I suspected might not really like me but was just stringing me along, I wouldn't be hanging out with that person. You need to be choosier when picking friends or recruiters or whomever.

I never said that I only work with candidates who are good matches for my clients. I wrote that I only work with stellar candidates (in my opinion) who are good prospects for my clients. Not every client agrees with my opinion. However, I am proud to represent each candidate who is being represented by my firm. No matter what happens in the long run with my candidates' interviews, my name is on the door and each candidate who interviews through my firm is representing my name. I certainly wouldn't want my name associated with someone I don't like.

And if along the way I stop liking someone? Well, I suppose everyone has a lapse of judgment at some point in their life, and perhaps there have been times when I have been sorry that I am working with a particular person. In the rare instance when that has occurred, I have been honest with the individual and said that I am not the right recruiter for him/her and s/he should probably find someone else for the job search. I will say that this has probably happened only once in my entire career.

Now, about the e-mail messages you are receiving once a week or so from your recruiter. Contrary to the way you are feeling (lack of communication), it seems to me your recruiter is quite conscientious. I frequently tell candidates who are not in active play that I will contact them as soon as there is something to discuss. I am not certain that sending out an e-mail once a week to them with nothing to report is really necessary. Not to mention that if I spent my time sending e-mails to all my inactive candidates, I wouldn't have time for my active candidates. As it is, I receive anywhere from 100 to 150 e-mails per day. There comes a point where I have to do my job for my clients and candidates. To send out an e-mail just to keep in touch seems senseless to me.

Don't stand on ceremony. If you want to know what is going on with your job search, pick up the phone and call your recruiter. However, I must tell you, if something is actively happening with your search, you probably will be the first to know as soon as the recruiter gets the news.

As to why your recruiter does not respond to your e-mail messages right away, well . . . I just can't answer that question. Perhaps they are going into a spam filter. Perhaps s/he doesn't check e-mail often enough. Perhaps you are being ignored, as you suspect. So, pick up the phone and ask what is going on. Don't stand on ceremony! My guess is that s/he receives as many or more e-mail messages than I do each day and it becomes necessary to "triage" the messages when deciding which one to respond to first. If there is nothing going on with your job search at the moment, your e-mail may not be the first one to receive a reply. The truth is that you do get a reply within a few days. Again, pick up the phone and ask why there is a delay.

It is difficult to determine whether your recruiter is a "bad" recruiter or if you are not a viable candidate for the opportunities available to this recruiter. Perhaps the firms where you have been presented are taking an unusually long time to decide whether or not they want to meet with you. Maybe your recruiter isn't excited about representing you. Who knows? It could be so many different reasons. Whatever the case may be, you need to be more in charge;

stop believing that recruiters are just stringing people along and find out what is really happening. Pick up the phone, call your recruiter, and express these concerns. You may be pleasantly surprised at the outcome. Best wishes!

Sincerely,
Ann M. Israel

City: San Francisco

Dear Ann,

I am currently working with a recruiter I really like. However, so far she has not presented me with a lot of good opportunities. I have seen positions on various law job websites that I would like to apply for, but you have to go through another recruiter to apply. I would like to be able to apply for these positions. What is the protocol as far as working with more than one recruiter? I don't want to adversely affect my relationship with the recruiter I'm currently working with, but obviously I want to increase my chances of finding a good job. Your advice would be very much appreciated. Thanks.

Appreciative

Dear Appreciative:

It's nice that you really like your recruiter but not so nice that she has not presented you with many opportunities. Why don't you take her out for lunch or a drink and become social friends? In the meantime, find a recruiter who will do a good job for you.

Seriously, you need to stop worrying about your relationship with this recruiter and start thinking about your future. Why isn't she finding opportunities for you? Have you had a heart-to-heart discussion with her about this? You certainly will not have an adverse effect on your relationship with her if you are honest about the situation.

Let her know that there seem to be a number of appropriate jobs available through other recruiters and you would like to explore these options. If she truly cares about your future, she is either going to get on the stick and get you out on interviews or release you and allow you to follow up on all other leads without any animosity.

Although I always caution people about working with numerous head-hunters at the same time, this does not apply in your particular situation. When your recruiter is not doing anything for you, that's the time to move on. Remember, this is your future and your career that we are talking about here. It is very endearing that you are so concerned about not hurting your recruiter's feelings. You clearly are a very loyal and dear friend. But this is about business and about your career. Do not stand on ceremony here.

In light of the fact that you do seem to have a good relationship with your recruiter, I would speak with her first and find out why she is not doing anything for you. Let her know what your intentions are and then follow up on the other leads. I would not suggest going after three, four, or five recruiters at the same time, but certainly talking to a couple of recruiters to follow up on what they have to offer seems to be a very good idea in your situation.

One word of caution: be certain to keep track of any place your resume is going to be sent so that there is no duplication of efforts!

Best of luck!

Sincerely,
Ann M. Israel

City: SF/SV

I am a junior associate and I just got laid off from my firm due to low volume of work in my department. I've been offered a severance package and assurances that the firm will assist in helping me find a job, including giving me the use of my office for three months, and that most people at the firm will not know that I did not leave voluntarily. I have begun to work on my resume and have started to talk to some headhunters. Should I tell any headhunters that I end up using that I have been laid off, and should I reveal the real reason for my departure from my firm to the other firms? To tell the truth, I have been thinking of lateraling anyway, as I have felt that this was not the right place for me. This is what I've been thinking of telling the other firms and headhunters, but I wonder if I am ethically obliged to tell the entire story.

Obligated

Dear Obligated:

There are some interesting issues at work here, and I suppose depending on how you define things, you can look at these issues several different ways.

My thinking here is that you need to be completely truthful with your recruiter and let him/her decide how to handle this situation when s/he is marketing you.

It is no surprise to me that the partners would like other people at the firm to think your departure is voluntary rather than a product of being laid off due to a low volume of work in your department; that really makes things look better for the firm, doesn't it? However, you should not be ashamed or embarrassed by the cause of your termination. These things happen and unfortunately, seem to be happening more frequently as of late.

It seems your firm is allowing you to remain "employed" there for the next three months while you mount a job search. Your headhunter can decide whether or not it is ethical to market you as still being employed at the firm during that time. The real question you will face in interviews is why you are looking to leave this firm and lateral over to a new employer. Obviously one answer—and a true answer—is that your department is very slow and there is not enough work to keep you busy. That is the truth, right?

Once the three-month period is over and you are no longer at the firm at all, there is no escaping the entire story, and even your resume will have to reflect your actual date of termination. Instead of saying that you are employed there through the present, it will indicate your last date of employment. Obviously this puts a good deal of pressure on you and your headhunter to try to find a new place of employment for you before you have to change the dates of employment on your resume. As I have stated many times before, you are much more marketable while you are employed than you will be unemployed.

But in the final analysis, layoffs are becoming commonplace happenings these days, and in a way, that is the good news for you because should you not find a new job by the time you have to indicate on your resume that you are no longer employed, you won't have to do that much explaining.

The bottom line here is if you want to have a good relationship with your recruiter, you need to be completely honest and open. If you hide the fact that you have been asked to leave and the recruiter finds out from another source (and s/he inevitably will), it could cause a disastrous rift in your relationship. Your recruiter will decide the right time to disclose this information to any potential employer, and probably it will be early on, because withholding this information might cause a disastrous end to your candidacy with an employer. As always, honesty is the best policy.

With your good references and a little luck on your side, chances are you will be able to find the right opportunity quickly. Fingers crossed! Best wishes!

Sincerely,
Ann M. Israel

❚▓❚

City: Washington, DC

I am an associate at a small firm and need to find another job as soon as possible because my team was downsized. While my academic record is unremarkable, I have ten years of experience in my field. Do recruiters only work with candidates with standout academic credentials like law review, or would they consider working with me? Thanks.

Standing Out

Dear Standing Out:

This is a good question, but it is somewhat complicated to answer. There are a number of reasons why you probably do not want to depend on recruiters to help you with your job search.

First of all, let me say that recruiters do not only represent candidates who have been asked to join their school's law review (although wouldn't that be nice for us!). Not every candidate we represent is in the top 5 percent of his/her class, nor does every candidate come from a top-10 law school or work at one of the top-20 BigLaw firms.

However, the major search firms do seek out candidates that have certain common threads. Their grades from law school are within a certain range, depending on which law school they attended. For example, if a candidate attended one of the top-tier law schools, most law firms will be interested in meeting him/her if his/her law school transcript has a lower final grade point average than that of someone who attended a second-tier law school. That is not to say that someone from a top-tier law school with Cs all over his/her transcript is going to be a recruiter's star candidate. That person is not going to have much luck with a recruiter.

But a candidate with a B+ average from a top-tier law school probably stands a much better chance of success with a recruiter than does the candidate from a second-tier law school with the same grade point average.

Of course, a major determining factor will be the candidate's class year and current employer. And those are some of the factors that are coming into play with your candidacy and the decision as to whether or not a recruiter will be able to help you with your job search.

Unless the small firm you are at right now is a well-known spin-off of a major BigLaw firm or a well-known small firm with a highly specialized practice area, this is yet another factor that will work against you when trying to get a recruiter's attention.

Last, but of great importance, is the fact that you are now a tenth-year attorney. When recruiters are representing tenth-year attorneys, they are generally representing junior partners with a book of business that is bordering on being significant. The firms that are willing to pay a recruiter's fee generally are not going to be interested in a tenth-year attorney unless s/he has developed—or is developing—a real book of business.

So many firms still have "up or out" policies and their tenth-year associates are either long gone or have moved into senior or permanent associate or counsel roles in the firm. The firms are not interested in paying recruiter fees for this level of attorney (except in very unusual circumstances).

I suggest that you forget about the recruiters and get your search going by your own devices. Get your resume out to every contact you might have. Start networking at every bar association event, every cocktail party, and any other place you might imagine. Contact your law school career services office to see what help and/or advice they might be able to offer to you. This isn't going to be easy, but you've got to get off your butt and do it now.

Please be clear that I didn't say you couldn't get a job because you have low—or unremarkable—grades on your transcript. I suggested that you probably will not have much success with a recruiter because your grades are not stellar, you have been downsized from a law firm—and a small firm, at that—

and you are at a point in your career when a recruiter's clients are going to want you to have portable business if they are going to pay a fee for you. You will fare much better without a fee attached to your candidacy. Best wishes!

Sincerely,
Ann M. Israel

Ⅰ▓Ⅰ

City: New York

Hi,

I'm currently thinking about making a lateral move and have had discussions with two recruiters. I disclosed this fact to one of the recruiters and he instructed me to not use more than one recruiter. Is this the standard policy? Or is this simply a case of a recruiter wanting to ensure that he's the one making money off of my search? Thanks for your help.

Sincerely,
Two for the Money!

Dear Two:

I have often advised job seekers to not spread themselves too thin between numerous recruiters. In fact, my advice has been to use only one—or at the most, two—recruiters at a time. If your recruiter cannot perform for you within a two-week period, then you should go on to the next search firm.

You were told by a recruiter that you should not use more than one recruiter and you wondered if this was simply because this headhunter wanted to ensure that s/he was the one who would make money off your job search. Well, that is a rather crude way to put it, but I suppose in the final analysis the answer would have to be yes.

Legal recruiters historically work on a contingency basis, meaning that unless they successfully place you, any and all work they have done for you goes unrewarded. For example, a recruiter may market you to just about every available opportunity out there. If you are working with a good recruiter, then s/he helps you to write an appropriate resume and spends time with you working on interviewing techniques and preparing you for each individual interview. The headhunter arranges the scheduling for each of the interviews and runs interference should there be any hesitation on the part of the potential client, smoothing over any reluctance on their part in bringing you back for advanced rounds if you are truly interested in this opportunity. The recruiter works on compensation matters if necessary, relocation if need be, and any other special needs, such as vacations, etc., prior to an offer being extended and accepted. All of this is taken care of by your recruiter, who acts as your agent/advocate for no compensation from you whatsoever.

And then, out of the blue, a recruiter that you have never spoken with before calls you about an opportunity that has just opened up and you give that recruiter permission to present your background. You hang up the phone and your faithful headhunter calls to tell you about this same opportunity and you say, "Oh, I have already been submitted there by another recruiter." The recruiter who has been working so hard for you is probably stunned that this has happened but continues to work on all of the other opportunities for you without a moment's hesitation.

And as Murphy's Law would have it, the other headhunter's job is the one job you like over all the rest and you accept that offer. All the time and effort the first recruiter has put into your job search has resulted in nothing. Well, that's the way our business works, and we certainly all understand that these things happen. But that is also why we ask our candidates to work exclusively with one recruiter whenever possible. You could have been represented by the first recruiter at the job you finally accepted, but you never gave him/her a shot at it.

Yes, it is absolutely true that we want our candidates to work with us exclusively because we want to ensure that we are the ones making the money off the search. I just wouldn't ever put it that way. I would say that I want a candidate to work exclusively with me so that I am motivated to work as hard as I possibly can to find the best possible opportunity for that candidate. If I don't, then the candidate will stop working with me and find another recruiter and I will have spent my time and energy for nothing—and I will deserve what I get.

But quite frankly, consider the following scenario. A candidate comes to me and wants me to represent him/her, so I spend an hour or two on an initial meeting and then another few hours doing research on the most appropriate opportunities for this individual. Perhaps I spend even more time redoing a resume. Then, I present all of this and am told that the candidate is working with several other recruiters, and many of the opportunities I am presenting are off-limits because the candidate has already been presented there. As you can imagine, my motivation to work with this individual is greatly diminished. And that is because I have other candidates who want my undivided attention and in return give me exclusivity. I am going to spend the most amount of time and energy on those candidates because it makes good business sense. And after all, I am a businessperson, not a social worker.

I hope you understand this from my side of the desk. If a client comes to you for representation but then wants to split the deal or the litigation with another lawyer, I can't imagine you would be inclined to take on this client. The only difference with recruiters is that we still end up working with candidates who have more than one recruiter on their job search.

I will say that if you are working with one recruiter and s/he is not getting interviews for you after two weeks, move on to the next recruiter. And don't be shy about this. Let the recruiter know that you are disappointed in the results and would like to know why you have not had any interviews set up. Tell him/her that no more resumes are to be sent out and that you are going to be represented by a different search firm. This is your career and your future and you need to be in control. At the same time, you need to understand our side of the story. I hope I shed some light on it. Best wishes!

Sincerely,
Ann M. Israel

IBI

City: New York

What advice would you give a BigLaw associate looking to break in to policy and government work—either at an NGO, think tank, or government research organization? Best resources for job hunting, differences between presenting yourself for these types of jobs versus law firm/in-house positions, etc.? While I found a recruiter to be very helpful in my lateral move between law firms, it doesn't seem like they are helpful for this kind of move. Are there recruiters who work in this niche?

Thank you,
Policy Wonk

Dear Wonk:

Yes, I would think you did find recruiters to be very helpful when making a lateral move between law firms; this is really the niche market for legal search consultants, particularly when they are working with BigLaw associates.

However, it is understandable why you are not enjoying the same type of success with recruiters as you try to break into policy and/or government work. Your basic legal recruiters are not going to be as helpful in this arena as you found them to be when making a move into another law firm.

There are specific search firms that work with government agencies or policy organizations, but generally these are executive search organizations and they do not represent candidates; they have specific searches where they seek out individuals to fill very specialized and defined spots.

But more often than not, you will find that the type of opportunity you are seeking is not going to be found through a recruiter. Rather, these positions will be listed on the websites of those organizations or through their papers of record.

The reason for this is that government agencies and not-for-profit organizations generally are not budgeted for paying search firm fees. Therefore, I strongly suggest that you do not rely on recruiters for these types of opportunities. You are going to have to get out there and network, speak with everyone you know, check the job boards at your law school career services office, read the Internet job boards and websites of the government agencies that are of interest to you, and basically look under every rock there is.

You might also want to speak with other attorneys currently working in the types of positions that you are seeking and find out how they were able to secure these opportunities. These people are probably going to be the best resources for finding out how to get the type of job you are seeking.

I hope this is of some help to you. Perhaps some of the readers of this column will be willing to share their experiences with me and I will be happy to pass them along. Best wishes!

Sincerely,
Ann M. Israel

City: New York

I am a third-year attorney, and recently I've been getting about a half dozen calls a week from as many recruiters. When they catch me in my office, I politely explain that I'm very happy where I am and have no interest in hearing about other jobs at the moment. When I'm not available to answer the phone, a few of them leave messages asking me to return their calls; sometimes they identify themselves as legal recruiters and sometimes they don't, simply leaving a name and number and asking me to get back to them as soon as possible.

My feeling is that I have no obligation to call them back; I have no interest in what they're pitching, and I'm a busy guy who doesn't have time to deal with all these minor nuisances. The other day, a recruiter who had left two messages over the last few weeks called back, caught me in the office, and delivered an angry lecture, telling me that I was unprofessional for failing to return his calls and saying that he thought I was a terrible lawyer and that he would be unwilling to represent me in the future because he couldn't, in good conscience, recommend to his clients someone too rude or disorganized to return phone calls. My feeling is "good riddance"; I had no desire to ever let him represent me, and with so many recruiters trying to get my business, I don't see any harm in offending one of them. I wondered, though, what you thought of this practice. Do you think it's appropriate for recruiters to leave such messages? If so, do you think it's inappropriate for me to ignore them?

Thanks,
I Want to Be Left Alone

Dear Mr./Ms. Garbo:

I'm impressed that you are getting so many calls from recruiters. You must have great credentials and be working at a really impressive law firm and in a very hot practice area to be receiving such attention from the headhunters as a third-year associate. And how nice that you are happy where you are working and have no interest in other jobs at this time. In these crazy times it is especially nice not only to have a job but to also be working somewhere that you really like.

It seems to me that you are handling the headhunter situation in exactly the best possible way. When you are available to take a recruiter's call, do so.

It is always a good idea to know a few search consultants because you just never know when you—or one of your friends—might need one. Developing a friendly relationship with two or three headhunters is a smart thing to do and a wise investment in your future. It never hurts to hear about what is happening in the marketplace—from recruiters you know and trust.

However, when you are busy and don't have the time to "schmooze" on the phone (you are at work, after all), no one should fault you for not taking a call. And an unsolicited voice mail message (or e-mail message) does not require a return phone call unless you are interested in doing so. It is exactly as you said—you are not obligated to return a stranger's call unless you are interested in what s/he is selling.

Some might consider the recruiter who left two messages for you to be verging on harassing you. Personally, I just consider it stupid. I think it is bad business to leave a message on a cold call. If the person doesn't return your message, then you have to call back again and leave yet another message and start to look like a pest. People who don't return cold call messages are usually sending out a message: not interested. It just isn't smart business to leave a message for someone you don't know when you are trying to sell them something for the first time. That's my opinion.

But this guy really took it to a new level. He got mad at you for not returning his calls. Now that's nerve. I wonder what he thought he was going to accomplish with that approach. Did he think that you were going to apologize and then ask him to represent you? Did he think you would be so impressed with his bravado that you would refer him to all of your colleagues?

I do not think it is appropriate for anyone—not just recruiters—to leave such messages and then to chastise you for not returning the call. Where does he get off calling you a bad lawyer? I really don't understand what that is all about. As far as calling you rude, well . . . I just think he needs to look in the mirror before he starts calling you names. Good riddance doesn't begin to express what I am thinking!

Lastly, no I don't think it is inappropriate for you to ignore this kind of phone call. If a recruiter with such a giant ego is upset because an associate (or anyone) doesn't return his cold call voice mail message, he needs to rethink his worth. Perhaps he isn't as terrific as he thinks he is. Don't give him another thought. This isn't someone you would want representing your future. If he treats a total stranger the way he treated you, I shudder to think about how he must treat his clients. Yikes! Best wishes!

Sincerely,
Ann M. Israel

CHAPTER 11

Becoming a Partner

I will never forget the senior associate I recruited for a specific opportunity at a major media network. He was perfect for the job, and everyone, including the VP/general counsel, loved him. After many rounds of interviews, a generous offer was extended to him. He clearly was having a tough time deciding what to do, but he finally confided in me. He informed me that he had been told that he was a "lock" for partnership within the next few years and he really wanted to be a partner at this particular firm. And so, he passed on the offer that would have propelled his career within a major Fortune 500 company. Several years later I happened to check in on him. He had been passed over for partner at his firm and asked to leave. He was now working at a small and unimpressive law firm, toiling away as a senior associate with no hope of a partnership in his future. He asked me about the media company, but there were no openings there any longer. And since he was now very senior and working at a firm with small and uninteresting cases, his resume was no longer one that all employers were grabbing. He had stayed too long at that first firm, believing that he was guaranteed a partnership when there really is no such thing.

So, what's the lesson to be learned here? Don't ignore the calls from recruiters and friends telling you about new opportunities. It never hurts to listen and it never hurts to take a look. There is no guarantee about making partner at any firm, but sometimes the chances are better somewhere else. Again, it never hurts to listen or to look—that doesn't mean that you have to move to another employer. The best thing to do is to develop relationships with a couple of legal headhunters and keep in touch with them through the years. When you are at your prime years for an associate move, you really need to evaluate your situation. Listening to someone describing new opportunities is the smart thing to do. As the expression goes, you never know . . .

▮▇▮

City: New York

I'm an eighth-year associate at a large firm that just completed a merger in the past year. At my annual review last year, before the merger, the managing partner told me that I was on target for the partnership track. After the merger, the firm came out with new partnership criteria that are much more difficult to achieve, and a new "up or out" policy (partner by ten years or out). I was just told at this year's annual review that I will not make partner under the new criteria, that there is nothing I can do to change this, and that under the new "up or out" policy, I will be officially asked to leave in two years. Gulp! They said they were basically giving me a heads up. I have two concerns that I'm hoping you can help me with. My husband and I recently decided to start a family. Should I get pregnant now and then find a new job after (or during) my maternity leave, since I have two years until I am kicked to the curb, or should I put starting a family on the back burner and focus on getting a new job? Also, what do I say when I am asked at interviews about why I am leaving my current job?

Curbed

Dear Curbed:

Yikes! How do I answer your question? This is one of the toughest questions I have encountered in all the years I have been writing this column. My heart goes out to you. This is a difficult situation and I am leaning in two different directions.

First, I do want to say that there is no way you could have seen this coming. Clearly you have been doing a great job at your firm and have been receiving strong reviews all along, or I would have to hope that you would have been looking for a new job a number of years before this.

I can only imagine the number of headhunter phone calls you received telling you that you need to make a move before you were too senior. However, you were loyal to your firm and, at the same time, were being encouraged to stay by partners who said you were on a strong partnership track. And then the unforeseen happened—a merger that changed everything.

I would never suggest that you should hold up starting a family in order to make a job change, but I spoke with a number of career female attorneys in your age group, some with children, some without, and some currently expecting children, and surprisingly they all basically had the same answer. You are a senior associate and the job market at your level is not plentiful. Should you decide to wait two more years before you get yourself out on the interviewing field, you are going to find your choices even more scarce as a tenth-year associate mounting a job search.

I wish I knew your practice area. If you are in the corporate practice area, then you might have a good chance right now as an eighth-year associate to line up a position with one of the major law firms. Are you willing to take a step back in class year? If you were to present yourself as a year or two more junior, then there would be more opportunities available to you at this time with those firms that are willing to do a step back.

Of course, depending on your practice area, you are at the perfect stage of your career to go in-house, and that would still be true two years from now. But the problem is that in-house opportunities can be few and far between, and as I keep saying, a lot depends upon your practice area.

All things being equal, I would say that you should get out and interview now if you are interested in looking at law firm opportunities.

On the other hand, what does your husband have to say about all of this? What are your plans for raising a family? Is it okay to wait a while until you start a family? This is not my place to make these decisions. This is something so very personal and strictly between you and your husband. I will say that I don't think you have to completely back-burner starting a family because if you find a wonderful job and get going sooner rather than later, I don't see why you couldn't start your family in the next year or so. Again, I am not advising you here, just sort of thinking out loud.

I am sorry that you are facing these decisions. If I had to trade places with you, I would get out of your current firm as fast as possible. Since you know that you are going to have to leave within two years, no matter what, I would want to leave sooner rather than later.

As far as what you should be saying on interviews, the only way to go is with the truth. Only a small percentage of associates make partner, and there is nothing to be ashamed of in terms of what has happened to your partnership chances. The merger changed everything. I can't imagine any interviewer not understanding your situation. Don't be defensive, and don't make a long story out of it, just tell it exactly as you have written it in your question to this column.

I hope this helps you a bit. I apologize that I can't be more definitive in my answer to you as to what you should do. I have a feeling you already know what you are going to do and just needed a little push in that direction. Best wishes to you, and please let us know how everything turns out.

Sincerely,
Ann M. Israel

City: New York

I was up for partner and was told that I was "deferred" for a year. Based on all of the intelligence I have gathered, the deferral appears to be for real, but of course no guarantees. Am I better off interviewing and trying to secure another position before or after the next decision is made?

Deferred

Dear Deferred:

Wow, how do I answer this question?

Are you a gambler? What do you think the odds are that you will be voted into the partnership next year? I have never done a study on how many deferred associates make partner the following year, so I really have no idea what the percentage might be. I only know that I see so many people who did not have good luck with the deferral process.

When I read your question, my first thought was that if I happened to be in your shoes, I would get my resume updated and start interviewing right away. To be up for partner tells me that you must be fairly senior at this point in your career. Being fairly senior, and no matter what your practice area may be, also tells me that there will not be as many opportunities available at law firms as there might have been three, four, or five years previously. You are at the right level for an in-house position, but depending on your practice area, they can be few and far between.

The only problem with waiting is that you will be one year more senior and the jobs that are available today will not be available in a year from now. Yes, the intelligence you gathered indicates that the deferral is for real, but you certainly don't know what is going to happen to your department over the next 12 months. There are so many variables.

For example, the firm might hire several new partners into your practice group during the coming year. The department might very well become top-heavy with partners and the firm could then decide not to elect any more partners into that group for the next few years. As an aside, if this did happen, they would need more associates working in the group rather than yet another partner.

Or perhaps the rainmakers in your group might be lured away to another firm and all of a sudden that department has no business to support a new partner. Unless you suddenly develop a big book of business (which I assume you do not have or else your firm would have elected you to the partnership this year), there would be no way that the firm would elevate you to partner status.

Another scenario, and one that is happening more frequently these days, is that the firm might suddenly merge with another firm and then everything would change. Your old firm may not have the same control it did and your chances of partnership more than likely would not exist any longer.

Or a year from now you could be elected to the partnership.

There is a slight chance that a new firm might bring you into their partnership, but unless you are coming in with business, that is unlikely. You might wind up coming into a new firm as counsel with a promise of a partnership vote in X amount of time (each firm differs in the amount of time you must be there in order to be considered). Or, you might have to come in as a senior associate and play the game with the other associates in the firm.

I once represented a very senior associate who had no business but was positive that she would be able to develop a large book within a year. She had top credentials, academic and law firm, and was very confident in what she was going to achieve. I marketed her to every BigLaw firm, but no one was interested in a senior associate with no business and the need to become a partner . . . until I found one managing partner who was willing to listen. After many meetings with me and with her, an offer was extended with very specific terms. She would come in as counsel, and if she had achieved the book of business she was claiming she would bring in by December, she would be made a partner of the firm. By the way, she did it. But the point of retelling this story is to emphasize that you need to have a lot of confidence in what you will do for a new firm, along with a well-thought-out plan as to how you will achieve your goals. There are hiring and managing partners out there that are looking for up-and-coming superstars—are you one of those? Show them how and why.

Again, if I traded places with you, I would go out looking to see what my options might be. What do you have to lose? The only way to answer the question of whether you should stay at your firm without taking a look at what else is out there is to ask, are you a gambler? Good luck!

Sincerely,
Ann M. Israel

I would love to hear from any of you who have been deferred for partnership—what was the final outcome?

City: New York

I read your response to the question from the associate who stated that he had a 50/50 chance of making partner. My only issue with your response is that I think it is dangerous to put any faith in "guarantees" of making partner two years from the date of the statement. Don't you?

Faithful

Dear Faithful:

Um, yes, I surely do. In fact, not only is it dangerous to put faith in those guarantees, I think you have to be in la-la land to believe in guarantees of partnership at all, especially those made so far from the election date.

The stories I could tell. . . . Over the years there have been many perfect opportunities for the midlevel to senior associates I was representing. They would be ready to accept the offer, but then they were told that partnership at their current firm was all but guaranteed and/or they were a "lock" for partnership, so they decided not to make the move after all.

Nine times out of ten when their turn for partnership came around, they were not voted in, and by then, they were too senior for the opportunities that had come their way several years earlier—those other firms where the partnership track was more realistic or the in-house opportunities where by now they would most likely be general counsel.

Your question happens to be very timely because just last week Tony Lin, one of the top reporters for the *New York Lawyer*, wrote about a New York associate's lawsuit that had to do with this very subject. It seems this associate claims he was *promised* that he would be brought into the partnership of his firm. Unfortunately, when the time came for the vote to be cast, not only was he not voted into the partnership, he actually was fired from the firm (*Hoeffner v. Orrick, Herrington & Sutcliffe*, 602694/05).

As Mr. Lin wrote in his article, "The highly unusual suit has attracted attention within the profession because large firms frequently hold out the carrot of partnership to associates, even as hundreds are passed over for promotion every year."

So, what does this all mean? The bottom line here is that nothing in life is for sure (I know, except birth, death, and taxes), so if you are smart you will always keep your options open. Yes, you may very well be a lock for partnership, but if an opportunity happens to fall in your lap, you owe it to yourself—and to your future—to take a look at it. Sometimes the grass isn't greener, and you will be glad that you looked and then came back to your firm and waited to see if that "guarantee" might be real. Because, sometimes it is.

But then again, what harm is there in taking a look? Perhaps Mr. Hoeffner might have thought twice about those two offers he turned down because he believed in that guarantee. Who's to know? Life really is a gamble. Best wishes!

Sincerely,
Ann M. Israel

City: New York

Ann, I am an senior associate at a large law firm that is ranked toward the middle of the Vault 50, and am in my partner year. Our firm has a single tier of partners and has traditionally been an "up or out," one-look firm a la Cravath, albeit with an eight-year, not seven-year, track, though this has been eroding in last year as at least one person was deferred. My specialty is lending and corporate finance, with strong credentials in bankruptcy financing, workouts, distressed debt, and other relatively hot areas. I have been relatively busy this year and believe I will finish the year off 5–10 percent from last year's billing total, and last year was a busy year. Looking at my chances for partnership, I would have expected to have a very high chance at partnership in a normal year, but I have no idea what normal is this year. That said, I do believe there is a strong possibility I will be made partner, but the gray skies are getting me down. To anticipate some questions, I have no business of my own, graduated in the top 20 of my class at a top-5 law school and with honors from a top college, if it matters. Four years ago I lateraled to my current firm from a top-10 Vault law firm. The question is, what should I be doing? I get calls from recruiters, thankfully, but I have a hard time imagining someone offering me a job that would be contingent on my *not* making partner. In addition, I don't want to spend time interviewing and the like if it is too soon. I doubt anyone is going to offer me a partnership outright, so what is the best thing to do? Sit tight, interview for networking purposes, lateral and get my partnership decision postponed to a better economy, hire a soothsayer?

Thank you.
Anticipating

Dear Anticipating:

This is really a time when a crystal ball would come in handy. Absent that orb, I don't know how else we divine what is about to happen to you.

This is a difficult position that you have found yourself in, and I am afraid that no one can really answer your questions for you. This is a situation you are going to have to work out yourself.

How can anyone predict whether or not you are going to make partner at your current firm? I can tell you that in the very best of times there have been senior associates who everyone said were absolute locks for partnership and when the announcements came out, their names were not on the list of new partners. What happened? Well, their practice group partners certainly were supporters for them, but the rest of the partnership didn't agree. There were other senior associates who were stronger candidates and had more powerful partners backing them.

In your particular situation, you have a very bad economy working against you. My guess is that if things continue as they are, very few people will be named to any partnership at the end of this year. Your billings are down, you have no business of your own, and you have only been with the firm for four years—not to mention that bad economy. How many other associates are there in your class year at your firm? Are there any who have been there since they were summer associates? Are they stars? What practice area are they in? Have they been busy? In other words, what does your competition look like?

You mentioned that you are still getting calls from recruiters. Are they asking you if you have portable business, or are they interested in you because you are in the financing, workouts, distressed debt practice area, which currently is a relatively hot practice area? My guess is they are looking for distressed debt people right now and they don't expect that you would have any portable business.

Being realistic, you should understand that any firm you go to at this time, without a portable book of business, is not going to bring you in as a partner, nor are they going to wait to see if you make partner at your current firm (as you suspected). They need a senior associate now to fill a need in their distressed debt practice group. And I am guessing that, just as at your firm, they probably have no intention of making a slew of partners perhaps in the foreseeable future due to the economy. But even if they are in a great economic position and are willing to vote any number of associates into the partnership, most firms have a steadfast rule as to how long an associate must be at the firm before they are eligible to be up for partnership. You certainly might be able to negotiate some kind of deal (i.e., two years instead of four), but you shouldn't be under the impression that going to another firm means that you will be up for partnership any sooner than at your current firm. This crazy economy has really messed things up, hasn't it?

So, what do I suggest? Have you spoken with the lead partner in your practice group lately? Have you asked him/her what your chances are of making partner? Perhaps even going to the managing partner of the firm might be in order here. After all, you really have nothing to lose. If the answer seems to indicate that your chances are slim to none at the present time, I suggest that you follow up on some of those leads offered to you by the headhunters. On the interviews, you can then ask those partners about partnership opportunities and exactly what it would take to become a shareholder. It might actually be a shorter road at another firm; another lateral move could end up being the right thing to do at this point in your career.

Without exploring options and speaking to all the powers that be, you really are just guessing at what might be happening down the road. You need to find out as much as you possibly can at this time and then try to make an intelligent decision based on whatever information you are able to gather. Once you do have some details, write back to me and fill me in. I might be able to give you better advice at that time and that also would be helpful to more people. Best wishes!

Sincerely,
Ann M. Israel

City: New York Metro

I am a midlevel associate at one of the nation's largest firms. I graduated at the top of my class from a law school at the bottom of the top 50. I love my job, my colleagues, and my clients, but despite my best efforts, I am having trouble figuring out my long-term prospects at my firm. The partnership process here is completely opaque and the length of the partnership track is getting longer with each passing year. I meet my billing target each year but do not exceed it by much. I would rather stay at my firm than move, but not at the cost of failing to make partner. Should I tough it out or move to a firm that will be more transparent about partnership selection?

Tough

Dear Tough:

This is a difficult question to answer. You are in one of those "damned if you do and damned if you don't" positions, and probably only a coin toss will provide the answer you are seeking.

Here you are at one of the top BigLaw firms. Your transcript is great, although your law school is second-tier. In a good job market, you would be a viable candidate, but the way things are right now, you are competing with candidates from first-tier schools, and that puts you in a tough position.

You love your job, the people you work with, and your clients. Do you have any idea how rare that is? I hardly ever hear that. It is the perfect trifecta; you are very fortunate.

But here's the problem: you can't figure out if you have a future as a partner at the firm. Well, welcome to the real world. Sadly, that is the state of the law firm today, whether you work in BigLaw or in a boutique firm. In an article published in 2010 in *Bloomberg Businessweek*, Caroline Kolker wrote: "Making partner, the brass ring for law firm associates who toil slavishly for a decade after law school, has become an elusive dream as shrinking revenue cut promotions at some of the largest U.S. firms. Partner compensation is derived from profits and isn't fixed. With less money to divide among them as the recession forced clients to cut costs, partners have grown reluctant to increase their own ranks by promoting salaried attorneys or even non-equity partners who can get some of their pay from profits."

The truth of the matter is that even in the best of times, partnership has pretty much always been an opaque process and never a certainty; I can remember trying to recruit associates who told me that they were an absolute "lock" for partnership and then receiving a phone call from them a few years later telling me that they had been passed over. Nothing was ever guaranteed.

Today, the chances of making partner are just not in your favor, no matter where you work. Caroline Kolker cut to the bottom line—there is simply less of that pie to divide, making it more and more difficult for the existing partners to open up their door to bring in more partners to share the slim pickings. Or not so slim, as the case may be, but they just aren't willing to take the risk. After all, even equity partners without big books of business are being thinned from the ranks.

So, should you tough it out or move to a firm where you believe there is a more visible—and attainable—shot at partnership? I believe in this day and age you need to base your decision on whether or not your current firm, or the firm you might join, has an "up or out" policy. For me, that is the key factor for your future, not whether or not you are going to make partner, because right now the odds of making partner are not in your favor.

As I frequently advise, sit down and speak with the head of your department and have a candid conversation regarding your future with the firm. By the way, if no one has told you that you would be smart to think about a different home for your future, you probably are in good shape at this firm for the foreseeable future. Nevertheless, you need to know whether, if you are passed over for partnership (which is the norm for most associates these days), you will need to move on or if there will still be a place for you at the firm.

It certainly never hurts to take a look at what else is out there. However, I think there is a lot to be said for the "devil you know," particularly if there is no "up or out" rule at your firm. If you have a home for your foreseeable lifetime career and you love the work, the people you work with, your clients, and the firm in general, I say you have got a great thing going for you. I don't know a lot of associates who can say the same thing. Best wishes!

Sincerely,
Ann M. Israel

▌▒▌

City: San Francisco

Ann—I have heard from my supervising partner that I am about to be promoted to partner. While I am delighted to become a partner, I am a little reluctant to manage some of my friends who are associates in my section (especially those who are not being promoted this year). What advice can you give me about making the transition to partner and dealing with associates/friends?

Lonely at the Top

Dear Lonely at the Top:

First and foremost, congratulations! You should be delighted, and very proud of this tremendous accomplishment and vote of confidence from your soon-to-be partners.

The sentence above contains a very important sentiment. You are about to face some major changes and adjustments in your work life and your personal life. One of those changes is learning to adjust to the fact that your former bosses or supervisors are now your *partners*. Wow, that is earth shattering, isn't it?

The other adjustment is recognizing that this promotion was well deserved. While you don't want to act as if you are the greatest thing since sliced bread and make the associates you are leaving in the dust feel like dirt, you can't act as if you didn't deserve becoming a partner. False modesty doesn't serve you well here. Obviously the associates who are not being promoted this year (most likely being passed over or, at the very least, deferred for another year) are having a tough time grappling with their own issues right now; seeing their friend make partner only brings home their own lack of promotion—not that they aren't happy for you . . . sort of.

And now comes the big issue—suddenly you are on the "other side." You are no longer one of them; instead, you are now a partner, one of the bosses. You go to the partner meetings; you vote on matters that will directly impact their work life.

Interestingly enough, management consultants are split down the middle on how people should behave when they are promoted and suddenly are supervising former peers. Do you continue to deal with your friends in the same manner as always, or do you end any social contact altogether? It's really a very difficult decision to make. If you continue to pal around as if nothing has changed at all, it is liable to be very difficult to supervise your staff, which will surely be made up of some of your friends. And yet, if you detach yourself completely from your friends and build a wall between yourself and them, morale will deteriorate and those once-friends will turn on you faster than you could ever believe possible.

The best solution would probably be to try to be a little of both. In other words, you still want to be friendly but not quite as buddy-buddy as before. However, I do think it is important to sit down with each friend as soon as possible and talk about the fact that the two of you are friends but you are now also a partner and the boss too. You need to explain that because of this there will be times when you can't talk about certain things and also there will be times when you will have certain expectations from each person on the team. Letting each friend know what your expectations are from day one can help to keep a friendship but also establish the correct boundaries at the same time.

No matter what, your friendships are going to change in some way. It's wise to remember that no matter how happy your friends may seem to be about your promotion, there is going to be some anger, jealousy, and/or envy on their part. That's human nature. Be careful and be smart about how you handle things going forward. Don't stop spending time with these friends, but when/if you go out for a drink with them, just have one drink and then leave. Go back to the office or go home instead of staying out for hours and partying with them as you used to do. After all, you are a partner now and your responsibilities are much different from this point forward. It is possible to still be friends *and* the boss, but it has to be clear from the beginning what that friendship is all about now.

Just remember, you did it—you made partner! Congratulations and best wishes!

Sincerely,
Ann M. Israel

CHAPTER 12

Problems in the Workplace

I t isn't easy being an associate. There's no question that you have to be very political and very savvy and understand how to deal with partners. After all, your future depends on what they think and say about you. Unfortunately, there isn't always much you can do about partners who treat you unfairly or harass you, whether it is verbally or sexually. Or is that not the truth? As you will read in the following questions to the column, there are situations where there is no other choice but to speak with someone in power, or else find a new place to work. For the most part, I encourage people in compromised situations to find a partner—a seemingly objective partner, that is—to discuss the problem with and try to find a solution. Unfortunately, sometimes there simply isn't a solution, and when that does happen, it is time to find a new employer. We have all heard about the partner who drinks too much and then starts hitting on associates—and as you will see in this chapter, it isn't always a male partner hitting on a female associate. When something like this does happen, the associate is definitely put in a very precarious position, which sometimes ends in litigation and almost always ends with the associate needing to find a new job, whether it is due to his/her own decision or being forced out of the firm. Problems in the workplace are particularly difficult for associates, simply because of the hierarchy of law firms or legal departments. No matter what, it is always best to try to find an unbiased ear to discuss the problem—if possible.

|||||

City: North Jersey

Hi Ann:

I accepted a position that will start in September, after the end of my clerkship. Recently, my friends surprised me with a cruise for my 30th birthday (four months after I start my new job). How do I let my firm know of my vacation request (five days)?

Some background is that the firm is midsized and located in North Jersey. I was told that while associates are expected to bill a certain number of hours yearly, the firm culture expects them to take time off. Specifically, after I was hired, the hiring partner told me that he expected me—in fact, wants me—to take at least two weeks' vacation a year.

Should I call and tell him now? Wait until July or August? Or wait to tell him after I start?

Thanks for your help in advance,
New Associate in NJ

Dear New,

What nice friends you have! You must have been very surprised to receive such a generous and wonderful gift. Clearly you are a very special friend to have people remember your birthday with such an amazing gift!

I don't see that you really have a problem here, except that I don't suggest you wait any longer to inform the firm about these plans. Since you know about the cruise now, there would be no reason to withhold this information.

Over all the years that I have been headhunting, there is rarely a time when I place someone that s/he doesn't have some kind of trip planned for the coming year. These upcoming trips are generally prepaid—as is yours—and almost always are for a special occasion—as is yours. When an offer is about to be accepted, or is accepted, I always inform the employer that the candidate will need these specific days off as a condition of employment. It has yet to present a problem.

If the planned trip takes place soon after the candidate starts his/her new job, it is fair to tell the employer that there is no expectation of pay for the missed workdays. However, if it is after the six-month mark of employment, generally there is already accrued vacation time and there is no missed pay.

In your particular situation, it is going to be up to the employer whether or not this time off in your fourth month of employment will count as vacation days, meaning whether or not this will be a paid vacation for you. Nevertheless, you are going to be taking off these five days and you need to let the firm know as soon as possible.

I would suggest that you speak briefly with the hiring partner, as well as the person who extended the offer to you, letting them know that your friends have honored you with this gift to take place on these specific dates. Let them know that you will certainly give them those dates again once you start your employment in the fall, and that you will certainly give the dates to the head of your practice group as well, but you just wanted to make sure that you told them about this trip as soon as it had been planned.

This is no big deal, and probably it would be just fine if you waited until you started work at the firm to tell the hiring partner. I just think it looks a lot more straightforward to let him/her know right away. He sounds like a great guy, at any rate. I love a managing partner that wants, no, expects his associates to take at least a two-week vacation. Believe me, I know plenty of associates that haven't had a vacation in years! Have a great time on your cruise and best of luck with your career!

Sincerely,
Ann M. Israel

❚▨❚

City: Unknown

Hi Ann:

Just an update—I recently submitted a question that you answered on the Daily Buzz about being a minority woman trying to find a job after not receiving a summer offer. Well, you were right! I landed a great position in a Vault 100 firm. The only thing that I'm concerned about is that there are *no* minority female partners in the office that I am working in (and

it's the HQ office!), and there are only five minority male partners out of the approximately 350 attorneys. Should I be concerned?

Cloud 9

Dear Cloud 9:

I am so pleased that you are up there floating—what a happy ending! I frequently ask people to keep in touch and let us know how things worked out, and I am happy that you did so. Just as a reminder about your situation, here is the question you had originally submitted:

> I didn't get an offer. I think it has been haunting me, and the only reason I can think of is not something I can say in an interview. I graduated from a top-20 law school, with honors, and was on law review. My work product was excellent, and my midterm and final reviews were excellent. The managing partner at the final review told me to be optimistic. When the hiring partner came to my school during OCIs to recruit the next year's class, he told me, "The word on the street is good." A senior partner wrote on my reviews that I was the best summer associate there. In all honesty, and I'm not searching for a whiny reason, I suspect I didn't get an offer because I am a minority female. I felt very out of place and unwelcome. I honestly felt that I was filling a quota of some sort. To top it off, I was working in a city that is considered to be one of the most liberal cities in the United States, so this came as rather a shock.
>
> I didn't go to law school in the same region as the firm, so it wasn't until later that I found out from attorneys at other firms (both big and small) that the firm had a lot of question marks surrounding it regarding its treatment of minorities and females. Nobody was surprised about how I felt; some were even the first to ask me how I liked the firm, being a minority female. On top of it, my supervising attorney left in the middle of my summer with less than graceful good-byes (she hated the place), and my second supervising attorney left the same month my summer ended (with even less graces than the first). Needless to say, I didn't want to work there, but I was willing to stay for one to three years to gain experience before moving.
>
> After graduating, I found a job with a solo practitioner who called up a senior partner at the firm I summered as a reference. The senior

partner said that I was an excellent summer associate and had no idea why I did not receive an offer. The solo practitioner, who has practiced in the area for over 30 years, also made a remark that I didn't get an offer because of "internal problems" with the firm. I've had lunch with another junior partner and a senior partner that I worked with, and they both said that work product was spot-on. The firm gave me some excuse about overestimating how many people they could hire and something about an LLM student coming back to work and a senior associate coming back from maternity leave, even though the next year, they hired more summers than they did for my year.

The problem is, I would like to find a job at a BigLaw firm. I don't have much work experience and my resume just screams "I didn't get an offer." I have three partners and one associate from the old firm as references as well as the solo plaintiff attorney and a professor. However, I haven't received one phone call. In fact, rejection letters come in as early as two days after I send my resume.

So, in a nutshell, my questions are: (1) What's going on?! (2) Am I ever going to get my foot in the door at a BigLaw firm? (3) If and when I do finally get an interview, what should I say when asked why I didn't get an offer? Needless to say, I can't say that the firm was conservative and an unfriendly place to work if you are a minority female. Should I just say they over-hired and leave it at that? (4) Also, wouldn't staying at a small plaintiffs' firm hurt me the longer I stay?

All's well that ends well in your case—you are now at a top law firm and not only that, you are at the main office. Clearly this firm saw your potential and didn't care about the insanity that went on with your 2L employer. Congratulations!

I certainly can understand your concern over the fact that there are only five minority partners at this firm and of those five, none are female. Unfortunately, although your firm has fewer minority partners than the national norm, I suspect that they are not that much different from other firms of their size. Get ready for some startling statistics. According to a study done in November of 2006 by the National Association for Law Placement (NALP), "minority women constitute just 1.48% of partners in the nation's major law firms . . . [and] minority men . . . account for just 3.53% of partners."

The NALP's study is an analysis of the small gains made nationally of the addition of minority partners—male and female—to the major law firms. It's an eye-opener and something you should read: http://www.nalp.org.

Now, let's address your specific concern. Do I think you should be worried at this point in your career about your partnership potential at this particular law firm? No, I think you have other matters to focus on at this time. Based on what you have told us about yourself, you are a very junior attorney, someone who is really just starting out on your career. You are correct to be wary about this firm; partnership is elusive enough, and your firm has a bad track record with female minorities. But the good news is that you have time on your side. Be the best that you can be and learn as much as possible in your first few years of practice there. Three or four years from now, you will have a better sense of your position at this firm, and at that time you will be ready to make a lateral move to a firm where your partnership track will be more solid.

For now, keep floating on Cloud 9! You did it! You succeeded just when you thought you were never going to get into a major law firm. Keep focused on that and remember where you are headed. Quite frankly, based on what you have done so far, it wouldn't surprise me to hear that one day in the future you will be asked to be the first female minority partner at this firm! But that's a long way away, and you have so much to do before you cross that bridge. There are so many opportunities that will come your way in the next seven or eight years before partnership looms before you—take it one day at a time! Best wishes and definitely stay in touch!

Sincerely,
Ann M. Israel

＊

City: New York

Dear Ann,

I just started work as a new associate this past September in a big NY law firm. It is not quite a lifestyle firm, but there are many female partners and associates, many of whom have children. I didn't go directly to law school from undergrad, and I've been married for a few years. My husband and I do not want to wait too long to start a family, but I am concerned that having a child within the first two years of starting this job will be bad for my career. Will the firm view me as unserious? Will taking maternity leave so early on derail my career permanently?

Thank you.
Serious

Dear Serious:

I'm starting this column out with my usual close of a column: the bottom line is that you need to do what you want to do with your life. If you and your husband want to have a family in the near future, and nothing could be more important to both of you than starting a family at this time, then you can't be concerned as to how you will be viewed by the partners in your firm.

On the other hand, if you suspect that your firm's partners will believe you are not serious about your career because you take a maternity leave during your second year with the firm, and your career is the most important thing in your life, then perhaps you need to rethink whether or not you want to have children at this time.

In other words, you need to think about your priorities and what you want.

But let's talk about realities. First of all, you have already told us that there are many female partners (and associates) with children at your firm. Right away we know that these women are able to balance their careers with being mothers. And clearly their career paths were not derailed when they took time out during their maternity leave.

By the time you are completing your second year with the firm, you will have established some sort of reputation. If you are serious about your career path with the firm, it should already be somewhat evident that you are a serious young attorney within the first two years of your practice. Taking a maternity leave *might* put your partnership track back a year, but it certainly won't cause it to disappear if you are serious about your career. And really, what are we talking about here? Three months away from the office?

Not that I am telling you to do the following, but I do know so many mothers who take on some work from home during their maternity leave. In fact, toward the latter part of the leave, they welcome the distraction! A mother's helper or nanny is out taking the baby for a walk and the mother uses that time to stay in touch with the office by taking on some work. No partner is going to think you are "unserious" about your career with the firm as you are working from home!

What you do need to be aware of is the fact that as a career-minded associate with a newborn at home, you may have a hard time juggling everything in the beginning. But if you have a good nanny at home, you focus on what you need to do at the office, and the baby's father is willing to take on his responsibilities as well, you can have it all.

Clearly there are many women at your firm who have it all figured out, and when it comes time to announce your pregnancy, you might want to sit down and discuss how they handled their maternity leave and then their initial time back at the office with a newborn at home.

Incidentally, we are seeing more and more firms that are making child care arrangements at the facility itself. As more women dedicate themselves to a full-time career and are voted into the partnership, firms realize that they can get more work product out of them—and create a happier work environment—if they provide child care facilities right there at the office.

Who knows? Your firm might offer such a program or have one in the planning. At any rate, just as I wrote in the beginning of this column, you need to sit down with your significant other and figure out your priorities. No matter what you decide, the immediate future says that you should be the best associate you can possibly be so that you are noticed by senior associates and hopefully some of the partners. In that way, when you do decide to take your maternity leave, you will be sorely missed and greatly welcomed back upon your return. Best wishes!

Sincerely,
Ann M. Israel

I

City: New York

I work at a BigLaw firm. I am also a minority female junior associate and feel as if the firm I work for is trying to push me out. What I mean is that there is a certain type of junior associate in my class that is sought out by partners. These associates are always busy and always have work from a myriad of partners for no substantive reason. I have worked with these associates before (we are in the same class), and their work is quite lacking and the questions they ask me are quite elementary, yet they are chosen over me and the other minority associates time and time again. I have talked to other minorities, and our experiences are the same across the board. Perhaps the firm isn't intentionally trying to push us out, but it is definitely ignoring us and favoring others.

As a first-generation child of refugees, I have no political connections or powerful relatives. My father is not general counsel at one of my firm's clients like other associates' fathers are. My uncle is not managing partner at another BigLaw firm like other associates' uncles are. I feel like I am hitting my head against a wall. I am told time and time again my work is good, but this uphill climb is starting to look more like a vertical wall then a hill with footholds.

I believe the law firm management believes in diversity and is very interested in retaining minority associates; however, the day-to-day partners that we interact with feel differently or don't care.

If I lateral, will it be any better at another BigLaw firm? Getting out of the law is not an option; going to a small firm is selling myself short. I would like to make partner and not just go in-house in my fifth or sixth year, but I'm daunted by the obstacles that are put in my way. Am I stuck in a "grin and bear it" situation?

Daunted

Dear Daunted:

Your question has me at a loss for words, which is not a common predicament for me.

I really am not clear on how to respond to your situation, for I would choose not to believe that your firm is intentionally trying to push out and/ or ignore all the minority associates and favor some dolts—or, as you put it, a certain type of junior associate—simply because they are not minorities, or perhaps because they have political connections or powerful relatives.

Certainly it doesn't hurt to have a father who is a general counsel at a Fortune 500 company or a relative who is the managing partner of an AmLaw firm or an uncle with powerful political connections. However, if every nonminority associate in your class year has this type of connection, it is an unusual group of associates indeed.

I am not trying to belittle your interpretation of what is happening to you, but is it possible that there are other reasons that these associates are sought out by the partners? Is it possible that they are more aggressive in seeking out assignments from the partners? Could their work product be better than you are giving it credit for? It does not seem credible to me that a major law firm would allow their clients to pay for substandard work time after time, as you are suggesting.

It is unquestionably true that a number of years ago many firms were guilty of exactly what you are accusing your firm of now doing, but perhaps not always for the reasons you might think. A partner would be assigned an associate and like this individual for one reason or another, or just get used to this person, and then request this associate for the next assignment and the next and the next. What would then happen is that other associates would never have an opportunity to work with this partner and, on the other side of the coin, this associate might be stuck with this partner for years on end.

Fast-forward to today and you really do not see this happening in the BigLaw firms any longer. The assigning process is much more rigid and structured and follows a certain pattern where assignments are handed out in a manner so that all associates have an opportunity to work with each partner and have equal time and shares. This is why there are now assigning partners in each practice group and why I am disturbed by what you seem to be observing.

Additionally, law firms are under strict orders from their clients to staff up with minority/diversity associates and partners. The partners in the law firms are desperate to keep minority attorneys within the firms, not push them out, in order to appease their in-house clients.

My advice to you is as follows: Step one is to sit down with the assigning partner in your practice group and express your concerns. You need to let him/her know that you are not getting the experience and/or the assignments you want and in fact, you believe that other associates are continually chosen over you. You need to find out that if indeed this is the case, why this is happening.

If the answers to this sit-down are not satisfactory to you, and/or if the conditions do not change as a result of this meeting, then of course you need to change firms. Your BigLaw firm may be one holdout from the cave ages, and if this is the case, get out of there, and fast. Move into a firm that is practicing in the twenty-first century and attempting to run an assigning process that is fair to all junior associates. Good luck!

Sincerely,
Ann M. Israel

Dear Readers:

Thank you for an overwhelming response to last week's column about the associate who was hit upon by the "well-respected" senior partner. I thought I would reprint several of your messages this week that were representative of the many received.

###

The dilemma:

Dear Ann,

I am a fourth-year associate at a BigLaw firm. I recently traveled out of town with a senior, well-respected partner at my firm to conduct depositions for a case I am working on with her. We had a few drinks with the client after the deposition, and then a last drink in the bar just the two of us. Then the partner tried to get me to come back to her room for a nightcap. I made an excuse, but what do I do the next time?

Is this every guy's dream or am I being sexually harassed?

Dreaming

From Name and City Withheld:

This is in response to Dreaming. Obviously, please keep my response anonymous if you use any part of this. I was at a satellite office of BigLaw and regularly worked with and for a married and later divorced female partner who was on BigLaw's managing board. She would regularly host board games after midnight in her office—which was always fully stocked with cases of wine. While I remain convinced she both carried on an affair with a married, nonattorney subordinate and had a fling with a married partner, she never made any specific advances on me. However, I was pretty regularly chided for not staying and playing dice and drinking. Although I was not against drinking on principle, the need for sleep and the desire to avoid a DWI on the way home would send me running for the door after the final drafts had been turned in. Basically, my MO was always to make sure I was with her with at least one other person, even if it was nonfirm personnel. We had a similar experience with her on a firm retreat. Not being able to beg out because of work the next day, each of the male associates turned tail once we realized there were no female associates around and might be stuck as the last one in the room following the nightcap. This stuff definitely happens, and the ridiculous hours put in at law firms can easily hide affairs as well as flings. While the question and answer were stilted because of the wacky facts, it was a worthy read and will probably provide good counsel to both new and experienced lawyers.

From S. B. in New York:

I have seen this situation before. The best thing to do is refuse politely and act like it never happened. If it is ever mentioned again, allow the partner to save face by blaming it on the alcohol and/or stress.

If it happens a second time, do the same as before, but avoid working with the partner in the future—and don't breathe a word of it to anyone.

If it happens repeatedly, speak to HR and consider a harassment suit, while looking for another job.

From Anonymous in New York:

Unfortunately, this is a scenario that I hear about from associates from time to time. It certainly puts the associate in a bit of a pickle. This associate really handled a tough situation well. For the future, I agree that the best course is to try to steer clear of this partner, but if the situation re-presents itself, the associate should let the partner know how flattered he is, but that he wants to keep their relationship at a professional level. The key to pulling this off without ruffling the partner's feathers and potentially creating a situation that would make the associate want to jump ship for another firm is to do it lightly, quickly, and with a smile. And never to speak of it again.

▌▓▌

I was quite surprised at how frequently this type of situation seemed to occur but happy to learn how the associates handled it. What an awful position to be in, but how impressive and mature you all are in the way you have dealt with it.

It is my hope that you never have to be put in an uncomfortable position of harassment such as what we dealt with in this column.

Sincerely,
Ann M. Israel

CHAPTER 13

When Good Things Go Bad

Being employed is always a good thing—it's just where and how you are employed that makes the difference as to whether or not it is a good situation as well as a good thing! As you will read, even in the most difficult of job markets, there are times when it becomes necessary to make a move. When you figure out that your employer is not exactly the best person in the world and does not have the best intentions for your future, don't hang around—dust off your resume and get on the job market.

And sometimes you can get the idea of what it would be like to work for a firm or for a specific person simply by how they behave in the interviewing process. If things are not going smoothly in the process, take it as a sign as to how things will be if you actually work for that firm or that person. If things are bad during the interviewing process, you can pretty much count on things being bad if you should be an employee there.

During the interviewing process, you will usually find people to be on their best behavior. That just makes sense, doesn't it? After all, if a firm were interested in you, then they would want to put their best foot forward. But if the behavior of a firm—or even just one person—leaves you questioning the personality of the firm or the person, trust your gut and get out of there while the getting is good. As you know, I have always believed that things happen for a reason. If a firm is dragging their feet in getting you back for an interview, or if a partner makes you a promise that never materializes, take it as a sign that this place isn't meant to be for you and move on to a place that is.

⚊

City: New York

I am a midlevel-year associate looking to make a lateral move to another firm. A firm has offered me an interview. However, I was offered this interview a month ago and no interview has been scheduled. I called at the two-week mark to see what was going on and was told that they were still working on the interviewing schedule. I did not get this interview through a recruiter, so I do not have a go-between who can inquire for me. Can I inquire again? Is something wrong, or does the interview process often get drawn out like this? Thanks!

Inquired

Dear Inquired:

Oh, boy, I get to put a plug in for using recruiters! Okay, I'm just kidding . . . sort of kidding, that is.

Once in a while when I am discussing an opportunity with a potential candidate, s/he will tell me s/he knows someone at that particular employer and would just as soon apply for the job on his/her own rather than have a fee involved in the mix. My response to that reply is always the same, based on far too many years of experience.

First of all, and truly very important, if a firm gives an opening to a recruiter, they are already budgeted for the fee. Would they prefer not to pay a fee? I'm sure they would, but one less recruiter's fee spread out over the entire year is really not going to have that great of an impact on their recruiting budget. The types of firms that work with recruiters have the fees built into their recruitment budgets. They expect to pay these fees, and that is why they count on the recruiters to bring them the best candidates.

Secondly, a recruiter can—and will—call the client frequently to get the interview process going. You would never be in the situation you are in right now if you had a middle man or agent working for you.

Next, once you secure an interview date, the recruiter will prep you on each person you are going to meet and after the interview will debrief both you and the people you met. You will receive feedback as to why you are a strong candidate or why you are not being called back. You will also learn about any hesitations the client might have about you and discuss strategies on how to overcome any concerns the client might have.

Once an offer is extended, the recruiter is able to negotiate certain points for you and work out the fine details—everything an agent does for a client.

Incidentally, I had lunch today with the managing partner and the director of recruiting of an AmLaw 100 law firm. During our meeting I discussed this week's column and asked whether or not a recruiter's fee ever stood in the way of hiring someone. They were both quick to answer that the recruiter fees were built into their budget at the beginning of each year; fees were never a factor as to whether or not they would hire an individual. The director of recruitment actually admitted that she preferred to see candidates through recruiters since she knew those candidates were already prescreened.

Now, on to your situation . . .

Trying to piece together your time frame from the date on your question, it would appear to me that you first started hearing from this firm around the holiday season. Based on that assumption, your two-week call probably came at the end of the holiday season or right after it ended, and partners were still not all back at the firm.

So now it is the end of January and interviewing schedules certainly can be made. But what happened to you?

I don't see any reason why you shouldn't call the recruiting department again and ask when you will be scheduled for your interview. The interviewing process sometimes can get drawn out like this, particularly around the holiday season, when there just isn't anyone around to interview the candidates. But the holiday season is over and we are back to business as usual. This isn't just drawn out—this is ridiculous now.

Unless something out of the ordinary has happened, it would seem to me that your paperwork has fallen into a black hole of sorts and someone needs to pull it back into the system. Since you don't have an agent or recruiter to do it for you, you need to take action. I suggest you take a proactive stance here and get on the phone right away and speak with the recruiting department. Let the person on the phone know you were told over a month ago that you were being scheduled to come in for an interview and as of this date, you have not heard back from the firm. If necessary, let them know that you will get another copy of your resume over to the firm as soon as possible.

Of course, there is always the possibility that this potential employer has had a change of heart and is not really interested in you after all. And if that is the case, then they are showing their true colors by leading you on, and you should be thrilled that you are not going to interview with them. This definitely is not the kind of employer you would want to be working for, is it?

In any event, just in case you really are a candidate they are interested in interviewing, I do recommend you act with a sense of urgency before another candidate fills the position. Best to know one way or the other and as soon as possible, wouldn't you agree?

Please let us know what happens. Best wishes!

Sincerely,
Ann M. Israel

City: Boston

I graduated and passed the bar last summer. I've been working for a solo practitioner as her "legal assistant" since my third year of law school. The attorney knows I want to leave and work for a midsized firm. Although she has said she doesn't want me to leave her office, she claims she can't afford to keep me either. I am trying to aggressively search for a job, but she keeps dumping more cases on me in the meantime without bumping me up to an "associate" with higher pay. Although I know the experience would be good, my first reaction is to decline these offers because she is taking advantage of me without offering me decent pay and without covering me under her malpractice insurance. What should I do? Take the experience, or tell her to back off unless she wants to make me a serious offer?

Dumped but Not Bumped

Dear Dumped but Not Bumped:

Yes, I definitely understand your dilemma. It's a tough situation you're in, especially considering the state of the job market right now.

On the one hand, you've got a real job that brings in a real paycheck, even though it isn't paying what you believe is your true worth. On the other hand, if you had the time to get out there to do a job search, you might actually find a position as an associate and earn an attorney's wages.

But here are some issues that you must deal with when trying to decide exactly what to do in your situation. First of all, based on what you have told us, we must assume that you did not spend your 2L summer at a midsized firm or, if you did, you didn't receive an offer of permanent employment to begin working there upon law school graduation. We have to assume this simply because you have been working for a solo practitioner since your 3L year as a legal assistant even though your ideal job is to be employed at a midsized firm.

Without that 2L summer employment on your resume, you are already missing a key element when you go out on your interviews. Next, you have been working as a legal assistant, not as an associate, since last summer, which also puts another question mark onto your resume.

These two factors are going to make your job search a bit more difficult than that of the typical lateral associate out there trying to make a job change. Nevertheless, I still think you need to think seriously about the situation you are in.

I am concerned your current employer keeps you up in the air by telling you that she doesn't want you to leave and yet she can't afford to keep you either. My feeling is that she has no intention of naming you as her associate but rather that she is taking advantage of the salary situation by keeping you on as her assistant. It doesn't matter whether or not she could afford to keep you because she continues to give cases to you and you continue to work on them. She's got a sweet deal going on. By the way, if she is entrusting you with so much work, it's time for her to reward you by naming you as her associate . . . duh. This relationship really does need to come to some kind of conclusion, one way or the other.

You need to sit down and have a heart-to-heart discussion with your boss, and soon. She needs to be honest with her intentions and let you know as to what your future is with her and the firm. Either you have a future there or you don't. And if she intends to keep you employed there (and it certainly seems to be the case, as she piles on the cases), then she needs to promote you to associate—after all, you have now graduated from law school and have passed the bar. Fair is fair.

I suggest you ask to have a meeting with her to discuss your position with the firm as soon as possible. Much like the compensation conversation we discussed in a recent column, this is not something to talk about while standing in the hallway. Make an appointment to sit down face-to-face in her office. And soon.

However, if she continues to complain that she cannot afford to keep you employed, you need to face reality and understand that she has no intentions of ever making you a full-time, fully paid associate and will probably continue to underpay and overutilize you as a legal assistant. If that turns out to be the case, you have several choices: accept the situation (bad choice), immediately quit and devote all your time to a job search (not a great choice since it could take some time to find a new job and you would be without a paycheck), or continue working and collecting a paycheck while at the same time doing a serious, thorough, and motivated but discreet job search until you find a job as an associate.

My advice to you is no matter what happens in that meeting, you should start a discreet job search. The way she has treated you says so much about her and about your future at this firm. You have been warned and now know who you are dealing with—I say get moving on that job search now. Best of luck!

Sincerely,
Ann M. Israel

CHAPTER 14

Resigning from Your Job

It's a small world, and don't ever forget it. I mention this because properly resigning from a job is an art, and if it is done improperly, it might haunt you for the rest of your career.

Sure, it would be a wonderful world if you could tell that partner who has been such a bully that you really hate him/her and you have a wonderful new job, so basically, take this job and shove it—I quit! Wouldn't that feel really great to be able to say what you are feeling? Oh yes, that would be such a liberating feeling . . . that is, until that partner you told to shove it decides to leave his/her current firm and winds up as the head of the department at your new firm. It happens.

Leaving an employer is a delicate task. You must suck it up and be as gracious and complimentary as you can possibly be. You might need this person for a reference or, as I noted before, s/he might turn up at your new firm the day after you start there!

So, what is the best way to give notice? Be sure to thank the person you have worked for and do it sincerely. Let him/her know that everything you have learned up to this point is thanks to his/her mentorship and generous time. Tell him/her that you are sad to leave but that the proverbial opportunity you cannot refuse has been offered to you and you could not turn it down. Make sure you give good and proper notice—nothing short of two weeks, and make it three weeks if you possibly can.

Lastly, no matter how hard it is to give notice, do it in person first and then submit your letter of resignation. Burned bridges cannot be rebuilt—remember this whenever you must give notice!

▮▮▮

City: New York

I am looking for a new position. While I may be jumping ahead of myself, I am concerned about informing my current firm that I will be leaving. I have a huge amount of responsibility and know that the firm will be in a rough spot. However, it is best for my career to move on. What is the best way to approach the inevitable conversation with the partner in charge?

Jumping Ahead

Dear Jumping Ahead:

While you have not told us anything about yourself, in this particular situation it really doesn't make much of a difference. I am going to have to assume that you are not at a partner level, basing my assumption on the way you phrased your question and basically by the question itself.

The best way to approach giving notice to the appropriate partner in charge is to first wait until you have received and accepted an offer from your new employer and a start date has been established. Depending on which person you are going to choose to be your reference(s), you might also want to wait until references are checked and all conflicts are cleared. Then, and only then, can you go ahead and give notice.

The most important factor in giving notice is to make certain you do not burn any bridges. You never know when that partner you'd like to tell where to get off ends up at your new firm or just happens to be the cousin of the managing partner of your employer-to-be. So, think it through before acting or saying anything you might regret.

Personally, I think the best thing to do is to thank the partner for giving you the opportunity to work at the firm and learn all you have up to this point. After all, you wouldn't be the attorney you are today without the training provided by this firm. Say that this is a very difficult moment for you, but the proverbial offer that you cannot refuse has been presented to you and after much soul-searching, you are giving notice that you will be leaving the firm in two weeks, etc.

Now, here comes some reality from me. I know you are concerned about leaving your firm in the lurch, and I certainly admire you for your loyalty and sense of responsibility. You certainly are right in being concerned for your own career, and presumably that is why you are about to mount a job search. However, please do not think that the firm is not going to recover when you give notice.

I understand that they have piled you on with a good deal of responsibility but I suspect they will somehow muddle through after you leave. You are not going to leave them in a "rough spot," so kindly remember this fact if they start to lay on a guilt trip and ask you to reconsider. They will miraculously recover. Go back a couple of *Lawlorn* columns ago and read about accepting a counter-offer. Don't even consider it!

We would all love to consider ourselves indispensable to our employers, but that just isn't the real world. Companies, corporations, and law firms are all set up to recover from the loss of employees. Just remember, you are thinking about your future, your career. Give notice as a professional and then move on to your new employer, where I am certain you will start receiving just as much responsibility as you currently have—if not more! Best wishes!

Sincerely,
Ann M. Israel

City: New York

After a month between jobs I received two offers. I likely would not have accepted either one had I been employed, but I did accept one (a) because I had to and (b) because I was promised various opportunities to practice in new areas. After a week it's clear the promises will be broken, that I was hired to be a body to fill a seat. Also, to say things are disorganized in the office is an understatement. My question is, how long am I required to stay?

Employed

Dear Employed:

Interesting, very interesting. Well, I guess the answer to your question really depends on whether or not you have a contract, and since you didn't mention one, I suspect a contract is not involved. Therefore, you are only required to stay as long as you want to stay. In other words, if you want to quit today, go ahead and do so.

However . . . before you do anything rash, I would think it over.

In this tight job market, it is really wonderful that after only one month, you received two job offers. Yet, you tell us that had you been employed at the time, you wouldn't have accepted either offer, so we have to assume that neither employer was really the greatest in the world. It is a sad state of affairs to say that you accepted a job because you "had to."

Really? You had two job offers after just one month of unemployment and you didn't like either one. Didn't you think you could hold out any longer to try to find something that perhaps you might like just a little bit?

Actually, I don't believe in passing up offers in these economic times, but I also don't believe in going to work somewhere that will make me unhappy.

So you took this job because they made you promises about practicing in new areas and you can tell after only one week that these are empty promises? Have you spoken to the person who hired you about this situation? Why would anyone hire someone just to fill a seat in this economy? What firm or company has that kind of disposable income?

You asked how long you were required to stay and I told you that you could leave straight away. Sure, you can quit right now. But since you took this job as recently as last week simply because you "had to," I assume your situation hasn't really changed and you still need to be employed. Therefore, I wouldn't jump ship so fast unless you have another job offer—and for something guaranteed to be better—waiting for you as you walk out the door. Otherwise you are liable to be on that proverbial—and possibly literal—breadline for many months to come. It's a tough job market out there right now, and you need to face that reality. We have no idea whatsoever about your credentials or experience or situation, but it really doesn't matter; the candidate pool right now is big and your competition is tough. You had better face up to the fact that you are fortunate to be gainfully employed and collecting a paycheck.

Before you do anything hasty, go to the person who hired you and find out exactly what your responsibilities are supposed to be. You should be proactive in your job—sitting around doing nothing isn't fun, and perhaps they are waiting for you to jump up and ask for work. Who knows what the office procedure is there? But whatever it is, sitting on your duff and thinking that you have made a mistake is not going to make it any better for you. You need to find out if they actually did misrepresent the position or if they are just getting everything ready to move you into new practice areas and a load of work is about to be thrown on your desk (wouldn't that be great!).

It is possible that there has been a great miscommunication here and you can rectify it after just the first week. Or maybe you did make a mistake by joining this firm. Whatever. You need to find out before you just up and quit. And don't quit without having another job! Hang in there whatever you do end up finding out. Remember—it's better just filling a seat and collecting a paycheck, if that is what they hired you to do, than sitting at home without that paycheck! Best wishes.

Sincerely,
Ann M. Israel

⬛

City: Silicon Valley

Dear Ann:

I am a junior associate who is contemplating leaving my current firm for greener pastures. I need to formally accept my "greener" opportunity soon, but I would not start until [late August]. Should I give notice to my current firm now, or should I wait until closer to the time I would (ideally) be departing? I have no concern about the security of the future position.

Greener

Dear Greener:

First and foremost, congratulations on your new opportunity. How wonderful that you have found an exciting new position that is better than your current job, especially considering that (1) you are a junior associate and (2) this is a very tough job market. You should be very pleased with yourself!

If you are certain that this is the very right opportunity for you—and it does sound as if you are very sure about this one—then go ahead and let the new employer know how excited you are about the offer and that you accept! Don't let any more time go by before accepting so that they don't think that you are having any second thoughts or start looking for a better candidate.

What you want to keep in mind is that your offer and acceptance will be pending references, and since you have not given notice to your current employer, the last thing you want to happen right now is to have your references checked before your current employer has any idea that you are about to leave.

As you accept the new offer and reconfirm your start date of late August, explain to your new employer that you plan to continue working until you start your new job and do not intend to give notice until the traditional two weeks prior to your last day of employment. Because of this, you do not want your references checked until you have officially resigned from your current position. You will call in and let them know as soon as you have given notice and will sound the all-clear as to when they can check references. You certainly can let them know that you completely understand that your offer is pending the reference check and you have no problem with this matter (as long as you *don't* have a problem with this!).

Two weeks before you have determined the date that will be the last day you will be employed at this firm is the day you will give your notice. At this time you will go to the two to three people that you believe will be the best references for you and say something along these lines to them: "I have given your name as a reference for the new job that I have just accepted. What you say will determine my future. I hope you are willing to be my reference."

Of course, you should know well in advance the people you will be asking to represent you as a reference, right? As soon as you have notified these individuals that they will be called as your references, give your new employer a call and let them know that you have given your notice and it is now time for them to check your references and let you know as soon as possible that the job offer is finalized.

I see no reason for you to give notice to your firm now unless you want to leave in two weeks and have a nice four-week vacation until you start your new job in late August. By the way, if you can afford to do that, go for it! It will be a while until you have a vacation once you start a new job, and August is a great month to have some time to relax and chill. Best wishes!

Sincerely,
Ann M. Israel

City: Columbus, OH

Example resignation letter for an attorney resigning from a small firm.

Resigning

Dear Resigning:

Well, one thing is for sure—you are succinct. And your resignation letter should be written in the same manner . . . but perhaps with a bit more feeling.

Resignation letters need to be succinct and must cover certain points about your specific resignation. However, it is so important to make sure that you are positive and that you thank your partner or supervisor for giving you such a wonderful opportunity (whether or not you really do feel this way). Remember, your resignation letter is going to be included in your personnel file, and what you write in it will more than likely follow you in future references and job opportunities.

So now that you have decided that you are leaving your current employer, there is no good reason to write anything negative in your resignation letter, no matter how much you finally want to get it all said. All this letter should include is the fact that you are resigning, the date of your last day of employment, and an expression of how grateful you are for all that this employer has done for you (seriously, you need to include this in your letter). You've made the decision to leave, you (hopefully!) have a great new job, and what do you really believe you will accomplish by writing down all of the things you hated about your job or boss in this letter?

By the way, hopefully you have resigned in person and your resignation letter is simply proper etiquette (and a proper paper trail that you need to leave). You really do not want to simply send an e-mail out to your partner or supervisor the day before you are leaving with the words "Surprise! I am out of here!" Giving notice is critical (usually two to three weeks' notice is standard), not only because you need to tie up loose ends but also to help your current employer prepare for your departure. Sometimes the loss of someone from a department can be momentarily crippling, and you want to be certain that everything is in order before you leave (remember those future references!).

It's never easy to resign, whether or not you like your job, but it is critical to remember that you must leave with everyone believing that you left as a professional. A well-written resignation letter will help to foster that impression. Don't forget that you are going to need this past employer as a reference for many years to come; in fact, before you leave, make sure you have mentioned that you will be using your partner/supervisor as a reference (if, in fact, you will be doing so) and you hope that s/he understands that what is said will determine your future.

Don't forget to return any firm or corporate property; in some cases, your final paycheck may be withheld until that property is returned. Just recently one of my clients has been harassed by an ex-employee (*big mistake!*) through continual e-mails and phone calls demanding her last paycheck when she had been specifically told during her hiring orientation and her exit interview that her final check would be mailed (or could be picked up) upon receipt of specific company property. Hopefully she will eventually return the property, and when she does, she will get her check. However, I hope she never intends to use this employer as a reference, because after what she has done over the past two weeks, I suspect it won't be a good one.

A couple of hints about things to do prior to giving notice. Clean up your computer! Delete any personal e-mail messages and/or files you have stored on your *employer's* computer, and make sure you have updated your contacts before you walk out. And finally, let human resources/personnel know where you are going as well as saying good-bye to your colleagues and assistants and letting them know where you are going too. Not only do you want your calls, e-mails, and mail forwarded to you, but it's a good practice to stay in touch— you just never know . . . Best wishes!

Sincerely,
Ann M. Israel

City: Pittsburgh

I just received an offer from a larger firm and am concerned about resigning from my current firm. I plan to give my current employer two weeks' notice, but I have scheduled a vacation that will fall in the middle of those two weeks. Should I quit early and take the vacation on my own time, or should I take the vacation on the firm's time? And, if the latter, when do I submit my letter of resignation?

Thank you.
Vaca-ting

Dear Vaca-ting:

So, first of all, congratulations on your offer. This sounds like good news for you and your career. But obviously you need to make some clear-cut decisions here, because as you know, this offer is pending your references, and those references are not going to be checked until you give notice at your current firm. Clearly, when and how you give your notice is going to be critical in terms of how it might affect the feelings of your references.

Let's play out a few different scenarios.

1. Not a word is spoken, and no one at your firm has an inkling that anything is going on. You leave for vacation with everyone assuming that you will be back and life will resume as normal. Right after you leave for vacation, you call your partner in charge and tell him/her that you will never be returning and please accept this phone call as your two weeks' notice. No, that isn't a good idea at all. And I don't believe you posed this scenario for us, so let's move on.

2. You give the firm the traditional two weeks' notice but remind them that you have a vacation due to you, so you will only be physically at the firm for another week and the last week of your two weeks' notice will be spent in Tahiti (or wherever) on your paid vacation that you have had calendared for the past six months. Your partner stands there slack-jawed for a few moments and then walks away, headed toward the HR office, trying to control him/herself from throttling you.

An hour later s/he returns with another partner and calls you into his/her office. You are then told that there will be no need to give two weeks' notice because your employment with the firm is being terminated as of now. Since your state is an at-will state, this would not be a surprise; there is a 50/50 chance that this actually might happen.

Of course, your partner might say to you that s/he hopes you can get everything finished up before you leave for your very well-deserved vacation and s/he hopes that your new position will provide you with everything you are looking for in your future. Yeah, what are the chances that this will be an honest wish for you?

3. If you quit early—without giving the minimum two weeks' notice—you risk the chance that this is going to reflect on your references as well as burning some serious bridges with the partners and senior associates at the firm. As I have written about so many times before, you never know when you are going to be working with these people again. For all you know, your old firm and your new large firm could be in merger discussions, and by the time you start at your new firm, your partner in charge could be the partner from your old firm that you just burned by giving short notice.

4. The most painful—to you—choice would be to give two weeks' notice and work through the vacation time that you were planning on taking. Let your firm know that you have certainly enjoyed working there and this was a difficult decision for you to make, but it truly was an offer you could not refuse. Explain that you do not want to leave them in the lurch and so instead of taking your vacation, you will work for the next two weeks and make sure that everything is in order before you move on.

There is no guarantee that your current firm won't tell you to forget the two weeks, leave now and take your vacation, but by giving notice in this manner, you are absolutely not burning any bridges. My guess is that they will appreciate your professional attitude and when it comes time for references, this will play into them.

The last choice would be to delay your start date at the new firm for a bit longer than usual, say nothing to your current firm for a while, go on vacation as scheduled, and when you return give two weeks' notice then. I think you might annoy some people at the firm with this scenario, but it resolves a lot of your issues. I don't think the new firm should have a problem waiting an extra week or so for your start date.

Whichever scenario you choose, you certainly do want to get some vacation time in prior to starting at the new position because once you start there, it is going to be a while before you have some serious time off. Let the new firm know that you do have a vacation scheduled and that is going to delay your start date (and possibly also checking your references, depending on when you decide to give notice). Again, this is not abnormal; the large firms are used to associates taking a vacation before starting with them.

I like the option of giving notice and then taking a vacation on your own time because I think that is the most honest and professional option and also the one that will present itself in the best light to your current employer and to your new employer. You need to decide how to play this out. I hope you will let us know what you have decided to do. Best wishes!

Sincerely,
Ann M. Israel

CHAPTER 15

Being Terminated

What a way to ruin a day. What could be worse than being told that you are fired from your firm? Even though this isn't something that is happening to me personally, I get a pit in the bottom of my stomach when I read the submissions to my column from those people who have just been cut loose. Is there any way to find some silver lining in this cloud?

The most important thing I can say about being terminated is to try to pinpoint what went wrong. It is human nature to blame the boss or the employer for what has just happened, but it is really important for you to be honest with yourself and try to figure out if you did something to cause this drastic action. You want to make sure that whatever went wrong will never happen again; the only way to do that is to figure out why you were fired and how you are going to change things around so that history will not repeat itself.

Another reason why you need to do some deep soul-searching to come up with the reasons why you were let go is so that you will be able to discuss what went wrong in any interviews for your next job. It is so important that when you are stating your reasons for being let go, you do not sound defensive and are succinct and to the point.

Sometimes it is very difficult to figure out where things went south leading up to your termination, but in these cases you really need to dig deep to figure out where you started to slide down on the job. This is not meant as an exercise to beat yourself up but rather as a clarification that you can use when you meet with potential employers and they ask the inevitable question, "Why were you let go from your last job?"

There are some employers who are benevolent and will let you stay on at the firm for a specified period of time while you hunt for a new employer. This allows you to give off the appearance of still being employed during the job search. If you have been terminated but your employer allows you to stay on and use your office as head-quarters for your job search, consider yourself very fortunate and in a position to have dodged a big bullet. You might want to request this favor if it hasn't been offered as you receive your pink slip. But don't expect it as your due, because it is not the usual pattern. However, there is a fine line here between telling the truth and telling a lie. If asked whether or not you are still working at your firm, you need to think about how you are going to answer this telling question.

I do want to emphasize the importance of speaking with your supervisor or part-ner in charge when you have been fired and asking what they will be saying when called as a reference (and trust me, they will be called). They might be willing to say something as benign as the department was slow and the last people hired were the first to be fired. Or perhaps they might say that it was your idea to leave and they were sorry to see you go. Well, who knows what they are going to say, and that is why it is critical that you ask. What they have decided to give out as the reasons for you leaving the firm might very well work in your favor, and that is why you absolutely must ask what is going to be said.

Remember, by law they cannot give a bad reference over the phone, and so you might really luck out if you take the time to speak with the powers that be and ask them point-blank what they intend to say. You never know . . .

███

City: New York

I have worked as a contract attorney doing document review in New York City for approximately six years. I have worked with many of New York's best firms and have often received promotions and worked as a team lead, done quality control work and privilege reviews. This summer I worked on an antitrust project for an agency I had not previously worked for. This agency is getting a lot of work since it started here. I am HIV-positive and while on the project became ill and needed an accommodation for a reduced work schedule. I explained the situation to the project manager. The agency seemed more than happy to accommodate me and allowed me to work a reduced schedule for the remainder of the project. Two days after the project ended, they demanded my building pass and locker key. I never received any negative work reviews and only received praise. The agency now will not respond to my inquiries about new projects, even though they continue to advertise for new projects. I know people who work there, and so I know that they are still hiring new people because they are so busy. How do I deal with this situation without becoming blacklisted everywhere? I would like to resolve this without an EEOC complaint.

Unresolved

Dear Unresolved:

Yes, I understand exactly what you want . . . you just want to get back to work instead of starting a lawsuit with the EEOC and perhaps even risking the chance of being blacklisted by all of the other temp/contract agencies out there. I can appreciate that. I would feel exactly the same way.

However, I don't think you will be blacklisted if your end result is filing a complaint with the EEOC. That should be the very least of your worries at this time.

I am not the person to give you legal counsel on this matter. I can only give you my personal opinion or viewpoint on what I think might have happened and what I believe you should do from this point forward. Remember, this is *not* legal advice and is only my personal opinion, nothing more.

In reading over the description of what happened to you, the only thing I think went wrong here is TMI—too much information. You were working for an agency that did not know you or your work, and based on what you have written, it sounds as if they were a fairly new agency or at least fairly new to New York. While you were working on this project, you suddenly became ill and had to work on a reduced schedule. So, here is this new-in-town agency that suddenly has to add on to its work force or extend its contract with this client because one of its workers cannot fulfill the full term of his/her work schedule. The client is probably annoyed and perhaps does not want to use this agency again (maybe/maybe not), but in any case, the agency is probably nervous.

And you, because you are used to top reviews and great relationships with all of the agencies you have been working for, decide that instead of saying you have just returned from the doctor, who has advised that at this time you need to reduce your work schedule, determine that it is better to give full disclosure and say that you are HIV-positive and can no longer work full-time on this project.

From everything I have read on the subject, I understand that there is no reason to disclose that you are HIV-positive unless you are in a job that requires some exchange of blood or semen. Brett Grodeck, the author of *The First Year—HIV*, writes,

> Sometimes it's best not to disclose your HIV status. For example, in a work situation there's no good or rational reason why you should have to disclose that information. Among friends, and perhaps in a dating or social situation, again, there's very little good reason to disclose that information unless you want to, unless you want people to get to really know you and know what's going on with you. Early in the epidemic there was a lot of fear and misinformation. People weren't really clear how HIV was transmitted. Now they know. It's basically blood and semen. That's it. So unless you're sharing blood or unless you're sharing semen, there's not a lot of rational reason to disclose that information unless you want to, unless you're compelled to.

More specifically, Mr. Grodeck speaks to the very issue of informing your employer that you are HIV-positive in a specific instance, such as the one you faced with reducing your time at work. And, as you will read, even then he believes you shouldn't be disclosing your HIV status:

> You don't need to tell your employer that you are HIV positive unless you are a surgeon or a prize-fighter. Unless there is the potential for exchange of blood or semen, there is no good or rational reason why your employer needs to know that you are HIV positive. Unless of course you need accommodations because of being HIV positive—if you need to go to a doctor's visit often. But even in that case, there has to be some compelling reason to tell them that you are HIV positive. I don't think they deserve to know that an employee is HIV positive and I think the right to privacy is far greater than the right for an employer to know.

If you truly believe this agency is not responding to you because you disclosed that you are HIV-positive, I do believe you should consider going to the EEOC or to an attorney. Mr. Grodeck writes, "If you can prove that the employer denied you a position that you were capable of doing because of your HIV, you can sue that employer not just on your own behalf, but to make a larger point to society." Unfortunately, in your particular situation, you are going to have a difficult time proving that the reason the agency is not hiring you for new assignments is due to you being HIV-positive. Maybe they don't have any assignments at this time that will accept workers on reduced hours (I am not defending their actions of not speaking with you—I am just thinking out loud). You really don't know why they aren't returning your calls. Pretty stupid if it is because you are HIV-positive.

You need to make a decision here. Either go speak to someone who can give you some legal advice on this matter or else move on and go back to all those other agencies where you have been working for the past six years—or do both. Think about the promotions and reviews and all the other wonderful things that were said and written about you from those agencies and forget about these idiots who are not calling you back. Or apply for jobs at these other agencies while pursuing legal remedies against this one agency.

But whatever you decide to do, I would take Mr. Grodeck's advice from this point forward: it's nobody's business what ails you. Just continue to feel well and try to keep busy through all those other agencies. Best wishes!

Sincerely,
Ann M. Israel

▮▮▮

City: New York

Dear Ms. Israel,

I am a midlevel associate in a large New York firm and graduated from a top-5 law school. I have been with my current firm for several years and have decided that I would prefer to work in-house, as large New York firm life and my current practice area are not for me. I have a review coming up this fall, and I am expecting it to be neutral to negative, and perhaps I will be told to move on. As I am already looking for a new job, would it be wise to sit down with a few partners before the review, explain that I think it is time to leave, and ask for a few weeks' time so that I can conclude my job search rather than be fired? Thanks very much for your advice.

New York Lawyer

Dear New York Lawyer:

The short answer is *no!*

What are you thinking? Do not even consider mentioning to the partners that you are looking for a new job and that you will be leaving the firm in a few weeks.

First and foremost, this is one of the tightest job markets that we have ever seen. In-house opportunities are few and far between. If you leave your firm within the next few weeks, you will be unemployed while you are conducting your job search. The candidate pool that competes for the very few in-house jobs is quite competitive. I can assure you that the credentials of the other in-house hopefuls will be every bit as good as yours, but with one exception—they will be employed and you will not. Who do you think the potential employer will want to see in an interview?

Yes, perhaps you will be told to move on, but generally the firms are rather generous with their time allotments, and you might very well be given enough time to actually find an in-house opportunity that offers you a good career path rather than just a job. However, if your review is simply neutral instead of negative, perhaps you will not be asked to move on and will continue to be gainfully employed. That would be the best situation of all. Then you would be able to proceed with your job search and could tell future employers that you still work at your firm and, most important of all, that no one at the firm knows that you are looking.

If you tell the partners that you are looking and would like to stay on at the firm for just a couple more weeks until you find your new job, you are setting yourself up for a very bad situation if you don't find that job right away. Two years ago, you would have been able to garner two or three in-house job offers in a short period of time. Unfortunately, things are quite different today. The job market, as I said before, is quite tight, and practically nonexistent for midlevel attorneys looking to go in-house.

Another point I forgot to mention: you did not tell us if you were a corporate attorney or a litigator. If you are in the corporate practice area, then you really need to try to hold onto your job until things turn around on the job market front. If you are a litigator, then it is even more difficult to find in-house opportunities because even in the best of hiring climates, litigation positions in-house are not plentiful.

You mentioned that your current practice area is not for you. I would say that it is a bit late for you, as a midlevel attorney, to start thinking about switching practice areas as you commence a job search for in-house opportunities. And in this economic time, when the job market is so tight, going to a law firm to start over in a new practice area might come very close to being considered career suicide. It just isn't going to happen right now.

Mind you, I am talking about the major midsized and boutique law firms. Granted, the smaller law firms, solo practitioners, or suburban law firms might be interested in hiring you. But none of this matters because you are not looking for a law firm, whether it is large or small. You want to go in-house at this time. So, the best advice that I can give to you is to go ahead and start your job search. Just remember, this is no time for a heart-to-heart with the partners. You need to keep your job at the law firm for as long as it takes you to find a new opportunity. As I have emphasized throughout my answer to you, this is a very tough job market and you really don't want to be unemployed at this time if you can possibly avoid it.

Words to the wise: Try to focus on your work so that your reviews might change from the not very desirable "neutral to negative." When you do receive a job offer from a new potential employer, you are going to need your current employer to give you a decent reference. Best wishes!

Sincerely,
Ann M. Israel

∎∎∎

City: Unknown

Ann:

I am an attorney who was recently laid off. I interviewed with a firm prior to being laid off and did not indicate that my layoff was imminent, even though my firm had already given me the news. I have now been called back for a second interview. On this second interview, I am scheduled to meet with the partner I will be working for directly (I interviewed with him on the first interview as well), but not until after I meet with certain other partners. What is my responsibility to divulge the fact that I was laid off at this second interview? Should I ask to speak with the partner I met on the first interview and will be working for directly prior to meeting with the other partners to divulge the layoff? I should note that I have a reference at my firm who will confirm the fact that I was laid off and will provide a very good recommendation.

Responsible

Dear Responsible:

Here's the problem as I see it. You are going to be meeting with some people whom you had not met during the previous interview round with this particular firm. They will want a copy of your resume (although they may have a photocopy of the one used on your first round of interviews). You have to make a decision here. Do you want them to be interviewing you with a resume that is not exactly the truth? Wouldn't you rather have everything out in the open prior to the interview so that you don't have to lie or, just as bad, have to tell them that the resume is inaccurate when they ask you why you want to leave your current employer?

I assume that when you tell us that you have a reference at your old firm who will confirm the fact that you were laid off, you mean that you have someone who will verify that you were not fired but laid off due to economic reasons or some other non-work-product-related reason. So then what are you so worried about? You have a good reference from your old firm, and I hope that you have lined up at least one other reference to give you another strong recommendation.

It seems to me that the biggest issue you must face right now is if someone asks you if you knew that you were going to be laid off when you came in for your initial interview. If that question is asked, you need to answer it honestly and without being defensive. In our current economic climate, there are more than just a few associates that are currently unemployed because of a slowdown at their firms. You do not need to feel as if you are going to be singled out as someone who was not up to the task, especially since you have already lined up a strong reference from your past employer.

It is clear that you did a good job on your first round of interviews, as evidenced by the fact that you have been asked back for an advanced round. I think you have a good idea to speak with the partner you would be working for directly prior to meeting with the other partners. You might ask to come in a few minutes early for the next set of interviews to sit down and talk with this particular partner to let him know that you have been laid off from your firm since the last time you met with him. He may very well ask you if you knew about this when you initially met with him, and if he does ask the question, you need to answer it truthfully. This would be the time to explain that the layoff was not due to dissatisfaction with your work and that you have references to back up this claim. Make sure you let him know that you were still employed when you first met with him and that you need to update the resume that was initially submitted. In fact, this would be a good time to hand him your new resume with the revised dates of employment.

I think that it is dangerous to not "fess up" when you go in for this next set of interviews because the truth is going to come out eventually. For example, if the firm makes you an offer, they will want to check your references. Imagine how it would look for you if they called the firm and asked to verify your dates of employment, only to find out that the firm no longer employed you. I suspect that you might end up with the offer being rescinded because you did not represent yourself honestly. I know that you do not want to have something like that happen to you.

Or what if you go to work for the firm and somehow they find out that you were unemployed when they hired you while they had thought all along that you were still employed? This is a terrible risk to take, and one that more than likely will leave you unemployed, and this time for cause. I am certain that you do not want to take such a terrible risk.

Because you are about to go in to the firm for the second round of interviews, I don't think that the matter of you being laid off is going to be as big of a deal as you think it might be. If this partner liked you on the first round, hopefully he will feel the same during this set of interviews, and the fact that you were laid off in the meantime should not present too much of an issue. You do stand the risk that there are other candidates coming back for advanced rounds of interviews and that they may still be employed at their firms, which might give them a small edge over your candidacy. But what can you do if that is the case? There is no sense to try to pretend that they will never find out, and if you let the partner know right now—and not make a big deal out of it—then perhaps it will not affect your candidacy in any way.

If you are working with a recruiter, make sure you tell him/her about your employment status. S/he will be able to contact the main partner and let him know your situation while at the same time discussing your references and the reason for the layoff. This would be the best of all situations because your headhunter will know exactly how to handle this matter.

No matter whether you have to divulge your status yourself or you have a recruiter to do it for you, the truth needs to be told. You will feel much better not having to hold your breath, wondering if the firm will find out, and hopefully you will find that your interviewer is far more interested in you and your experience than the fact that you are no longer associated with your old firm. Best of luck and please let us know what happens!

Sincerely,
Ann M. Israel

Afterword

I often think about the fact that if I had to start my career as a legal headhunter all over again, I don't know if I could do it. It is hard being a new recruiter, and the level of rejection is intense. But when I think about how I wouldn't want to start all over again in a career in the attorney search field, I then remember how wonderful this career has been for me. Yes, the financial rewards are tremendous if you make it through that first difficult year in the profession. But it is far more than just the commissions that have kept me in this business since 1979 (yikes!). There is nothing better than that whoop of delight when you tell a candidate that an offer is being made for a job that s/he really wants. And what a wonderful reward it is when an associate you have placed into a great firm calls you to tell you that s/he has been elected into the partnership. Nothing compares! And I can't begin to tell you what it feels like to watch someone you have placed become internationally famous as the top rainmaking partner at his/her firm. You could burst with pride! How about when that bouquet of two dozen roses arrives as a thank you for placing someone in a great job? It brings tears to my eyes! Even a simple thank-you note after someone has been placed makes all of the rejections and disappointments disappear. Yes, it is a really tough—and sometimes thankless—business, but one I wouldn't trade for anything. The wonderful friends I have made over all these years—both candidates and clients—are worth more than any commission could bring.

But let's not forget how tough this business can be. What could be more devastating than when your candidate really wants a job and you get a phone call from the client stating that they are going to pass on this person—with no explanation.

And the same goes for dealing with disappointments that affect your client. They go all-out for a candidate that they really want as a new employee and do everything in their power to convince this person that they will be the best place for him/her, and then, without warning, the candidate pulls out of the process. It is not a fun moment to break this news to the client.

How about cold-calling? Hanging up on a recruiter seems to be the norm. Hanging up on someone? How rude! And how do you think we feel when we are just calling to tell you about appropriate opportunities? Wow, I never will be able to understand why someone hangs up on me.

Oh, but when you connect with someone on the phone, and they are a really great potential candidate, it is such a wonderful feeling. You are about to start on a journey with someone who hopefully will become a friend for life—someone who is about to embark on a job search that will irrevocably change his/her life for the better, as well as that of the client. It's the best feeling ever and the reason that someone becomes a legal recruiter.

What you have just read is the culmination of more than 35 years of advising legal professionals like yourselves on managing their careers. This book has been nothing if not a labor of love for me. Your questions motivate, challenge, and inspire me. I hope that I, in turn, can motivate, challenge, and inspire you to be the best that you can possibly be in this most exciting—and yes, oftentimes frustrating—profession. The legal industry is constantly changing and has perhaps experienced more ups and downs than almost any other profession I can think of, with the exception perhaps of finance and banking.

Advice for the Lawlorn is my gift to you. Keep the questions coming and keep pursuing your dreams.

Best wishes,
Ann M. Israel

Acknowledgments

I would like to thank all of my faithful readers for sending me their thoughts, fears, and hopes that continue to give life to this column after all of these years. Tremendous gratitude is extended to Judge Steven S. Honigman and Judge Andrew P. Napolitano for their kind and beautifully written preface and foreword. I can never forget Edward Adams, Editor at *Bloomberg LLP*, who suggested I write this book many years ago and never gave up on me. Very special thanks is given to the wonderful team at the *American Bar Association*, especially my amazing editor, Jonathan Malysiak - this book never would have been written without his fabulous editing abilities and the phenomenal support and encouragement he extended to me at all times.

Ann M. Israel
June 2014